FORESHORTENED TIME

Andrew Marvell and Seventeenth Century Revolutions

FORESHORTENED TIME

Andrew Marvell and
Seventeenth Century Revolutions

R. I. V. HODGE

D. S. BREWER · ROWMAN & LITTLEFIELD

First published 1978 by D. S. Brewer Ltd, 240 Hills Road, Cambridge
and PO Box 24, Ipswich IP1 1JJ
and by Rowman and Littlefield, 81 Adams Drive, Totowa, N.J. 07512

ISBN 0 85991 037 7 (hardback)
ISBN 0 85991 040 7 (paperback)
USA ISBN 0 8476 6089 3 (hardback)

British Library Cataloguing in Publication Data
Hodge, R I V
Foreshortened time.
1. Marvell, Andrew – Criticism and interpretation
I. Title
821'.4   PR3546

ISBN 0–85991–037–7

Photoset by Galleon Photosetting and Printed in
Great Britain by Redwood Burn Limited
Trowbridge & Esher

CONTENTS

Introduction		1
1.	The Logical Basis	7
2.	Images that Live	27
3.	Rational Magic	68
4.	'Thorough his own Side'	96
5.	Appleton House	132
	Notes	159
	Index	169

ILLUSTRATIONS

1. Thomas Cockson: Charles Howard of Effingham   29

2. William Marshall: Sir Thomas Fairfax   31

3. Pieter van den Keere: title to Norden, *Speculum Britanniae*
   Part I, 1593   33

4. G. Glover: title to *The Antipathy betweene the French and
   Spaniard* by R. Gentilys, 1641   35

5. H. Hugo: Emblem 14, Book I, from *Pia Desideria*, 1624   37

6. F. Quarles: Emblem XIV, Book III, from *Emblems*, 1634   39

7. H. Hawkins: 'The Platforme of the Garden', 1633   43

8. R. Hooke: Scheme XXXV from *Micrographia*, 1665   45

Introduction

This book began as a conventional enough task for a literary critic, a study of a poet, Andrew Marvell, and his 'background'. But as I attempted to take this relationship and its terms and possibilities seriously, I stumbled on some disconcerting truths about literary criticism, the discipline I had been trained in. If writers ought to be studied in relation to their background, then literary critics obviously have to know history. How do they acquire it? It soon struck me that there was something very curious about the history they knew, and the way they knew it. Where historians of a period myopically pore over records, and anxiously read other historians' books and articles, literary critics seemed to fly, like gods of the intellectual world. They appeared not to read historians, nor even the evidence historians draw on, yet they could talk confidently about an Age as a whole, if not Life itself. What was the secret of this enviable facility?

Looking closer at examples of criticism, I realized the potency of certain specialist terms, words like 'sensibility', 'modes/structures of thought and/or feeling'. These words are practically incomprehensible to students of a period from any other discipline, so they allow statements that these other disciplines would find unfalsifiable. But I saw that this does not make the terms totally vacuous. Critics write for other critics, and to educate neophytes in the mysteries of their art. The unspecific terms transmit a particular version of history, one however which proves highly resistant to change, since it is insulated from influence from outside and remains implicit within the discipline.

The fate of Andrew Marvell in literary criticism served me as a peculiarly illuminating case to show the function of the English literature version of history, and the potency of its operation. Since T. S. Eliot's influential essay of 1921 Marvell has been established as an interesting minor poet, the last authentic follower of the metaphysical mode.[1] This status, however, was peculiarly dependent on the Version of History, its strongest confirmation and finest product, the evaluation generating the corresponding historical account so automatically that both seem unassailable. Time and again, for instance, it is asserted that his fragile talent could not make the transition into the coarse world of the Restoration. Patrick Cruttwell's influential book 'The Shakespearean

Moment' asserts baldly: 'On Marvell the effect (of the Civil War) seems to have been a total destruction: the end of what had been one of the most delicate and exquisite sensibilities in the language' (p. 199). A more recent book on Marvell is equally confident: 'It is . . . well known that from the Restoration until his death in 1678 . . . Marvell wrote only social and political satires in rhymed couplets.'[2]

This is a limiting judgment on the poet. But the whole account has no evidence at all in its support. Very few of his major lyrics can be dated, and most of them could easily have been written after 1660.[3] The 'facts' on which the evaluation rests so confidently have been generated by the evaluation itself. Behind this evaluation is the Version of History, which has a nostalgic myth of a 'fine civilization' which similarly could not survive into the Restoration. Reading Marvell I felt that this general picture was badly wrong about his work. He seemed a much more powerful poet, strange, disturbing, enigmatic, not at all about to fade away like the last rose of the Elizabethan summer, certainly not to be preserved dismissively in the canon as a 'minor talent'. But to challenge the particular evaluation meant to question the Version of History itself. I came to feel that the complex of current notions about Marvell and his age is so subtly but pervasively misleading that the whole account, and even the terms it is conducted in, needed to be revitalized for literary students by fresh contacts outside the discipline.

A central belief of the Version of History still seemed to me to contain an important truth: the seventeenth was a decisive century for the development of English culture. Although Eliot's phrase 'dissociation of sensibility' is now unfashionable, most literary critics accept that major changes in forms of art and language occurred over this period, that went far deeper than the normal shifts in fashion from generation to generation: and a grasp of these deep processes is essential to an appreciation of the full significance of any poet. I am surer than ever that this is right, and that what needs doing is to define this change more adequately: which means, less imprecisely and more openly, in more public terms. The change at issue was so far reaching, touching on spheres of life studied by so many different disciplines, that literary criticism has made a grave mistake trying to go it alone.

The history of science was clearly one field to look to. The rise of science, at the expense of the poetic imagination as many suppose, is such an important fact of the century that any critic working in the seventeenth century needs to acquaint himself with the history of science. For me the study was especially rewarding, because in the work of T. S. Kuhn, a historian of science, I found a way of studying intellectual history which proved immensely helpful. Categories he developed specifically to describe developments in science seemed to make new sense of other aspects of the age as well. The following study makes use of some of his terms, so this is a proper place to summarize his theory.[4]

Science is often thought of as a kind of knowledge-machine, invented in the seventeenth century, which since then has systematically demolished ignorance and accumulated truth. Kuhn challenges this 'Whig' view of science, and sees the progress of science in other terms, as an alternation of 'paradigms'. For science a paradigm refers to a complex of models and methods, instruments and techniques, facts, theories and commitments, usually associated with the achievement of a great scientist. Paradigms are communicated by example as much as by explicit teaching, so that the paradigm is prior to any particular rules, theories etc. that may be derived from it, and can direct research in the absence of any formulated programme. Every paradigm defines a particular scientific community, and binds it together in essentially harmonious activity, in spite of a range of opinions on individual matters of fact and theory.

So far the term refers to a kind of framework, and belongs to the same family of ideas as 'modes of thought'. It is with his account of the typical pattern of development of a paradigm that Kuhn's term becomes really illuminating. Only some periods of science are dominated by a single paradigm. These he calls periods of 'normal science'. A paradigm does not remain static. In its initial form it seems totally comprehensive to its adherents, but this is largely an act of faith, and succeeding generations of 'normal' scientists can work at the further articulation and extension of the paradigm, this rather than the acumulation of new facts being their characteristic activity. But eventually a paradigm will outlive its purpose. Having explained all that it can, it begins to create problems that it cannot solve. The cause of the breakdown is not simply hard facts, for facts are not usually hard enough to impinge on a paradigm. Fact and theory alike can be manipulated to preserve more fundamental principles. But finally the accommodation is felt as excessive by a sufficient number of scientists. Science then enters what Kuhn refers to as 'crisis'. Theories and critiques are thrown up of an ever more fundamental character, until a new paradigm emerges to win the allegiance of a new community. Another period of normal science then begins.

But paradigms which are in open conflict at some points can be actually incommensurable at others. A paradigm is at bottom a way of looking at the world, so a change of paradigms is a far-reaching qualitative change. The result can be a discontinuity so radical that it is not even perceived at the time. Kuhn refers to the phenomenon as the 'invisibility of revolutions'. Out of a deep misunderstanding of the nature and achievements of former paradigms, a new normal science characteristically rewrites the history of science in its own terms. From this arises the illusion of steady progress.

This account has necessarily been schematic. Naturally Kuhn's presentation is fuller, and in any case the theory needs further extension and articulation, (like any other paradigm he might add). Kuhn's ideas have been objected to on particular points by other historians of science,[6] but for my purposes the development the theory most needed was a way of locating and analysing paradigms. Kuhn is at his most interesting on the ways paradigms develop and conflict with each other. However, disagreements and differences can take place within a paradigm as well as between paradigms. How do we know that a different paradigm is involved? How can we describe the evolution of a new paradigm?

One obvious way is to look at basic assumptions at the core of the paradigm. Here the work of C. S. Peirce proved extremely valuable. Peirce, a logician and philosopher of science, developed the concept of what he called leading or guiding principles of inference.[7] These are basic, habitual assumptions about truth, and the nature of language and reality which thinkers make *before* they proceed with any particular piece of reasoning. Peirce thought that these principles of sound reasoning vary from community to community – exactly like paradigms. These principles are what must be assumed if an argument is to be valid. So when someone's argument seems illogical or inexplicable to us, the cause might simply be a different set of leading principles. Instead of calling the man a fool, we ought to ask what assumptions seem to underly his reasoning. We may be in the presence of a different paradigm.

This opens up a number of possibilities for analysis. If paradigms are specified in terms of leading principles, we might be able to show precisely where one is continuous with another and where there is a break. For instance, we might see exactly what fundamental assumptions were shared by poetic and non-poetic thinking. We might also hope to locate areas of conflict between competing paradigms, areas where particular arguments will inevitably meet with blank incomprehension or hostile or contemptuous disbelief, where no appeal to common reason could work and only force of a kind could prevail, and revolution becomes the only possible adjudicator. We may have arrived at a means to represent the deep structure of an intellectual revolution.

The rest of the book will proceed within this general framework and programme. I will use 'paradigm' to indicate a particular set of characteristic assumptions clustering around a central core of leading principles. An account of Marvell's significance in these terms inevitably establishes a relation between the poet and his age, and carries the study into areas outside the usual range of reading of a specialist literary critic. The strategy I have used in recognition of these limitations in my own education (and perhaps my reader's) is to offer studies of versions of a paradigm rather than a comprehensive account of the age. Marvell

4

remains at the centre. Qualities of his language and thought were the starting point of every enquiry, as I tried to arrive at the form and sources of the relevant paradigm by every means I could. From there I worked outwards, and supplemented the central study by less exhaustive but still particular studies of writers in different fields of thought; logic, art, science and politics. Naturally I relied on specialist studies for guidance and have used them to sketch in very general maps of the relevant areas of study, but the exposition generally proceeds through individual analyses. I have been told that this makes the book hard to follow: the focus is remorselessly sharp, the effect an almost continuous foreground, part of which is meant to be interpreted as background. I am sorry about these difficulties, but I hope readers will appreciate their reason. It seemed better to give readers a first hand experience of how the paradigm at issue was embodied in the complexities of actual thinking than to present generalizations tidily wrapped up in convenient packages. Similarly I have wanted to suggest and even demonstrate interrelations between thinking in diverse fields, science, politics, art and poetry, but some of these interrelations are much more direct than others, and I have tried not to force connections and impose a simplistic unity on the age, or on the book.

I have also been accused of a kind of determinism, of claiming that paradigms determine thought. However, that is a misleading account of the process as I see it. I do not think that paradigms descend from above, with mysterious powers over an innocent community. Paradigms are very much the product of the community, rules of thought which have been reinforced in innumerable ways by that community. A normal scientist is the result of years of training. A paradigm is the field of an individual's complicity with his community. Paradigms do not determine thought so much as institutionalize it, prescribing the proper forms in which socialized thinking must proceed.

If most people cannot in practice think effectively or argue persuasively outside prevailing paradigms, this is not because paradigms exert an irresistable power. Nor is it the case that only the unintelligent accept paradigms. Kuhn's insistence that the normal scientist is not a blinkered dolt is to the point here. But real innovators and genuinely creative thinkers also exist, people who act not only with but on these leading principles, reshaping paradigms at their core in a profoundly critical and creative activity. A necessary part of their achievement will be a peculiarly active grasp of the prevailing paradigm, an acute sense of its limitations and potential. A study of such thinkers is invaluable in understanding any paradigm.

Marvell emerges from this study as an artist of this special kind, his greatness a personal achievement, of course, but also and indistinguish-

5

ably a function of his location in history, and his vantage point on his age. Marvell's reflections on history and Cromwell in 'First Anniversary' seem to me to describe his own privileged position. At a period when historical processes have briefly accelerated, a reflection on immediate experience can penetrate to a profound level of explanation of history, and a creative response can contain within it tendencies which may not become dominant and recognizable for centuries. In Marvell's words, 'foreshortened time the work of ages acts'. The greatness, the sheer range of the poetic vision, is dependent on the revolutionary context out of which the poetry grew. A major poet does not have to be a revolutionary, but he must be the poet of a revolution: or so the example of Andrew Marvell would suggest.

Acknowledgments

This book has profited greatly from helpful and well informed criticism from many people whom I have consulted on specific sections in their areas of expertise. What I have learnt from three individuals in particular is not confined to any one section, or even to the book: Professor L. C. Knights, who supervised the thesis out of which the book was written, Dr Michael Long of Churchill College, who read early drafts of most of it with exuberant acuity, and Professor John Wallace of Chicago University, who was imposed on for most of one sabbatical without losing his patience or withholding his expertise.

Ingenium nobis ipsa puella facit.
(Propertius II i 4)

Chapter 1

THE LOGICAL BASIS

Seventeenth century logic textbooks are liable to seem boring and simple-minded to our complex twentieth century intellects, yet a study of these dry texts can illuminate the paradigms of seventeenth century thought. Poets, scientists and philosophers all studied logic from these books, and carried out exercises associated with them which were designed to develop certain powerful and general intellectual skills. Conversely, logicians were more likely to describe the assumptions about the mind and the world that underlay prevailing forms of thought. Logic texts are a natural place to look for contemporary articulations of leading principles of paradigms.

The crucial development to understand here is the role of Ramism, the form of logic developed by the Frenchman Peter Ramus in the sixteenth century. Ramist logic was initially offered as a tidier version of scholastic logic, so it had continuities with earlier logics, and as the seventeenth century progressed it developed in divergent directions, so the beginning and end of Ramism is hard to fix.[1] Even so a number of things can be said. Ong's massive study shows that fairly pure Ramism had enormous currency[2] and Miller has demonstrated its profound influence on early seventeenth century puritan thought.[3] When Ramism is interpreted as a carrier of a major seventeenth century paradigm the well known facts about its development and influence in the seventeenth century acquire deeper explanatory power. Its initial form, what we can call simple Ramism, had the overwhelming simplicity of the initial form of a typical paradigm in Kuhn's account. Later and more sophisticated forms still bear traces of their origins in simple Ramism, their diversity stemming from contradictions latent in the parent form. So writers as apparently different in their mature intellectual styles as Marvell, Milton and Hobbes all shared a basic Ramist training, which provides a key to differences and underlying relationships that might otherwise be missed.

(i) Simple Ramism and Miltonic thought

Simple Ramism is characterized by its love of dichotomies, that is, its preference for dividing any subject matter up into a series of paired categories. This makes it strongly dualistic in tendency. The categories in the dichotomies normally were kept absolutely distinct. Simple Ramism was obsessed with boundaries. These qualities are clearly displayed in the major intellectual techniques associated with Ramism, the Ramist forms of method and invention. Both these techniques rested on and reinforced assumptions about reality and the mind, as any successful intellectual technique must. Kuhn insists that a paradigm can be transmitted through characteristic methods and techniques as well as through conscious instruction.

Ramist method was a means of classifying material and presenting it in tabular form. The simplicity and power of method can be seen from Ramus's diagram for his own logic, which he reduced to a two-page scheme (see fig. i).[4] The fascination and potential danger of the method derives from this massive simplification. The method imposed neat symmetries on phenomena that might be much more complexly organized. It also required sharp boundaries round the categories, otherwise there would be problems of categorization. Because it solved the problem of organization before the collection of material began, it predisposed towards a priori thinking: a Ramist was likely to apply unexamined categories with total confidence. Ramists formalized the assumptions that facilitated this activity as three laws: the law of justice (that categories should be distinct), wisdom (that the general should precede the particular), and truth (that the contents of categories should be homogenous).

The operation of Ramist 'invention', the process of filling out the scheme with particular material, was determined by Ramist method. The power of method left the mind with only a simple task, to scan material to see if it belonged to the predetermined category or not. Invention was a good way to accumulate large amounts of vaguely relevant material under predetermined categories over a long period of time: good for a composer of speeches or sermons or poems. However the procedure did not encourage a testing of categories against material, since the material could only fill the category not challenge it.

Ramism as a logic had to have a section on syllogisms, or forms of valid argument. In place of the four Aristotelian moods of scholastic logic, Ramism had two, both important intellectual habits of Ramism. These two syllogistic forms, which became signatures of simple Ramism, were the disjunctive syllogism (either-or) and the connex syllogism (if-then). These correspond to the two basic actions of the mind in the forming of a Ramist table, separating, and joining. These two basic actions are reflected in Ramus's other logical categories. The basic unit of a Ramist proposition was called an 'argumentum' or 'that which is apt to the arguing of something'.[5] The underlying idea here is of pairs of categories

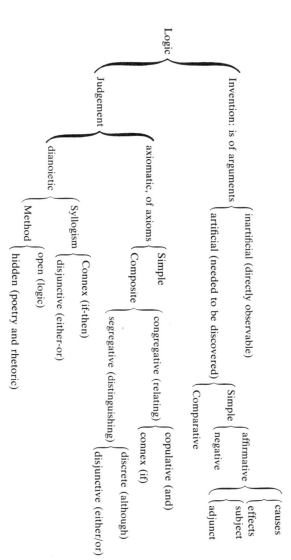

Fig. i

9

that automatically go together, like subject and adjunct, or cause and effect. The unit of judgment, the 'axioma', is divided into two, 'simplex', where a relation is affirmed or denied, and 'compositum', further distinguished into 'congregativum' and 'segregativum'.[6]

Simple Ramism looks an absolutely coherent if limited system of thought, but the two basic syllogistic forms, and the contrary actions of the mind they represented, contained the seeds of a contradiction which was to transform Ramism unrecognisably. The growth point concerned the connex syllogism, the 'if-then' form. This form had been called the hypothetical syllogism in scholastic logics. The Ramist name emphasized connection, but the syntactic form signalled its conditional status: a certainty that was not certain, axioms attached to each other but not to reality. When the confidence of the simple Ramist wavered, a doubt was bound to arise about the relation between the method and reality.

Alexander Richardson, the influential early commentator on Ramus, faced this problem and gave an unequivocal answer.

> Marke this, that Art is the Law of God . . . Marke this well, for the Schooles runne into many absurdities, whilst they have thought that Art is in a man's head, and not in the thing.[7]

Art, the Ramist method, corresponds exactly to the nature of things. God not Ramus, it seems, composed the Ramist categories – which is another way of putting the categories out of reach of human criticism. The result is that the mind is represented as completely neutral, as though it is simply reflecting the nature of things. 'The soule is "tanquam tabula abrasa"' as Richardson puts it, in words that foreshadow Locke's more famous dictum.[8]

However, even a simple Ramist can notice that there is not an easy match between a Ramist table and the reality which that table reduces to order.

> The Genesis of every thing is Gods, and man must see the rules of Art, therefore man must see them from singulars, by analysis. This art of reason . . . is fitly called invention. And this teacheth man thus much, that he is to seeke out, and find this wisdome of God in the world, and not to be idle; for the world, and the creatures therein are like a booke wherein Gods wisedome is written, and there must wee seeke it out . . . We are by this Art to sever them, and to look at them simply . . . (and) as in mists to look at the elements.[9]

The source of this knowledge is not books but nature conceived of as a book, from whose jumbled pages creatures can be extracted like quotations. All the energy is in the busy Ramist, who is 'to seeke out and find . . . and not to be idle'. His main intellectual action is to 'sever' things from their order in nature, to isolate them. But 'invention' is immediately followed by 'judgment' whose function is to connect them in a more natural and inherent order.

10

Invention teacheth us to find out simples, judgment teacheth us to lay them together; we may compare invention of arguments, to the hookes and nayles in a thing: judgment to the fastening of them together.[10]

A remarkably transparent example of the simple Ramist paradigm in action can be seen in the writings of Milton. Milton's connection with Ramism is easy to demonstrate, for he published a version of Ramus with a commentary in 1672.[11] Even without this, his 'de Doctrina', the unpublished work in which he formulated his essential religious views, shows clear signs of the leading principles of Ramism shaping structures and forms of thought and even particular arguments, as he grappled with problems that he regarded as of the first importance.[12] The organization of the work as a whole can so easily be represented by a dichotomous scheme that this must have been its original form. The first chapter is not about God, who is metaphysically prior, but about Doctrine. But Milton spends no time on the epistemological foundations of his system, which are treated only in chapter 30 of the first book. The pre-eminent place of doctrine is not due to any consequential relationship between knowledge in general and God; 'Doctrine' is simply a category which includes God. So Doctrine is divided into its two parts, knowledge of God and love of God. Chapter 2 deals with God, again dichotomized. His two parts are Nature and effects. The effects are internal and external. The internal are general and special. The external have three parts, generation, creation and providence. Providence is general and special. Special is of men and of angels. This takes us up to chapter 9 of book 1 (see fig. ii). An interesting feature is that the clarity in the summary is not felt in the work itself, because the progress of a book is linear, and since the categories are not causally connected and their contents are not entirely homogeneous, a reader does not have a strong sense of consecutiveness. This illustrates how intermittently logical the system is in effect. The contents

Fig. ii

of each category are confined to that category, so that things potentially contradictory or related in some way can be insulated from each other. The range of the treatise is the typical product of the method and a main source of its appeal, but it was achieved at some cost. The method provided a simple structure, so Milton's great energies could be absorbed in 'invention', collecting texts to fill out his doctrine, which the method allowed him to do piecemeal using a common place book. We can see the effects of the procedure in the first chapter. A definition is given, which is then divided and supported part by part with texts.

> Christian Doctrine is that Divine Revelation disclosed in various ages by Christos.[13]

'Divine Revelation' is supported by Isai. 51.4: 'a law shall proceed from me'; John vi.46: 'They shall be all taught of God'; John ix.29: 'We know that God spoke unto Moses'; and three other texts. A definition orders its constituents. However, this definition is not examined or supported as a whole; only the two components are, in isolation from each other and from the definition. Moreover, the quotations under each heading argue slightly different positions. Since he assumes that categories are homogenous, he ignores diversity. Two of the quotations are prophecies, which look forward to a time when God's purposes will be known. This implies that the previous revelation was seriously incomplete, though Milton's point is the certainty of the doctrine. The third quotation is detached from a context that negates its force as evidence. The words in fact are said by Jews to a blind man cured by Christ. The passage as a whole in the Authorized Version reads: (vv.28–29).

> Then they reviled him, and said, Thou art his disciple; but we are Moses' disciples. We know that God spake unto Moses: but as for this fellow, (i.e. Christ) we know not from whence he is.

The context profoundly modifies the force of the phrase quoted, but Milton extracts and quotes it as though it were independent of its intention or source.

On matters of doctrinal importance the method operated differently. Milton's arguments for some of his more heterodox views show the process clearly. Texts were collected under the relevant head and examined with due attention to potential conflicts in meaning or implication. The individual texts, however, were still treated in isolation.[14] They were exclusively and unequivocally either true or not; so some were taken as simply and literally true and the others were wrested, sometimes unmercifully, to remove all contradiction. The process never aimed at a larger view which subsumed the apparent contradiction, or reinterpreted both to achieve a new unity. Ramist leading principles even affected his choice of what was to be axiomatic in crucial cases. On

12

the doctrine of the Trinity, for instance, one could equally well take as axiomatic either John 1.i: 'In the beginning was the Word, and the Word was with God, and the Word was God': or Christ's words in John 17.3: 'And this is life eternal, that they might know thee the only true God, and Jesus Christ whom thou hast sent'. Milton takes the second.[15] The section in which he argues for his view shows the grounds of this choice and of the conclusion. For instance he considers the key question of the creation of Christ, and decides that 'Generation must be an external efficiency, since the Father and Son are different persons'.[16] He then argues that 'the divines themselves acknowledge this' in their use of terms like emanation and procession;[17] but obviously the orthodox divines concerned would say that it is impossible to talk of the divine nature in human terms without contradiction.

Milton considers and rejects the possibility that God the Father and the Son are identical because

> according to the one hypothesis there would be two infinite Gods, or according to the other the first or efficient cause would become the effect, which no man in his senses will admit.[18]

There is no appeal to the Bible here. Milton splits contending theologians of previous centuries neatly down the middle with a disjunctive syllogism, an either-or, and then relies on the self-evidence of his reason. The arguments of Cause and Effect can be attached by hooks and nails into a universal connex syllogism, but the two categories must remain for ever distinct. The concealed assumption in refutation after refutation is that the Ramist law of justice applies universally, even to God, who therefore must be either one or two (or more) distinct entities. He can be uncircumscribed in space and time but He cannot be in two categories at once. In a subtle but total way Milton cannot understand the arguments of the orthodox divines, and his refutations continually miss their point. Their statements offend against the principles of valid inference of his paradigm, and have to be translated into terms that they would repudiate, even to be meaningful to him; while his objections would seem to them only an incomprehension of the appropriate way to reason about the Divine. It is especially vivid case of paradigm difference. When he repeats the formulations of the orthodox theology (as less independent-minded Ramists did to a far greater extent) they remain mere words, whose content is irrelevant to what he really thought. For instance, Milton ends his section on the Trinity with a repetition of the principle that underlay the orthodox paradigm, the incomprehensibility of God to human reason: 'Let us then discard reason in sacred matters'[19] – but this is after he has already used reason to discard the Trinity.

Further analysis would only reinforce the conclusion that 'de Doctrina'

13

is continuously and decisively shaped by Ramism. So also are the views of the nature of society and the mind underlying the argument of his most admired work in prose, 'Areopagitica'. The view of truth essential to his argument is similar to that of Richardson discussed above. Good and Evil 'in the field of this World grow up together almost inseparably', but they are like seeds,

> those confused seeds which were imposed on Psyche as an incessant labour to cull out, and sort asunder.[20]

Richardson called them 'simples' or 'elements', but the pellet-like nature of truth is the same. The powers Milton attributes to the mind would not be beyond an industrious hen. There are, however, some important differences between Richardson and Milton. Though Truth sorts out the seeds, Milton is aware that 'in the field of this world' the seeds grow into more complex forms. Along with this goes the greater effort implied by Milton's 'incessant labour' against Richardson's invocation 'not to be idle'.

Another passage from 'Areopagitica' brings out revealingly how Milton's view of society was connected to his Ramist conception of the structure of ideas. He describes the Sects:

> These are the men cry'd out against for schismatics and sectaries; as if, while the Temple of the Lord was building, some cutting, some squaring the marble, others hewing the cedars, there should be a sort of irrational men who could not consider there must be many schisms and many dissections made in the quarry and in the timber, ere the house of God can be built. And when every stone is laid artfully together, it cannot be united into a continuity, it can be but contiguous in this world; neither can every peece of the building be of one form; nay rather the perfection consists in this, that out of many moderat varieties and brotherly dissimilitudes that are not vastly disproportionall arises the goodly and the graceful symmetry that commends the whole pile and structure.[21]

This image was more usually used for the reconciliation of diverse interests in society. Milton uses it to talk simultaneously about ideas and people: the 'schisms' in the ideas define groups of people. Sects are composed of persons, not just types of doctrine, and this is what makes them dangerous. But Milton is implicitly supposing that the relation between the persons will exactly parallel that between the ideas. The reference of the image to a view of society still acts through 'brotherly', but a Ramist view of the structure of ideas underlies the conception of society. It was not normal to stress that stones 'can be but contiguous', though this is an essential feature of the categories in a Ramist table. Nor was it usual to stress the act of cutting or dividing. The more common emphasis was on the diversity which was reconciled, but discreteness takes the place of diversity in Milton's use of the image, and he

14

underplays the extent of the diversity. The most important feature of both ideas and men is that they are separate, as inert as stones and therefore innocuous.

We have not considered Marvell's guiding principles yet, but this passage from 'Areopagitica' gives us a good opportunity for some initial observations by way of contrast to Milton. In 'The First Anniversary' of a decade later Marvell uses the same commonplace image and even applies it to the Sectaries, or at least to what the Sectaries had grown into by then.

> All other Matter yields, and may be rul'd;
> But who the Minds of stubborn Men can build?
> No Quarry bears a Stone so hardly wrought,
> Nor with such labour from its Center brought;
> None to be sunk in the Foundation bends,
> Each in the House the highest Place contends,
> And each the Hand that lays him will direct,
> And some fall back upon the Architect; . . .
> The Common-wealth does through their Centers all
> Draw the Circumf'rence of the publique Wall:
> The crossest Spirits here do take their part,
> Fast'ning the Contignation which they thwart;
> And they, whose Nature leads them to divide,
> Uphold, this one, and that the other Side;
> But the most Equal still sustein the Height,
> And they as Pillars keep the Work upright;
> While the resistance of opposed Minds,
> The Fabrick as with Arches stronger binds.   (lines 77f.)

Almost every point of contact is one of contrast. The passage starts with a statement of the mind-matter polarity, but the relation between these is neither identity nor difference. 'All other matter' implies that Mind, too, is a species of matter, though with unique properties. Marvell's stones are far more difficult to remove from their place in the quarry, and the cutting action is not just a simple splitting along natural lines of cleavage. Stones must be 'wrought' to be usable in his temple. Potential discord is at its maximum in Marvell's use of the image, and is only reconciled by Cromwell's almost supernatural power. The stones are as wilful as the minds they represent, and there is no assurance that they will stay put as readily as Milton's. Where Milton's temple is weightless and static, in Marvell's the lines of force are almost visible, and every stone has a potential for invading the area occupied by another which only a carefully planned, highly complex and powerful structure can order and control.

But the relation between the two poets, even though one of contrast, is still a relationship, unlike the lack of contact between Milton and his orthodox divines. Marvell's passage is built on an underlying dichotomy,

15

spirit and matter, which is simultaneously denied and used. ?gories are not used vaguely. The Ramist law of justice, which at every category must be discrete, is deliberately transgressed, 'A Dialogue between the Soul and Body' the structure and imagery is generated by the tension between the ultimate discreteness of the categories, and their actual inseparability 'in the field of this world', as Milton puts it. Moreover, the organizing principle for the state in Marvell is clear and hard and mathematical, not organic. Milton's and Richardson's worlds had nothing of the organic either, but they were barely even machines; the elements were not joined like hand to body, but nor were they related as cog to cog. At best their universe was like a vast commonplace book, become that simplest of intellectual machines, the filing cabinet. Marvell's state looks like a Gothic cathedral, but it is a Gothic cathedral seen as a complex and dangerous feat of engineering, capped by the metal dome of the apotheosized Roundhead. This discussion can only suggest what later analyses of this passage in its context and of Marvell's modes of thought will more strongly confirm. Marvell (born 1621) was not an attenuated survival from a previous mode of thought, exemplified by Donne and decisively though perhaps unfortunately supplanted by Milton. It is Milton (born 1608), Marvell's friend, colleague and early patron whose modes of thought Marvell developed to a degree of sophistication and complexity that makes them barely recognizable. The dates are not misleading after all.[22]

(ii) Extension of the Connex syllogism

The connex syllogism, or if-then form, was the focal point of a major instability in simple Ramism. We have seen how simple Ramism emphasized the isolated coupling of elements in a unit of certainty, but the grammatical form tugged in an opposite direction. Milton, for instance, observed in his commentary on Ramus that with connex syllogisms:

> the necessity springs from the necessary connection of the parts, which can appear even in false parts.[23]

Ramist logics, moreover, were fond of logically correct but untrue examples from poets. The example from Ovid used by Ramus is, in Milton's version:

> When Paris deserts Oenone, let Xanthus turn back.
> Paris has deserted Oenone. Therefore let Xanthus turn back.[24]

The connex syllogism was also open to another development which if carried far enough would transform the Ramist paradigm. Ramus' use of the term 'axioma' invited comparison with geometrical axioms, and their place in an extended chain of reasoning that could lead to new or surprising knowledge. If the connex syllogism of simple Ramism was loosened from its point-by-point correspondence to reality, this development became more likely. The result would be a mode of thought that has been seen as essential to the scientific method, hypothetico-deductive reasoning.

The seventeenth century thinker most closely associated with such a revolutionary development was Hobbes, whose conversion to Euclid in middle age was famous, and whose 'Leviathan' was offered as something of a model for thinking of this kind applied to politics and morality. Some representative statements show both how his method grew out of the Ramist paradigm, and how considerably it modified it. He summarizes kinds of knowledge as follows:

> There are of KNOWLEDGE two kinds; whereof one is Knowledge of fact: the other Knowledge of the Consequence of one Affirmation to another. The former is nothing else, but Sense and Memory, and is Absolute Knowledge; as when we see a Fact doing, or remember it done: And this is the Knowledge required in a Witnesse. The later is called Science; and is Conditionall; as when we know, that, 'If the figure showne be a Circle, then any straight line through the Center shall divide it into two equall parts'. And this is the Knowledge required in a Philosopher; that is to say, of him that pretends to Reasoning.[25]

The chapter is followed by a classic Ramist table summarizing the whole of science. It is arranged entirely dichotomously except for some of the lowest categories. His scheme of Knowledge, and the form of the passage quoted above, is determined by successive disjunctives, either-ors, but science for him is constituted by connex syllogisms. But in contrast to the Ramist emphasis on connection, Hobbes' term insists on the conditional nature of such reasoning. For him, the connex syllogism is neither certain nor self-contained; it is only a stage in a chain (or 'trayne') of reasoning that can proceed unerringly to surprising conclusions but will not certainly correspond with reality. A chain of reasoning of this sort can be validated at either end. If the initial premises are admitted, the conclusion is entailed. However, one can disprove the premise by showing that the conclusions are wrong or absurd. Hobbes summarizes the position:

> By this it appears how necessary it is for any man that aspires to true Knowledge, to examine the definitions of former Authors; and either to correct them, where they are negligently set down; or to make them himselfe. For the errours of Definitions multiply themselves, according as the reckoning proceeds; and lead men into absurdities, which at last they see, but cannot avoyd, without reckoning anew from the beginning.[26]

His 'Leviathan' was offered in its most revolutionary aspect as an argument of this kind. Starting from premises about the nature of knowledge and man he comes to some startling conclusions about politics and morality. Simple Ramist conceptions would make the point of the procedure hard to grasp, for the Ramist emphasis on the isolated self-evidence of arguments and axioms would minimize the need for the strategy. It might also conceal the amount of effort needed to match the conceptions of the mind to reality exactly enough at the crucial starting point of thought. A Ramist might be more easily satisfied that the clarity of his first (and later) conceptions was sufficient proof of their validity.

Hobbes's thinking retained leading principles from simple Ramism but his idiosyncratic development isolated him in two directions. Milton treated his scholastic opponents as rational men like himself who had, however, made a large number of obvious mistakes. Hobbes regards them as simply mad.

> Let (any man) take a Schoole-man into his hands, and see if he can translate any one chapter concerning any difficult point; as the Trinity; the Deity; the nature of Christ; Transubstantiation; Free-will, etc. into any of the moderne tongues, so as to make the same intelligible . . .

he challenges. Then after quoting from Suarez, he comments:

> When men write whole volumes of such stuffe, are they not Mad, or intend to make others so?[27]

A reaction like this may have lain behind Milton's heterodoxies in 'de Doctrina' as well as the more entertaining and eccentric views of the last two books of 'Leviathan'.

But a study of the refutations of Hobbes over the century reveals how opaque his own paradigm was even to fellow Ramists. Two of these refutations bring us closer to Marvell. Both Bishop Bramhall and Samuel Parker wrote against Hobbes,[28] and the fact is an important part in understanding the conduct of the argument of Marvell's ' "The Rehearsal" Transpros'd', of 1672, his most famous prose work. Marvell was intervening in a debate between Parker, later to be Bishop of Oxford and supporter of James II, and John Owen, a moderate Puritan. Parker began with 'A Discourse of Ecclesiastical Polity' (1670), urging persecution of non-conformists. Owen had replied with 'Truth and Innocence Vindicated' (1671), to which Parker responded with two works, 'A Defence . . .' (1671) and 'A Preface to Bishop Bramhall . . .' (1672), a long preface attached to his reissue of a work by Bishop Bramhall. Parker's choice of Bramhall is at first sight strange, but it may have had something to do with Bramhall's reputation as a critic of Hobbes. Bramhall's 'The Catching of the Leviathan', of 1658, was regarded by contemporaries as one of the most effective of the replies to Hobbes. A modern critic, J. Bowles, has endorsed this verdict, praising Bramhall's 'trenchant good sense'.[29] It was entertainingly written, based on shrewd

18

observation of political life, though Bramhall did not enter deeply into Hobbes's basic assumptions, his leading principles.

There is no place for liberty in Arithmetic and Geometry, but in policy there is, and so there is in tennis play.[30]

This is simply a flat denial of Hobbes's most basic premise, dismissing it as not to be taken seriously.

Bramhall's status as Hobbes-slayer would have made his book a useful vehicle for Parker's 'Preface', for Parker's relations with Hobbism were equivocal. His 'Discourse', which started the battle with Owen and then Marvell, was organized in a deductive fashion clearly modelled on Hobbes, and started with one of Hobbes's conclusions, the absolute supremacy of the magistrate, as its first premise. However, in the early part of the work he refutes some of Hobbes's more pernicious tenets, consciously using Hobbist methods of argument against Hobbes. After a perfunctory refutation of atheism along conventional lines, he adventures on a more original line of attack. He tests a possible corollary of Hobbes's view of religion, as he sees it; that is, that since all religion is a cheat a sovereign should leave his subjects to their delusions in peace. He starts off:

Only let me observe that this Discourse (i.e. the corollary) lies under no less Prejudice than this, That if any of the Principles of Religion be true, then is all these mens Policy false; but waving this too great advantage, I shall content myself only to discover of what noisome and pernicious consequence such Principles are to the Commonwealth, though it were granted that all Religion were nothing but Imposture.[31]

It was a curious tactic to use against non-conformists, his ostensible opponents, none of whom would think of calling religion an imposture. But clearly he is captivated with the thought of using Hobbist deductive reasoning against a Hobbist argument. He continues:

If all Humane Laws have their main force and efficacy from the Apprehensions of Religion . . . then let Authority judge, how much it is beholden to those men, who labour to bring it into Publick Disreputation;[32]

and he concludes:

So that though Religion were a Cheat, they are apparently the greatest Enemies to Government, that tell the World it is so.[33]

Unlike other refuters, he is not meeting Hobbes' words merely by repeating conventional truths. He appears to be arguing entirely in Hobbes's terms, dispassionately testing consequences of a doctrine and showing them to be intrinsically self-defeating. He uses a series of connex syllogisms clearly marked by 'ifs' and 'thens', bonded by an initial disjunctive syllogism, (Religion is either true or a cheat). The whole

19

argument is presented as purely hypothetical, independent of his own religious beliefs.

Marvell's strategy in his attack on Parker's argument is to assume that it is more truly Hobbist than it is. The most systematic possible representation of Parker's argument, preserving his order, would be:

1. The Magistrate is supreme in religious affairs (Chapter I)
2. Religion consists of morality (Chapter II)
3. Conscience is internal in its authority (Chapters III and IV)
4. Religion is politically potent (Chapter V)

Consequently,

5. The magistrate may and must punish fanatics – even more than vice (Chapter V)
6. Anarchy is worse than tyranny (Chapter VI)

Consequently,

7. Obedience is a higher duty than integrity (Chapter VI)

Numbers 1–4 and 6 have the status of axioms, which Parker supported by appeals to commonsense or precedents, showing that they did not conflict with the Bible as suitably interpreted. It is not logically very powerful, but Parker was only interested in the single conclusion, 5. Marvell, however, reorders the argument more tightly into six heads, under which he collects some lengthy quotations. His rewriting is as follows:

'1. The Unlimitted Magistrate'. (Parker's No. 1)

'2. The publick Conscience'. (i.e. the elimination of private conscience, as in Parker's 3 and 7. Marvell sees it as the necessary consequence of the elevation of the Magistrate's claims).

'3. Moral Grace'. (i.e. religion as morality, Parker's 2, which Marvell sees as a redefinition necessary within the system).

'4. Debauchery Tolerated

'5. Persecution Recommended

'6. Pushpin Divinity.'[34]

For No. 4 Marvell has elevated Parker's frequent parenthetical remarks about the relative innocuousness of vice – which were probably intended mainly to amuse the court and irritate non-conformists – into a separate proposition, which he then inserts where its contradiction is most apparent. Since Parker has made religion to consist only of morality, remarks of this sort effectively contradict even his limited definition of religion. But Marvell concludes with a sixth head, 'Pushpin divinity' or the absolute claims of the State Church. He derives this from Parker's 4 and an uncharitable interpretation of his motives. But he points out its essential incompatibility with the original premise, which he suggests it really supplants as the 'syntagm' of Parker's system.

20

Marvell's pose of negligent wit was incompatible with a display of logical expertise, but his comments on the connections between the various parts of the thesis show unmistakably his sure sense of the system as such and of how such systems are to be approached. On the role of the main thesis, he observes (after eight quotations, some lengthy, to show that Parker is not being misrepresented):

> This being the magisterial and main point that he maintains, the rest of his assertions may be reckoned as corollaries to this THESIS, and without which indeed such an unlimited maxime can never be justified. Therefore, to make a conscience fit for the nonse, he says, p. 89 . . .[35]

The redefinition is presented as both a necessary consequence of such an initial premise, and also part of its justification. Marvell is being entirely hypothetical, not endorsing any of the arguments used, but he is more sensitive than Parker to the very different consequences that accrue in the rest of the system from changes in the range of reference of terms.

At a later state of the argument Marvell gives another brief account of his sense of the coherence of Parker's system:

> Having thus enabled the Prince, dispensed with conscience, and fitted up a moral religion for that conscience; to show how much those moral virtues are to be valued, page 53 of the preface to his Ecclesiastical Policy, he affirms that . . .[36]

He does not parade technical terms, but the account of the logical dependence of the propositions is precise and accurate. They are rearranged in a more tightly consecutive and elegant order than in Parker, but this serves to expose the confusion and inconsistencies in Parker's reasoning. The new ordering shows how the content of the redefined terms tends to zero. The disproof relies on drawing out the train of reasoning to a reductio ad absurdum, or in Parker's case to several absurdities. Marvell does not appeal to religious texts, nor does he take pains to refute any individual proposition. Parker's choice of his first proposition had seemed a shrewd gambit. Not even Royalists like Clarendon accepted the absolute supremacy of the monarch, but the tactic put the non-conformists at a disadvantage, for if they denied it or even showed reservations Parker would call them traitors and play on fears of the civil war. This is in fact what he did with Owen. Marvell had been a royalist sympathiser and so was less open to this riposte, but since the king was the main hope for a policy of moderation a frontal attack on this premise might have lost the cause without winning the debate. But no denial was needed. Under his analysis the system disintegrated, and Parker was left with the fragments in his hands complaining that Marvell had not even answered his main premise. This very protest shows how incompletely he understood the Hobbist mode of reasoning, for

21

absurdities in the conclusion are sufficient proof that the initial premise has been incorrectly defined. There can have been few more elegant demolitions in the history of pamphlet warfare. The materials for Parker's destruction were his own methods used against him with considerably more expertise. But Marvell's performance reveals a great deal indirectly about his own modes of thought. His insight into the foundations of the Hobbist method and his ability to move so easily around arguments of that kind show him far in advance of contemporary refuters, or such carping disciples as Parker. This does not make him a Hobbist; on the contrary, such expertise could allow a far more penetrating critique of Hobbes. But the analysis unmistakably reveals logical powers of a kind and degree not usually thought of in connection with Marvell: a virtuoso demonstration of the hypothetical deductive method of the new science, paradoxically deployed in defence of a pious simple Ramist. The intellectual alignments this suggests for Marvell are complex, but they are incompatible with any picture of him as a mid-century anachronism, a late surviving Elizabethan.

(iii) Logic and poetry

With a poet, the thinking that matters for his reputation must be embodied in his poetry. And even if Marvell had the formidable logical powers suggested above, an objector might feel that logic of this kind and degree is incompatible with great poetry. 'To his Coy Mistress' is a good test case for this prejudice, for the poem's form unobtrusively but unmistakably signals its roots in logic. But what logic? And how intrinsic is it to the quality of the poem?

The underlying logical form seems to be derived from the Ramist connex syllogism. The argument can be abstracted like this:

(If)	Had we but World enough, and Time,
(Then)	This coyness Lady were no crime . . .
(But not)	But at my back I alwaies hear
	Times winged charriot hurrying near:
(Therefore)	Now let us sport us while we may . . .

The form of this argument requires careful attention. Readers not trained in logic normally suppose it to be a valid argument. However, the form could be described abstractly as: 'If P then not Q; not P; therefore Q'.[37] This would be a logical fallacy which was recognized as such in seventeenth century logics. If this representation is correct we ought to acquire a sense of the invalidity of the argument as part of the experience of the poem. There are, however, certain features of the first couplet which suggest that the description is inaccurate. 'Had' implies not only the 'if' but the denial that is to follow twenty lines later. This suggests that this axiom is not the first step in the reasoning process, but that the poem takes up the argument after it has advanced to this point. More conclusive, 'not-Q' is a misleading description of the force of line 2, whose subject is coyness, not crime. 'No crime' in fact indicates neutrality, for the coyness is no virtue either. The whole argument could be re-written in the following form:

(1. If no time, then no coyness)
2. If time . . .
> (no consequence; i.e. coyness is permitted but not obligatory; it is 'no crime' though no virtue).
3. But no time
4.   then no coyness.

This is a valid argument, which the poem takes up at the second stage, 'in medias res' as is the right of a poet. The opening connex syllogism thus stands outside the poem itself but determines its course. So the poem opens with a gallant attempt by the poet to oblige the lady by entering her alternative connex syllogism, though his first word has signalled its fallaciousness.

The argument, though now valid, would still be open to an objection, for it seems to rely on an implicit disjunctive syllogism between time and no time. If, however, she had some time though not all she could be coy for a while. Marvell's argument is much more subtle than this. Both this subtlety and the implicative range emerge more clearly when we put it alongside a probable source, Cowley's poem 'The Dyet'. Cowley's last stanza in that poem is:

On a sigh of pity I a year can live,
> One Tear will keep me twenty at least,
> Fifty a gentle look will give;
An hundred years on one kind word I'll feast;
> A thousand more will added be
> If you an Inclination have for me;
And all beyond is vast Eternity.

The novel feature of Cowley's image is the cumulative arithmetic leading to infinity. In Cowley's arithmetic, Eternity is just the much longer time he will live if she bestows 'all beyond' on him. But the infinite has some unusual mathematical properties, which stimulated mathematicians of the mid-seventeenth century but which Hobbes among others was unable to understand.[38] Marvell's cumulative arithmetic seems to parallel Cowley's until the extension to the infinite, where his use of Cowley's 'vast eternity' thoroughly subverts Cowley's intended meaning. Cowley moves with a slow progression from 1 to 20 to 50 to 100 to 200 to 1,000. Eternity does not feel too big. Marvell's progression is from 100 to 200 to

30,000 to an Age to the last Age, a rapidly accelerating curve that has brought him to the day of Judgment in six lines. So the 'But' is not a simple adversative. The 'Deserts of vast Eternity' are the extension to the infinite of the logic of her wish, as well as the reality which makes it fallacious.

The reasoning is similar in form to a strange comparison in ' "The Rehearsal" Transpros'd' where he says that as 'a straight line continued grows a circle' so a prince's power extended to infinity becomes impotence.[39] Contraries meet not at their mid-points but at their extremities in the infinite. Marvell may have derived the idea in the first place from Nicholas of Cusa, modified by an understanding of this work in mathematics, or perhaps more directly from Giordano Bruno, whose formulation Marvell's more closely resembles.[40] But whatever its source for Marvell, he clearly found the notion important.

The second section of Marvell's poem seems to take up some of the arguments commonly found in 'Carpe diem' poems, but its use of logic and the nature of the logic it uses give it a very different quality. The normal poem in the genre was rhetorical rather than logical. The conclusion was usually stated first: 'Vivamus, mea Lesbia, atque ameamus', 'Come my Celia, Let us prove', 'Gather ye Rosebuds while ye may'.[41] Though the inevitability of age and death was the main argument it was presented in images of due delicacy, calculated to persuade but not to frighten the lady. Carew's 'To A.L.: Persuasions to Love' has so many similarities to Marvell's central section that it may have been in his mind; and in any case it serves well for a comparison. For instance, Carew has:

> That eye which now is *Cupids* nest
> Will prove his Grave, and all the rest
> Will follow; in the cheek, chin, nose,
> Nor lilly shall be found nor rose.[42]

Marvell writes:

> then Worms shall try
> That long preserv'd Virginity:
> And your quaint Honour turn to dust;
> And into ashes all my Lust.
> The Grave's a fine and private place,
> But none I think do there embrace. ('CM': lines 27–32)

The potential image of the eye becoming a grave-like cavity is blocked in the Carew by the interposition of the emblematic 'Cupid's nest', which discourages visualization with no corresponding increase in metaphysical awareness. The conventional lilies and roses again keep the physical facts of old age and death remote, and the very statement of the absence of the flowers leaves a vestigial fragrance. The quick, light movement of the verse like a salesman's patter does not leave much pause for thought.

Neither the physical reality nor the abstract significance of love and death are strongly present. The effect is predominantly decorative, though the intention to seduce remains.

There are no such distancing devices in the Marvell. 'Virginity' becomes like something kept in a bottle, and worms perform a parody of the sexual act, now rendered disgusting and absurd. The voice pauses with quiet but devastating emphasis on 'Quaint', and the line 'And into ashes all my Lust' completes itself almost redundantly, shut without its verb between a semi-colon and a full stop. Abstract and physical are fused in this resolution of opposites in the infinite of the grave. The energy of the erotic is far more present than in Carew but in a perverse form, acting through images that would disgust if not held taut by the tone. But the quality of the act of love is profoundly affected by the awareness that argued for it. By pressing the rhetoric of the genre to its logical conclusion Marvell has altered the delicate balance between the negative arguments, that life is brief, and the positive arguments, for the pleasures of fruition. The negative emotions of disgust and futility invade the act of love they argue for and painfully affect its quality. Marvell's has often been regarded as one of the greatest 'Carpe diem' poems ever written, but in an important sense it is the 'Carpe diem' poem to end the genre.

The problem is seen too acutely to allow the conventional solution, where the advice is to 'use your time' as though time will come and go independently, and during this time love will have taken place or not and will have been as pleasant as it always is. The promise of pleasures, like the arithmetic of kisses in Catullus's great poem, has been placed by the opening section as not the reward of seizing pleasures but the alternative, the fantasy that of its nature dissipates itself in the infinite. Marvell's solution does not renounce his logic, nor his insights into the quality of subjective time. But he is aware that subjective time at least can be affected, though only within terms of its own laws and logic. The pleasant fantasy of unlimited time leads to the painful contemplation of Eternity, but the process can be exactly reversed. The lovers can contract their strength and sweetness 'into one Ball', and through pain and aggression can 'tear (their) Pleasures with rough strife', in a miracle that blasphemously reverses Joshua's:

> Thus, though we cannot make our Sun
> Stand still, yet we will make him run.   ('CM': lines 45–46)

The logic is part of the poem's feeling. The very dryness of the terms and the inhuman rigour with which the logic unfolds are part of the experience, the logic an image of a remorseless causality whose main premise has been established before the poem begins. But paradoxically,

25

the thrust of the logic is to give supreme importance to passion, to make violent love a desperate necessity. The poet displays no simple wholeness of response, no blend or balance of intellect and feeling. A term like 'urbanity' which Leavis used so influentially of Marvell[43] misses this extremism, this lack of balance. Or to take another formulation, that of Eliot; the quality is, as he says, the 'quality of a civilization', not the remote and unproblematic civilization of Rome as Eliot thought, but the far from healthy civilization of which Marvell was a part, and which is continuous with our own.[44] And whatever Eliot meant when he called it 'not a personal quality', there is no useful sense in which the poem is not a major and profoundly personal achievement.

Chapter 2

IMAGES THAT LIVE

A paradigm according to Kuhn is ultimately a way of seeing. He means this in a literal sense, and in fact the work of Gestalt psychologists on perception contributed to the notion of paradigms.[1] Gestalt psychologists have shown that perception is not an automatic reflex act which passively records reality. It relies on visual habits, interpretative schemata, sets and expectations if it is to proceed effectively. At issue are what could be termed the paradigms of perception.

But it is obviously very difficult to study paradigms and paradigm changes at this level. Normally perception is taken for granted. We all naturally assume that everyone looking at the same scene sees exactly what we do. So in studying the past we cannot expect clear first-hand reports of paradigm-shifts or changes in modes of seeing. The most we could hope for would be occasional examples of confusion or incomprehension which suggest some cause. A small amount of carefully selected and tangential evidence has to go a long way: and even to have that needs a lot of luck.

With the near total lack of material on which to begin analysis, the images preserved in art and literature become an important source for habits of perception. Clearly, these images do not provide direct evidence of what people saw when they looked at the world. Picasso presumably did not see women refracted into cubist planes. Hilliard the Elizabethan miniaturist knew that people are more than three inches tall. But the images of art at least are fixed and available for analysis. The analysis cannot say much about the visual habits of everyday life, but it can attempt to arrive at the modes of perception behind the creation and appreciation of those images: the modes of perception defining the specific community for whom and by whom those images were created.

What I am suggesting here is that it may be illuminating to see the history of art in terms of paradigms. An account in these terms will at least allow the possibility of important connections being made with paradigms in other areas of thought. As with science, a period in art ('normal art') is normally dominated by a specific programme, which includes artistic aims and priorities, preferred subject matter and

27

characteristic techniques, all these often associated with the achievement of an exemplary individual. So certain major works as total images will carry the leading principles of the paradigm for the relevant community. The image will be the focus of a way of seeing and a way of creating, which if made explicit would be a theory of perception and imagination, an account of the mind and of the world which may challenge or confirm the accounts which are implicit in alternative paradigms.

Even if the history of art is seen in terms of paradigms there may still be no important connections with other paradigms. Kuhn suggests that in times of normal science particular communities and paradigms will remain distinct. Only in times of crisis and revolution do the barriers weaken. The histories of normal art, normal science and normal poetry may seem fully comprehensible in their own terms, but at times of rapid and revolutionary change in all of these fields, it becomes more obviously important to be able to see points of mutual contact and influence.

There was certainly a major change in arts forms over the seventeenth century, so fundamental as to suggest a change in modes of perception. It does not seem plausible to argue that paradigm change in art was a direct consequence of paradigm changes in logic and thought. There is no obviously Ramist art. Yet Ramist and anti-Ramist modes of thought would have been used to rationalize and explain the new modes of perception, and articulate the theories which were fed into new aesthetic programmes. In the rest of this chapter I want to suggest how the change in visual habits provided subject-matter for various forms of the Ramist paradigm, leading to new problems and new possibilities for a Ramist theory of the imagination. This will have important consequences for poetry, Marvell's included. But first it is essential to describe the changes in visual modes in their own terms, respecting the relative autonomy and fundamental nature of these changes.

(i) New modes of perception

Over the hundred years before 1660 English art altered course, accepting conventions and norms which can be categorized as Renaissance, to use a convenient short-hand.[2] This change went deeper than a change of fashion or taste. Renaissance art depends on specific visual habits as the basis of its illusionism. These habits have to be learnt and so totally assimilated as to seem natural before they become new ways of seeing.

This means to that to understand the change properly we need more than a study of the significant works of art painted in England. Such works were mostly painted by foreign artists, coming from different cultures, at different stages of development from the norm of the Italian

28

renaissance. We ourselves may understand the idiom of these works, and 'see' them properly, but there is no guarantee that this is how English artists or their public saw them. More reliable evidence comes from a more humble and indigenous art form, the engraving. Works by native artists for the home market survive in large numbers, covering the whole period. These engravers often used or adapted continental modes, which had been conceived according the norms of renaissance art. So we can superimpose these norms to see how far they apply, using apparent 'clumsiness' such as errors of perspective not as proof of poor craftsmanship but as a sign of different modes of perception. In these terms there is a significant though not invariable change in what these native artists were not able to learn or not interested in attempting. Over the period we can see England slowly, erratically, understanding the Renaissance.

The two equestrian engravings following serve to establish some general formulations.[3] Both are typical of their period and by artists of a comparable degree of competence. Cockson's horse is not drawn much less accurately than Marshall's, though its head is articulated with the body less naturally, and the rear off-leg reveals even greater difficulties with foreshortening. The differences do not stay at the level of technique. The two pictures work in a fundamentally different way. Both artists represent their subject as a great military leader. Marshall conveys this through a picture that shows Fairfax engaging in some kind of military and heroic activity. This picture could be regarded as representing a single image viewed from a single point of view in space and time. However, Howard of Effingham's horse rears against the background of something intermediate between a map and a scene. The compatibility of the two modes of representation is significant. The dates, 1588 near the horse's right fore-leg and 1596 just above his tail, show that the scene covers at least eight years in time, which reinforces the sense that no illusion of a single particular time is intended.

But Cockson has some naturalistic features. We have noticed the attempted foreshortening. The ships also diminish in size as they approach the horizon, and indicate the increasing distance as effectively as the blocks of soldiers do in Marshall's picture. But there is an interesting asymmetry in Cockson's space. The ships on the left are consistently larger than those which are on the right on the same horizontal, and therefore appear to be at the same distance. If this were taken as an accurate indication of size the ships on the left would swamp the island on the right. Size and scale are not of crucial importance in this linear style. Otherwise the contrast between ships and islands would seem obtrusive, which it is not. But the fact that the ships in each of the two engagements are consistently related to each other but not to the ships in the other engagement, on the other side of the horse, suggests another

30

William Marshall: Sir Thomas Fairfax

feature of the way the picture must have been looked at. Ship-size causes trouble if the eye takes in all the ships together and compares them. The clutter of the picture, however, gives no encouragement to this way of looking at the ships, and it is clearly the wrong way to respond. The correct method is to look at each engagement entirely separately, so that they do not interfere with each other. Visually they are independent, related only intellectually through their common reference to Nottingham. The whole picture is similarly composed. The optimum way to view it would be with the eye focusing sharply on it one area at a time, with virtually no use of peripheral vision. The centre of each such area soon becomes clear enough; for instance, the two dates, the shield, and the two rectangular legends. Other difficulties disappear if the plate is viewed in this way. If for instance the eye fixates at the centre of the circle formed by the horse's arched neck and its bridle, the problem of the articulation of the head to the body no longer obtrudes. Moreover, the inexplicable growth of mane apparently out of the side of the horse's face becomes merely the border of another fixation, as does the eccentrically-sited top-knot. Most of these areas are of roughly the same size. If the picture was viewed through a disc 8×5 cm. cut out of a plate of smoked glass, moving from area to area either randomly or from left to right as for a book, only the central figures of Nottingham would demand a slightly larger disc. Assuming that Cockson was regarded as a reasonably competent artist, this must be close to how the average Elizabethan would have responded to the picture.

Cockson's picture also communicates more information than Marshall's. All this could be communicated by words, and in fact much of it is. The picture is something of a visual code, designed to be read as much as looked at. Visually it oscillates between picture and diagram, and its function is both to represent and inform. Marshall has only a title rather than a text, and the pictorial is beginning to have some autonomy from the literary. The kind of meaning he can convey comes to be slightly different. He is restricted to a representation of a possible physical reality and what this can imply.

A contrast of this kind could be repeated in analysis after analysis. The two pictures following are less typical but illustrate the difference more strikingly. Van den Keere is not wholly a native artist, as his name implies; he came to England at the age of twelve.[4] In fact the interest of his work is its transitional character. Consider his two figures. They seem solid and naturalistic enough compared to Cockson's figure. However, the slab on which each stands disappears to a different vanishing point, as though the eye of the observer were directly opposite both. Moreover, beneath these slabs the columns lead into a central vanishing point, which makes three separate and incompatible spatial worlds within the one

32

Pieter van den Keere: title to Norden, *Speculum Britanniae* Part I, 1593

frame. As with Cockson, the difficulties are resolved if the eye concentrates with isolating attention on each centre of interest, which is more precisely located than for Cockson by the lines of perspective. Where this solution merely makes Cockson's picture more satisfactory, it is essential

33

for Van den Keere's to save it from absurdity. The difficulty does not arise with Glover, whose frontispiece represents a possible even if not highly functional single spatial context. Van den Keere's is an unusual case, where the incompatibility of the two modes of perception reveals itself by their coexistence in the one work. The effect, however, is an interesting one. A surrealist would have intended it. Van den Keere seems innocent of any such intention, but the quality leads to two observations. It is clear that no illusions relying on scale or perspective could work for someone for whom there is nothing wrong with this frontispiece. Conversely, however, someone sensitive to the cues of perspective and scale could, with a little perversity, create a bizarre world out of pictures like Cockson's, with ships nearly as big as islands, and a giant horse towering over trees no bigger than its hoof.

Van den Keere's figures are as naturalistic as Marshall's, but on closer inspection they work more like Cockson's, encoding a meaning that could be expressed in words. He indicates what he has to say about the figures through the equipment he suspends above their heads. Any naturalistic detail in these beyond what is strictly necessary for recognition adds nothing to the significance of the picture, and corresponds essentially to elaborate penmanship. His superior draughtsmanship merely gave him an advantage in stylishness over his rougher English competitors. Even his figures, for all their three-dimensionality, are static and inexpressive. They could as well be statues. The artist's skill has not gone into suggesting the difference in texture between the flesh, the clothes and the architecture. Glover, however, keeps the human distinct from masonry, and recreates something of the texture of the clothes. Moreover, his main means of conveying meaning is through images that convey the reality of the objects they represent. The point of the plate is the antipathy of the French and the Spaniard, so they act this out in dramatic terms. Accuracy of details accordingly can contribute to his meaning. In the faces minute details of expression can be significant of the national character or stereotype. Even the style of clothing can help define characteristics. The meaning of each figure is still as general; a Frenchman is hardly less generic than an English map-maker. The means of conveying this general figure have, however, changed. Glover even more than Marshall works with a particular used as a representative, recreated as a physical object for the senses to apprehend, where Van den Keere still relies more on an accumulation of particulars chosen for a verbal meaning rather than for their suggestive qualities.

A similar line of development underlies other art forms of the period. The major Elizabethan form was the miniature, whose greatest exponent was Nicholas Hilliard. Hilliard's miniatures are only slightly smaller on average than later miniatures, but his pictures tend to be more concen-

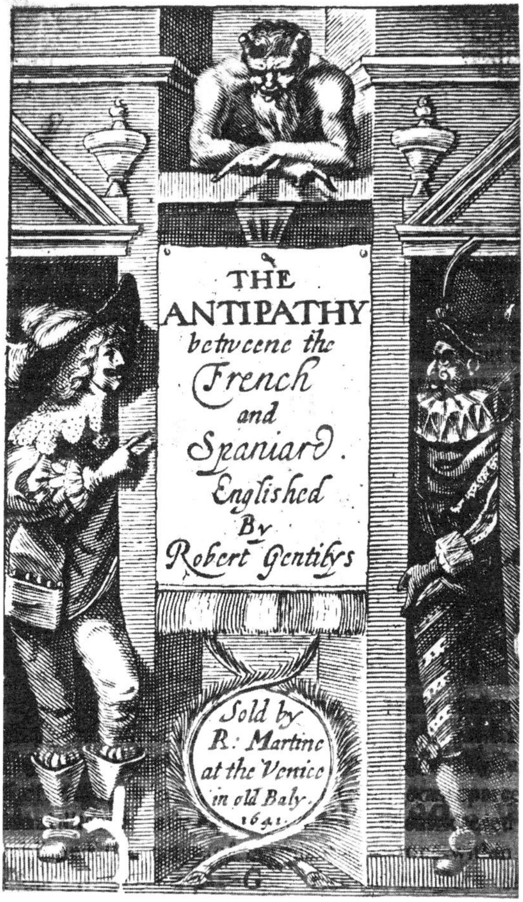
THE
ANTIPATHY
betweene the
French
and
Spaniard.
Englished
By
Robert Gentilys
Sold by
R: Martine
at the Venice
in old Baly.
1641.
G

G. Glover: title to *The Antipathy betweene the French and Spaniard* by R. Gentilys, 1641

trated, the detail more intricate, the patterns more complex, images of a world not just parts of a world. The average Hilliard is an oval disc of approximately the same size as the figures in Van den Keere, or the areas of coherence in the Cockson. It is as though Hilliard has put a frame round the Elizabethan unit of perception. Within this the trained eye could move easily and appreciate patterns of great precision and complexity. Later artists, like Samuel Cooper, the major miniaturist of the mid seventeenth century, altered the whole scale. Working on a slightly larger card, Cooper preferred to show just head and shoulders, where Hilliard gave the whole upper body, so that a Cooper head is three or four times larger than a Hilliard, and he is presenting only the faithful image of a part, not a compressed image of a whole. But with the miniature form no longer so organically related to primary visual modes, it was bound to become a less important and definitive form. The same point about scale can be repeated with other art forms. The intricate narrative patterns of Elizabethan tapestries give way to the monumental compositions of the Mortlake tapestries of the 1630s. Elizabethan portraits, designed to be read as well as looked at, gave way to the portraits of Van Dyke, Dobson and finally Lely, images of a single artificial but physically possible scene, to be taken in at a single glance. Works on the scale of Rubens' ceiling for Inigo Jones' Banqueting Hall have no parallel in native Elizabethan art. The overall pattern that emerges is consistent and significant, even though of course the change is not uniform in every form or for every level of society. Different forms at certain times are more advanced, and become agents of change rather than mere reflections. Even in these, the artists were probably not conscious that they were furthering a revolution in visual modes. They no doubt thought they were simply doing the same thing as their quaint predecessors, but much better. Such invisibility is the characteristic seal on the success of a perceptual revolution.

(ii) The Emblem tradition

To bring this topic closer to Marvell, poetry and the Ramist paradigm, it is useful to turn to Emblem books. Marvell's own interest in this genre is well known.[5] Two books in particular have been identified as probable sources for images he used: Herman Hugo's 'Pia Desideria' of 1624, and Henry Hawkins' 'Partheneia Sacra' of 1633.[6] This demonstrable connection is especially valuable because of the nature of Emblem books, in particular their hybrid status between visual and verbal. Emblems typically consisted of a motto plus illustration, often with explicatory verse or prose attached. That meant they often involved a multiple process of translation, from verbal to visual and back to verbal. They are an ideal form in which to trace continuities and discontinuities between the images of art and poetry.

The history of the form in seventeenth century England shows two interesting developments.[7] One concerns artistic modes. Elizabethan art, where details work semantically as well as visually, was well suited to emblem-forms. The affinity is such that Elizabethan art in general is often loosely referred to as 'emblematic'. The shift in perceptual modes could

Vtinam saperent et intelligerent ac nouißima
prouiderent ! Deuteron . 32.

14.

H. Hugo: Emblem 14, Book I, from *Pia Desideria*, 1624

be expected to destroy the equilibrium between visual and verbal which constituted the genre. Something like this seems to have happened over the seventeenth century, as we will see. Another development which affected the genre was its appropriation to religious uses, mainly by Catholic writers. This development made the form problematic for Protestants, provoking attempts to comprehend, transform or neutralize it. By studying these attempts we can hope to see basic paradigms of thought as they were deployed in the area of perception and art.

Herman Hugo's 'Pia Desideria' was at the centre of both developments of the emblem tradition. His book was immensely popular, and went through many editions over the century. Marvell was not his only reader. The plates used by Hugo were high quality productions employing the new visual modes. The book as a whole was designed as an aid to meditation, which was a distinctively Catholic form of activity.[8] The two developments were complementary. Ways of seeing are ways of

37

experiencing, and these are bound up with attitudes to reason and emotion, intellect and sense, or, to use seventeenth century terms, soul and body. The Marvell poem in which the passage from Hugo appears is, significantly, 'Dialogue between the Soul and Body'. Marvell there places Hugo in the context of a debate about the problems of a dualistic conception of the mind.

We can see what was involved in Hugo's use of emblems by contrasting him with Francis Quarles. Quarles was the English Hugo. His book of emblems was immensely popular, the definitive assimilation of Hugo to the English Protestant mind. Quarles re-used Hugo's plates as the basis of three of the five books that made up his major work, 'Emblems' of 1634. Take the two plates by Quarles and Hugo. Hugo has many details that work semantically, as in traditional emblems. Death is represented by a skeleton not a putrifying corpse, and it holds a sword and a palm. But even so the sensuous qualities of the picture are integral to its intended effect. The contrast between the light and the dark is used for its emotional and symbolic effect, and the barred shadows that lead to the final vision may be meant to suggest skeletal ribs. The perspective gives both distance and centrality to the figure of the skeleton. The sensory evocativeness consistently works to produce an emotional response which would intensify the meditative experience. The meditations following each plate are similarly effusions rather than lessons, organized into three books entitled respectively 'tears', 'sighs', and 'ejaculations'.

Hugo's plate was redone for Quarles' edition, clearly under the author's direction, by William Marshall or William Simpson.[9] The light effects are not so prominent and are no longer functional, either to make contrasts between light and dark or even to give solidity and roundness to the trees. The figure of death is slightly enlarged, in keeping with its significance but necessarily giving less sense of distance. The plant whose skeletal shape tends towards the sun (and death) in Hugo has been removed to make way for a figure who works in a more simply emblematic way. This is Flesh, in a topless dress but rather unseductive, with explanatory appurtenance in her hand. In Quarles' accompanying poems she engages in an increasingly unsuccessful debate with the Spirit. Neither the prism nor the optic tube are created as experiences. The picture is just a visual code, which invites only a series of statements. Hugo's has much that is emblematic like this, but he also has elements which invite a more total response, and the content of his picture for meditative purposes would be less strictly limited, since it does not consist so completely of a set of statements that make the contemplator independent of the picture once he has deciphered them. Quarles' emblem in comparison is unproblematic but inert. That was how Protestant England preferred its emblems to be.

Oh that they were wife, then they would
vnderstand this; they would consider
their latter end.Deeteron 32 . I P...ne scul

F. Quarles: Emblem XIV, Book III, from *Emblems*, 1634

Qualities similar to Hugo's can be seen in the other emblem book that
has left traces in Marvell's work, Henry Hawkins' 'Partheneia Sacra'.[10]
Hawkins displays a sophisticated knowledge of the emblem form. The
work consists of a series of meditations on various things most of which
can be found in or seen from a garden. Each object was ultimately
revealed to be an emblem for the Virgin. The dualism latent in the
emblem form, between abstract and concrete, picture and meaning, is
associated with the more fundamental dualism of spirit and matter by the
form of a religious emblem. Hawkins' emblems always have a spiritual
meaning, embodied in highly physical descriptions. Consider this part of
his meditation on a drop of dew:

> . . . a little drop of Deaw falling from the heavens, for example, on the
> Flower de luce, would seeme, perharps to you but a little round point of water,
> and a meer graine of Cristal, but if the Sun do but shine upon it, Ah! what a

39

miracle of beautie it is? While of the one side it wil looke like an Orient pearl, and being turnd some other way, becomes a glowing Carbuncle, then a Saphir, and after an Emerald, and so an Amethist, and al enclosed in a nothing, or a litle glasse of al the greatest beauties of the world, that seeme to be engraved therein.[11]

Hawkins' dew falls, as though accidentally, on a lily, an emblem for purity and of course for the Virgin. There is an attractive sensuousness about Hawkins' description as he tries to evoke the physical reality of the drop of dew in front of him. The effects of the light and the sense of wonder are an intrinsic part of his meditation. The comparisons with the jewels, however, take him away from the imagined drop of dew, which he treats as though it were solid. So he turns it 'some other way', and it changes colour as though it had been shifted from its site in the lily onto backgrounds of different colours. The effect at this point appears to be merely decorative.

This passage is reminiscent of Marvell's 'On a drop of Dew'. In some respects Marvell's poem is doing the same thing but better. He is less effusive but more precise in his observation, and details more consistently have a spiritual as well as a physical meaning. For instance, the light symbolism of: 'Dark beneath, but bright above' (line 31) has the obvious significance as an emblem, but also is visually precise. It records the minute gradations of colour which painters use to give the effect of translucence to a liquid on a coloured background. The balance of sensuous precision and spiritual significance of this line is a distinctive quality of Marvell's poem, and central to its theme. The opening of the Latin version of this poem, 'Ros', suggests the simultaneous difference and similarity of the Rose and the Dew:

> Cernis ut Eoi descendat Gemmula Roris,
> Inque Rosas roseo transfluat orta sinu.[12]
> (See how a little jewel of Orient dew descends
> And, sprung from the rosy breast of Dawn, flows onto the roses)

The dew is the soul and the Rose the world or the flesh, yet the dawn from whose bosom the dew is shed is 'rosy'. The two words 'Rosas roseo' are juxtaposed to make the connection unmistakable. The very sound of the Latin word for dew, 'Ros', suggests the connection with roses. The point which is conveyed through an intricate verbal texture in the Latin is transformed into a structural principle in the English. The physical drop of dew is described in terms appropriate to a soul in the first half of the poem, while the description of the soul in the second half evokes the drop of dew even more vividly than when the dew was being described. The poem apparently concentrates on the dew/soul and its longing to be separate. The resistance and attraction of the rose/body is only

40

occasionally present, but the structure is exactly poised between the physical embodiment and the spiritual significance, each of which is expressed in terms of the other. The two parts of an emblem, picture and moral, become an image for the more fundamental dualism of soul and body, but the antithesis between the two is denied by the very process by which it is asserted.

Marvell's poem clearly grew out of a profound acquaintance with Hawkins' kind of emblem. Marvell as a youth flirted with Catholicism and was only restored to godliness by his father, according to a well-attested story.[13] This poem is obviously the product of his maturity. The attraction of Catholicism must have been deeper and more lasting than is normally supposed. Marvell, however, is more conscious of dualities than the two Catholics, while at the same time being more concerned to overcome them. Catholic meditations typically did not raise doctrinal difficulties, but though this concern makes Marvell's meditation more philosophical or at least less simply pious, it involves no loss in intensity of the meditative experience. The poem is held between the poles of image and meaning, spirit and matter, focusing the identity and separation in images which reverberate inexhaustibly:

So the Soul, that Drop, that Ray
Of the clear Fountain of Eternal Day   (lines 19–20)

The lines fuse light and water into an image for purity and clarity that still remains unobtrusively beyond the imaginable. The drop of dew is transfused with light, and light and day are embodied and made visible in the transparency of water. The crossing of the attributes in a single image leads to an effect analogous to that of a hall of mirrors; water is defined as light, which is defined as water, which is defined as light, which is defined as water . . . The precision with which the drop of dew has been recreated tempts the mind to create the effect too, till the spherical shape nearly dissolves in a streak of light. The simultaneous refinement and defeat of the senses becomes an experience of the spiritual.

Hugo and the baroque engravers took one way with emblems to adapt them to newer modes of vision, but examples of the older kind of emblem naturally still survived, fixed in ink on paper. We could expect these to look quaint or even absurd to men of the newer modes who bothered to look at them. There are some indications that this in fact happened. Browne, for instance, in his popular 'Pseudodoxia Epidemica' of 1646, tries to expose the entymological and ornithological inaccuracies of certain common emblems, such as grasshoppers and pelicans.[14] The puritan poet George Wither indicates a similar kind of reaction in some lines he wrote in a book of emblems published in 1635. For this work he had used plates from an earlier book of emblems, excellently engraved

41

pictures in the naturalistic mode which, however, served simple emblematic purposes. This combination, realism of detail in an emblematic composition, is just the kind to emphasize the conflict of the modes. Wither, confronted with a typical multi-handed figure expressing 'Concord', commences with irritation:

> An Emblem's meaning, here, I ought to conster;
> And, this doth rather fashion out a Monster,
> Then forme an Hieroglyphicke: But, I had
> These Figures (as you see them) ready made
> By others; and, I meane to morallize
> Their fancies; not to mend what they devize.[15]

Such a reaction is of course quite opposite to the intention of the emblem. But Wither's lines clearly come from a sense that the way to respond to emblems is quite different from the normal response to pictures, and that absurd effects can come from the juxtaposition of the two. One needs to 'conster' emblems, construe their meanings as one would a Latin text. They work like language, and a foreign language at that.

Hawkins' book could give rise to a similar sense of disparate modes, for along with his evocative prose went emblems of the older kind. Consider the picture 'Platforme of the Garden', which contains within one frame all the emblems later meditated on at such length in the rest of the work. The quality of the drawing does not tempt the observer to see the scene as though it were before his eyes, as Hawkins' language tries to do, but if it were taken in this way the rose near the castle would be nearly 20 feet high, and the bee alongside it would be the size of a small plane. The meditation, of course, would be ruined by the tactic. But Marvell deliberately exploits an effect of this kind in his famous image of the grasshoppers:

> And now to the Abbyss I pass
> Of that unfathomable Grass,
> Where Men like Grashoppers appear,
> But Grashoppers are Gyants there:
> They, in there squeking Laugh contemn
> Us as we walk more low then them:
> And, from the Precipices tall
> Of the green spir's, to us do call.   ('AH' stanza XLVII)

At one level the image works emblematically, the grasshoppers standing for a political type. But the emblematic mode is itself the source of a disturbing visual experience that enacts the inversion of values represented by the Levellers' aims. The bizarre and frightening vision of the towering grasshoppers, their insect-noises amplified to a wordless minimally human expression of contempt, is created by a careful attention to comparative scale.

42

H. Hawkins: 'The Platforme of the Garden', 1633

In a real sense it is an image from science fiction, as we can see by comparing it with Hooke's engraving of a louse from his 'Micrographia' of 1665, one of the most significant scientific works of its age.[16] Marvell was clearly impressed by this particular picture, and refers to it in the opening section of his 'Last Instructions to a Painter' of 1667:

> With Hook then, through the microscope, take aim
> Where, like the new Controller, all men laugh
> To see a tall Lowse brandish the white Staff.[17]

Hooke showed his Louse gripping a hair to indicate the comparative sizes. Marvell indicates what must have been part of the virtuosi's reaction to Hooke's plate, amusement, but as in the grasshopper image of the earlier poem, he exploits the inversion of scale both ways. He professes to laugh but the poem is not light-hearted in its attack on corruption in Court and Parliament. The image of this louse, animated and placed in the speaker's chair, is as disturbing as it is funny. Hooke's original plate folded out to a drawing nearly two feet long. The size was clearly intended to astonish, as well as to display the anatomical features of the louse. Marvell's grasshopper may have sprung from some Elizabethan emblem book, but its multiple eyes stare out at the visual world of the new science and the new art.

Marvell's imagery represents an achievement of remarkable originality. Modern criticism, put off course by too much talk of wit and urbanity, has not come to terms with this equally distinctive and less easily explained quality of his poetry. The wit and urbanity are shared with others in the age, but no one else's images have the kind of penetration and sheer memorableness that Marvell so often achieves. Take his description of the Fawn, in 'The Nymph Complaining':

> Upon the Roses it would feed,
> Until its Lips ev'n seem'd to bleed;
> And then to me 'twould boldly trip,
> And print those Roses on my Lip.
> But all its chief delight was still
> On Roses thus its self to fill:
> And its pure virgin Limbs to fold
> In whitest sheets of Lillies cold.
> Had it liv'd long, it would have been
> Lillies without, Roses within.[18]

The last couplet has the unique potency of a great Marvellian image. Characteristically it is not an isolated flash of brilliance but grows out of its context in the poem. The flowers are as real as they are significant. They are in the first place the flowers the animal sleeps in and eats. But they have emblematic meanings as well, which are indicated and reinforced by the verse itself. As in 'Drop of Dew' the roses stand for a

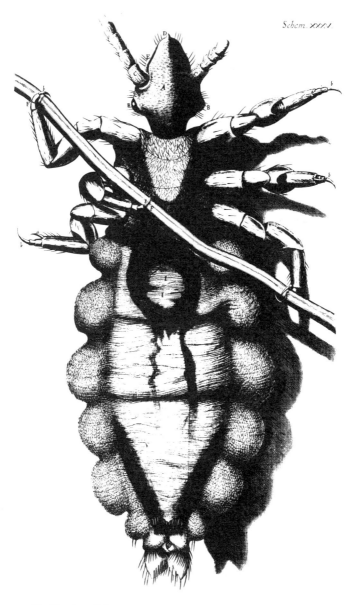

R. Hooke: Schema XXXV from *Micrographia*, 1665

45

kind of passion, and the lilies as in Hawkins stand for purity. The Nymph says that the roses are the Fawn's 'chief delight', while the lilies clothe 'its pure virgin limbs'. But the startling image of the bleeding lips and the ominous though fragrant coolness of the lilies, so reminiscent of a winding sheet, help to define the nature of this passion and this purity through the quality of the sensation. All this is focused in the final image, which begins to work in the mind by seeming too simple to be true, and so comes to draw into itself the equivocally sensuous definitions of the preceding twenty lines. The image repays a kind of attention akin to meditation.

Something of a context for Marvell's achievement can be given through a contrast between Spenser and Dryden, poets central for their respective ages. Spenser's Una, or Truth, is accompanied by an ass of the same colour as the Nymph's Fawn, perhaps with a similar significance:

> A lovelie Ladie rode him faire beside,
> Upon a lowly Asse more white then snow,
> Yet she much whiter, but the same did hide
> Under a vele, that whimpled was full low,
> And over all a black stole she did throw,
> As one that inly mourned: so was she sad,
> And heavie sat upon her palfrey slow:
> Seemed in heart some hidden care she had,
> And by her in a line a milkewhite lamb she lad.   ('Faerie Queene' I.i.2)

Dryden commences 'The Hind and the Panther' with an allegorical Hind who is probably a hybrid descendant of Una's ass:

> A milk-white Hind, immortal and unchang'd,
> Fed on the lawns, and in the forests rang'd;
> Without unspotted, innocent within,
> She fear'd no danger, for she knew no sin.   (lines 1–4)

The kinship of the Spenser with emblematic modes hardly needs pointing out. The ass's emblematic significance is indicated specifically by 'lowlie', while the significance of its colour is too obvious to need such a gloss. The stole requires comment. Black could indicate evil, so Spenser explains what it represents here, in relation to Una's essential purity. The stanza finishes with a purely emblematic animal, the notorious vanishing lamb, which ceases to exist once its emblematic function has been fulfilled.

As a sensuous experience this passage recalls not a physical reality but an art form, one much richer than an emblem book but working in the same way. The response to the entities as objects is minimal and contributes little that has not already been encoded into their significance. The snow, for instance, is compared to the ass and the lady for whiteness, but is not cold like Marvell's lilies, and the contrast of colours of the black and the white has some decorative effect, but is not part of the meaning of the picture as is the startling effect of the red on white in Marvell. But though the image as a physical entity contributes nothing to the meaning and lacks an independent existence, Spenser shows no irritation at the poet's duty to provide pictures. The repetition of whiteness, for instance, hardly adds to the moral meaning, but weaves in to the decorative effect of the 'w' sounds. The l's in 'lowly' follow those of 'Lovelie Ladie' of the previous line to make the quality of the words float together so that lowliness seems a kind of loveliness. The alliteration of the 'h's' in lines 7 and 8 is like a repeated sigh reinforcing the significance of the stole. The movement to this mood, from the whiteness and purity through the 'yet' and the 'but' is surprisingly swift. There is no single point, no image or line which concentrates the conflicting pressures of meaning or mood as there was in the Marvell. The pictures themselves are static but they are indeterminately located in time within the frame of the stanza, somewhat like the eight year span of the Cockson plate. The sensuous qualities are disembodied but constitute their own reality, which has its own laws and reasons. As a result there is something of a dissociation between the shifting mood and the ostensible emblematic meaning.

Dryden is clearly unhappy with the allegorical mode in general. The emblematic details are few, and the correspondence cannot be trusted to do its work. Since the Hind is unspotted on the outside, she is naturally going to be unspotted, or innocent, within. Both Spenser and Marvell take the relation of appearance to significance for granted, and use the relationship of inner to outer to express some further relationship. Dryden has to use it to give instructions on how to read emblematic verse. The outside is the physical appearance and the inside the significance. This sets up a dualism between object and meaning that does not arise in Spenser's two-dimensional world. So Dryden's Hind is milk-white, like Spenser's lamb and for similar reasons, but in the second line it does what Spenser's animals never do: it eats non-significantly. Where Spenser's lamb is physically irrelevant, Dryden's Hind has an irrelevant physicality.

But though the Hind is autonomously physical, it is not sensuously evoked. This is a typical feature of Dryden's verse. His preferred manner is to assemble a series of antithetical judgments which lean against each other within a line of verse, referring to a physical entity that remains outside the poem. This allows him his characteristic firmness of purpose and density of meaning, as he pursues his argument without the unassimilable intrusion of the physical. The strategy conceals the dualism between object and significance in his work by largely omitting the world of objects from the body of the poetry. Marvell handles a similar dualism

47

by giving both halves almost equal weighting within the poem, attempting to fuse the two into a single experience. So it would be a mistake to regard Marvell's imagistic quality as transitional in any limiting sense, although in fact his poem was written after Spenser's and before Dryden's. Spenserian modes were clearly more available and important for Marvell than for Dryden, but as a source of solutions to problems he shared with Dryden. Spenser's achievement was paradigmatic for his contemporaries. Marvell's and Dryden's work can be seen as competitors for a later community. It was undoubtedly Dryden's achievement that was accepted by his fellow poets as paradigmatic, his solution the one they found most congenial and imitable. The merits of Marvell's solution would only begin to be appreciated as the limitations of Dryden's became more evident.

(iii) Ramism and Imagination

If a poet's understanding of mind and imagination is definitively transmitted through the images he creates, then contemporary accounts of imagery ought to be an important repository of practical theories of the imagination. However, sixteenth century discussions of imagery are mostly disappointing. Rhetoric texts had a section on figures of speech, but this was normally an inventory of types. Metaphor was discussed, but briefly and mechanically. Ramist rhetorics are particularly uninformative.[19] This is partly because Ramists transferred 'Invention', the finding of content, to the logic, which left imagery with a merely decorative function. How could this be the age that produced Spenser and Shakespeare and Donne?

Frances Yates,[20] however, has drawn attention to a section of the conventional rhetoric texts which describes images of a more curious kind. These text books normally included a description of the classical art of memory. This art was designed to help a speaker remember details of his argument. Using its techniques he would find images to recall each detail to be remembered, and preserve the order of the details by imagining these images arranged around a well-known room or building or other environment with sufficient 'places' to contain them. The quality of the images recommended by the method can be seen from this description, taken from Wilson's influential traditional Rhetoric:

> The whiche Images muste be sette forthe as thoughe they were stirring, yea they must be sometimes made raumping, and last of all, they must be made of thinges notable, such as maye cause earnest impression of thinges in our mind. As a notable evill favoured man, or a monstrous horse . . .[21]

Such images were essentially private. This meant that they could be interesting and bizarre, without affecting the form or content of the actual

48

language used. The privacy released the maker of images from all external censorship. The process can be seen clearly in the quaint art of memory of Peter of Ravenna. Peter, a friar, used 'Junipere pistorien or of Pise which I loved greatly' to assist his memory. He gives this as an example of how he tries to member the details of a law case:

And set for the question the fayre Junipera beatynge her mayde. And for the consyderation I set a preste consecratynge the hooste. And for Penaunce I set Junipera shryving her to me of her lyght synnes . . .[22]

Sacred and erotic are mingled indiscriminately here in a fantasy which includes even a hint of pleasant sadism. In the creation of the image there is no distinction between speaker and hearer, who are the same, or between Reason and the irrational, both of which are used in an ad hoc fashion to make the image memorable. But Peter would obviously take good care not to let any details from the mnemonic technique enliven the court case he is arguing. Wilson is rather uneasy about the whole process:

thoughe it seme straunge and folyshe to them that know it not, yet the learned have taken this waye,[23]

he writes apologetically, but shortly afterwards mentions Erasmus's objections to the practice.[24] He clearly would not like his images to 'raump' in public. Images from the art of memory would often have been too memorable to be used.

But not all mnemonic images would have been of this extraordinary kind. The aim was practical, to remember details, not to indulge oneself. The striking or emotionally charged details that made the image memorable remained external to the significance of the item to be remembered. This would give value to conventionality in the actual image. Too great a novelty in the image might add to the burden on the memory. So, on the recommendation of another writer on the subject, knowledge should be represented by a book, vertue by a crown of laurel, Justice by a balance or a sword, and so on.[25] The kinship with emblematic visual forms is obvious. In both, the verbal meaning is primary, the image or picture only a visual code. Emblematic pictures must often have been used for mnemonic purposes, but no longer subject to limitations of the engravers' art they could be more sensitive to the irrational movements of the mind, exposed to a deeper level of the mind than usually went into the creation of images in Elizabethan poetry or art. If anyone had written them down the images could have had something of the shifting quality of Spenser's emblematic imagery.

But rhetorical theory over the period tended to eliminate the art of memory, not extend its range of application. Wilson's uneasiness was an accurate pointer, and the triumphant Ramist method was designed among other things to subsume the traditional art of memory. But 1583 saw the publication in England of an extremely interesting development of the imagistic potentialities of the traditional arts of memory, the 'de Umbra', ostensibly by Alexander Dickson but probably embodying the ideas of the Italian philosopher Giordano Bruno, who was in England at this time.[26] The ideas themselves are interesting enough, but a study of the work is given more general significance by an attack promptly made on it by a Cambridge Ramist, whose initials, G.P., probably stand for William Perkins, the father of the Puritan sermon.[27] Again an inconclusive debate illuminates the leading principles of a paradigm more precisely than a direct statement could; no other work so vividly reveals the simple Ramist assumptions about images and the action of the mind that creates them.

The Brunesque art of memory grew out of the traditional arts of memory and like them employs striking images. Dickson calls the process 'animation' and describes it as follows:

> Tum facta acria, & circumstantias insignes, superlatio praestet. Non sit autem a natura, neque forte temere, sed ex voluntatis praescripto judicatio. Tum vero quae fient, impulsum & affectus vehementes prae se ferunt . . . Hoc est animare; hoc est quod cogitatione perficitur, sic enim informata cogitatio, materiam deserens atque tempus, umbrarum illa quidem ideas & rationes arripit, in ipsam intelligentiam pro facultate propensa. Ac cum omnis solertia admiranda est; tum ea praesertim, quae efficit, ut inanima quae sunt, quasi vivere & spirare videantur.[28]

> (Then hyperbole must set forth notable details and things made sharp and piercing. Let the source of these be neither nature nor chance, but a judgment taken from the decision of the will. Force and powerful feeling manifest themselves in images so made . . . This is animation; this is what is perfected by reflection: for in this way trained reflection detaches itself from matter and time, and snatches up the ideas and reasons of the shadows/images, propelling them into the intelligence itself as far as it can. Skill is always admirable, but especially here, where things inanimate seem almost to live and breathe).

The end products seem similar, Wilson's 'stirring' and 'raumping' images, and Dickson's that almost seem to live and breathe, but the energies behind Dickson's are more fundamental and more fully understood. The difference centres in the role played by 'cogitatio'. Dickson's curious form of words, 'ex voluntatis praescripto judicatio', (literally 'a judgment out of the prescription of the will') implies that the judgment is derived from the will, which reverses the normal subordination of will to reason, and does not sharply distinguish the two functions. Corresponding to this, the images have an independent rational content. The word he normally uses for images, 'umbra', (literally a shadow) relates images to the Platonic distinction between mind and matter, but these 'umbrae' embody their own ideas or meaning. So the things to be remembered by this art are remembered through images that have a significance of their own. Unlike the usual images of the art of memory, which have only as much meaning as has been coded into them, Dickson's images could be more richly significant than either image or idea on its own. The 'cogitatio' is not merely cerebral either, but like the traditional arts of memory it releases emotional energies, 'impulsum & affectus vehementes.' Bruno describes the kind of activity of the mind the procedure involved both more precisely and more suggestively than his disciple. He writes of the 'receptable of the forms':

est subjectum formarum phantasiabilium, apponibilium, & remobilium, vagantium, & discurrentium ad libitum operantis fantasiae, & cogitivae.[29]

(It is the subject or container of imaginable, attachable and removeable forms that wander and stray at the will of the working and reflective fancy).

Reflection and imagination fuse in a single operative power that is the source of the movement of the images. A mind creating in this way would be allowing the play of its deepest desires without simply indulging in them like Peter of Ravenna. The images it would create need not be freaks like Wilson's 'monstrous horse', performing in the side-show of the memory but not to be exposed to the light of prosaic day. The split between private image and public memorandum is not so marked. The imagistic quality is more subtly remarkable, a particular kind of hyperbole whose aim is to make details penetrative, not just vaguely marvellous or extraordinary.

G.P. did not find this account either interesting or suggestive. The form of his attack was dictated by his Ramist assumptions, with revealing consequences. He summarizes Dickson's argument in a typical Ramist dichotomous table. Interestingly, the tabular form works very well, following Dickson's order almost exactly, and so it is probably the way Dickson organized the work himself.[30] But according to G.P.'s Ramism, the treatise should not have been written at all, in any form:

Logica inventio tradit doctrinam tam inveniendi umbram & imaginem, quam eruendi argumenti; eadem enim ratione & argumenta & umbrae rerum exquiruntur. Hic itaque peccatur in legem justitiae & sapientiae.[31]

(Logical invention gives instructions as much for finding out shadows and images as for educing arguments; for both arguments and shadows are sought for by following the same rule. Here then is a fault against the law of justice and wisdom).

The law of justice could have distinguished between arguments and images to allow a separate art of the memory, but the powerful synthesising tendency of simple Ramism has subsumed images into arguments. The law of justice then has the opposite effect, insisting on homogeneity within the single category. The law of wisdom, that the more general is prior, then gives an entirely logical quality to this whole. The result is that the logic has eliminated imagination.

The Brunesque art should not be contrasted too absolutely with the simple Ramist view. Prior to the last step, G.P.'s 'logical invention' could have become something like the Brunesque 'cogitatio'. Both are a single faculty concerned equally with images and ideas, combining the functions of Reason and Imagination. The law of justice could not allow both to coexist in a single category, but one possible development of the Ramist paradigm was to abate the rigour of the law of justice. This would make possible concepts such as a rational imagination, or 'fantasia cogitiva', where both powers are distinct but act inseparably. A potential development of G.P.'s form of simple Ramism could have looked similar to the Brunesque view of the mind. Dickson might have taken this route. So, we shall see, might Marvell.

In his critique, G.P. followed the typical Ramist practice of distinguishing style from content. His preface dealt with Dickson's style, criticizing it, justly enough, for needless obscurity and awkwardness of expression. But when he deals with the content in another section he paraphrases Dickson's argument, as though the uncouth style were entirely separable from its meaning. His paraphrases accordingly reveal the limits of what he could suppose Dickson might mean, which again helps to define his own paradigm. For instances, he summarizes the passage already quoted, on animation, as follows:

> Animatio nihil aliud est quam ratio quaedam efficiendi imagines vivas & actuosas. Hoc autem fiet, si imagini tribuemus facta aeria [sic], & circumstantias insignes: Si animatio non naturalis vel temeraria, sed cum judicio & voluntate fiat: Si faciamus imaginem excitare affectus, iram, odium . . . &c.[32]
>
> (Animation is nothing else than a certain rule for making images living and actual. And this is done if we provide the image with aerial exploits and notable adjuncts; if the animation is not natural or at random, but is done by the judgment and the will; if we make the image excite the emotions, anger, hate . . . etc.).

The phrase 'nihil aliud', 'nothing else', typifies G.P.'s reductive procedure. The complex and obscure relation in Dickson between will and judgment is simplified out to 'cum judicio & voluntate', by judgment and will, which separates the two qualities and gives the first place to judgment. Most of the other changes similarly demystify Dickson. The verb 'animare', with its suggestion of a creative power in the maker of images, is neutralized to a noun, which is then defined in quite other terms. The vitality of the creation, with its hint of a magical activity that makes 'things inanimate seem almost to live and breathe' is reduced to two adjectives, 'vivas & actuosas', living and actual. And when he comes to the role of the affections he not only reduces the force of Dickson's phrasing, he loses his Ramist calm in the comment he adds. Dickson's 'impulsum & affectus vehementes' emphasized the dynamic as well as the affective. G.P. mentions only 'affectus'. Simple Ramism is not equipped to deal with things that move, and the emotions that are a source of energy for Dickson are a distraction and worse for G.P. He comments:

> Animatio tota & cum umbris ac locis corruit, & per se insigni impietatis macula inusta est. Haec enim esse non potest, nisi in mente animantis excitentur affectus, ira, odium, metus, libido &c. (He then refers to the use of a youthful sweetheart as a mnemonic, with Peter of Ravenna in mind). nimirum eas imagines optimas esse & diutissime haerere in animis, quae petuntur ab iis rebus quae libidinem movere possunt, ut a foeminis a puellis &c.[33]

> (The whole of animation runs into a common grave with shades and places, and on its own account is branded with a notable stain of impiety. For there can be no animation unless the emotions of wrath, hatred, fear, lust, etc., are excited in the mind of the person animating them . . . surely the best images, the ones that stick in the mind the longest, are those which are sought from things which can provoke lust, as from women and girls etc.)

What perverse objects of libido lurk discreetly beneath that last 'etcetera' we shall never know. The looseness of phrasing is a symptom of the change in the quality of G.P.'s argument on this point. The tone has changed from crisp contempt for verbosity and offences against logic to a stern moral rebuke for the 'notable strain of impiety'. Normally G.P. eschews metaphor, but here he has two stumbling over each other in as many words, buttressed by 'insignes', notable, a vague word straight from the arts of memory. But though Peter of Ravenna's method may have confirmed G.P.'s worst suspicions of depravity in monkish minds, Dickson's method is altogether more serious in its purpose, and is not open to this kind of objection.

The images generated by the Brunesque art of memory might be too richly significant to be helpful as aids to the memory of any practising lawyer, however lascivious. The real purpose is a kind of meditation:

> Ecce ut ipsum infinitum, incomprehensum, ab effectis ostenditur. Infinita sunt hujus generis exempla . . .[34]

> (Behold how the incomprehensible infinite itself is revealed by its effects. Infinite are the examples of this kind . . .)

he begins a typical passage. This aim affects his description of the principle place in the traditional art of memory. Normally this was either a house with many rooms, or a small villa. Dickson writes:

> Cum sit autem ipsum universum, & ima tellus, & continens haec aut illa, & politeia, & oeconomica dimensio, & partes ejus: e proximis quidem tribus generibus absoluta subjecta pro occasione assumuntur.[35]

> (Since there is the universe itself, and the lowest earth and the different continents, and the spheres of the political and the domestic and its parts; for present purposes, absolute place can be taken from the three closest kinds of place).

G.P.'s paraphrase helps to focus on the distinctive character of Dickson's use of places:

> Locus principalis est vel maxime communis, ut sphaera mundi vel minus communis, ut terra, civitas, domus, & ejus partes, sed usitate ex tribus ultimis generibus loci petuntur.[36]

> (A main place is either especially general, like the sphere of the world, or less general, like the earth, a city, a house, and its parts; but usually places are chosen from the last three kinds.)

G.P.'s critique raises again the question of the relation between Puritanism and Ramism, or more exactly between a set of attitudes, a body of doctrines, and a logic. Whether or not William Perkins was also G.P. of Cambridge, he and the other founding fathers of English puritanism gave it a Ramist logical basis. Logic and doctrine were mutually reinforcing, disvaluing the whole affective side of man. Some influential Puritans in the seventeenth century tried to correct this unbalanced view. Most important here was the work of Richard Baxter, a Presbyterian minister whom Marvell was to defend against Samuel Parker. In his 'Saints Everlasting Rest', first published in 1658, Baxter tried to bridge the gap between Catholic meditative practices and Puritan habits of mind.[37] His work was immensely popular, which indicates the need he supplied, but its form reveals the size of the gap not simply between Catholic and Puritan but between the aspects of the self in Puritan thought. His title, significantly, does not suggest that this is a book on the art of meditation. Nor does he immediately disclose this aim:

> The duty which I press upon thee so earnestly, I shall now describe and open to thee: for I suppose by this time thou art readie to enquire, What is this so highly extolled work?

he writes – on page 695. After Baxter's relentless bludgeon-and-needle assault on his intellect the reader must have been more than ready.

A major aim of Baxter's meditation is to overcome the split between feeling and intellect. This is done by 'consideration', which 'doth, as it were, open the door between the Head and the Heart' (p. 720). The language he uses is revealing. 'Head' and 'Heart' encode significance directly, like emblems. The resulting image is a jarring mixed metaphor, part organic and part architectural. Paradoxically, this image for the resolution of the split tends to reinforce a sense that Head and Heart are fundamentally distinct compartments of the self, separated by a door which is usually locked. But the parenthetical 'as it were' indicates Baxter's uneasiness with the implications of his metaphor.

His view of the nature of 'consideration' is inevitably cerebral:

> The great Instrument that this Work is done by, is Ratiocination, Reasoning the case with your selves, Discourse of mind, Cogitation, or Thinking. (p. 720)

54

His 'cogitation' is nothing like the Brunesque 'cogitatio'. The view of the working of the mind has, like G.P.'s 'logica inventio', absorbed images under the category of ideas:

Mans soul, as it receives and retains the Idea's or shapes of things, so hath it a power to choose out any of these deposited Idea's, and draw them forth, and act upon them again and again: even as a sheep can fetch up his meat for rumination; otherwise nothing would affect us, but while the sense is receiving it.   (p. 720)

The connections backwards to G.P. and Ramus and forward to Locke are more obvious than any with Calvin. But such a position leaves little scope for the action of the feelings, though this was one of Baxter's chief concerns:

As Consideration draweth forth the weightiest Objects, so it presenteth them in the most affecting way, and presseth them home with enforcing Arguments. Man is a Rational Creature, and apt to be moved in a Reasoning way, especially when the Reasons are evident and strong.   (p. 721)

Reason is clearly dominant, and the meditator becomes a Ramist rhetorician working on himself, his mind divided into two parts accordingly. An important part of a Catholic meditation, the soliloquy, which for Hawkins could be an effusion on the beauty of a drop of dew, for Baxter is 'a preaching to oneself'. The description indicates the specific form of a meditation:

Therefore the very same Method which a Minister should use in his preaching to others, should a Christian use in speaking to himself.   (p. 744)

The method being recommended here is the Puritan-Ramist model for a sermon laid down by Perkins, which Baxter used to organize sermons, and treatises such as the present one. Reader and writer or speaker and audience are the same person, as in the art of memory, but both are almost equally public and rational aspects of the self.

Baxter has similar difficulties with the senses. On page 749 he assures the reader that the proper use of the senses has been 'the main work that I drive at through all', going on to say:

Sure it is both possible and lawfull, yea, and necessary too, to do something in this kind.

But the 'something' that has been so hardly won needs an immediate distinction to avoid the charge of popery:

I would not have thee, as the Papists, draw them (i.e. holy mysteries) in Pictures, nor use mysterious, significant Ceremonies to represent them. This, as it is a course forbidden by God, so it would but seduce and draw down thy heart; but get the liveliest Pictures of them in thy minde that possibly thou canst . . .   (p. 752)

Baxter's style again signals his sense of difficulty; 'sure' and 'yea' are anxiously assertive, and the progression from possible to lawfull to necessary is undercut by 'something'. The resolution is an unhappy compromise; the meditator can imagine a physical representation so long as there is no actual physical representation corresponding to it. Doctrine and logic have converged to make any communication from spirit to matter and Head to Heart immensely difficult. Baxter's art of meditation involves deeply inadequate notions of the self which are intrinsic to his paradigm and affect the quality of his responses. His awkward images and uneasy attitude to imagery are not peripheral accidents of style, but imply seriously distorting assumptions of a basic kind.

(iv) Marvell's theory of Imagination

Baxter's purpose was to resist some of the tendencies of Ramist Puritanism, but he still thought and argued from within an undeveloped version of the paradigm, whose leading principles constantly subverted the very terms in which he argued his case. The tome is a monument equally to the stultifying power of the paradigm and to Baxter's tenacious refusal to submit to its terms. Marvell's kind of development of the Ramist paradigm would not lead to such acute difficulties with meditation. So Marvell may have approved the aim of Baxter's book when it appeared in 1656, but he could have had little to learn from it. Baxter's difficulties only give a measure of Marvell's achievement.

In 1651 a book was published which helps to define Marvell's position far more exactly. William Davenant's epic poem 'Gondibert', with a preface by the author and a 'Reply' by Hobbes, was one of the most significant literary events of the decade. Marvell had a keen and intelligent interest in Hobbes' ideas, and he clearly had read both work and preface. Davenant is the only poet referred to by name in 'Appleton House'. Wallace finds many references to 'Gondibert' in Marvell's poem, which he even suggests is in ways an answer to 'Gondibert' and its preface.[38] But Davenant was a self-confessed disciple of Hobbes. Marvell must have been aware of Hobbes's presence behind the more interesting formulations, and the poem is a reaction to a Hobbist view of the mind as well as to Davenant's notions of the Epic. The connection makes these works by Hobbes and Davenant important documents in any account of Marvell's understanding of imagination and the creative process.

Hobbes figures in many demonologies as an early opponent of wit and advocate of judgment, for good reasons as we shall see, but some of his descriptions of the role of Fancy and Memory are very interesting and not at all limiting. In a central passage he writes:

> For Memorie is the World (though not really, yet so as in a Looking-glass) in which the Judgement, the severer Sister busieth her self in a grave and rigid examination of all the parts of Nature, and in registering by Letters their

order, causes, uses, differences, and resemblances; Whereby the Fancie, when any work of Art is to be performed, finding her materials at hand and prepared for use, and [sic] needs no more than a swift motion over them, that what she wants, and is there to be had, may not lie too long unspied. So that when she seemeth to fly from one Indies to the other, and from Heaven to Earth, and to penetrate into the hardest matter, and obscurest places, into the future, and into her self, and all this in a point of time, the voyage is not very great, her self being all she seeks; and her wonderfull celeritie, consisteth not so much in motion, as in copious Imagerie discreetly ordered, and perfectly registered in the Memorie.[39]

The mind here contains an image of the world, and in this world judgment and fancy are complementary powers. The slow deliberations of Judgment enable Fancy to act with greater rapidity and power. Nor is Fancy sharply distinguished from the order of such images. She seeks 'her self', so the Fancy is not an arbitrary power playing with ideas and images, but is in some sense an order which the Judgment discovers inhering in things. Judgment increases the range and penetration of this Fancy, and thereby enlarges the cosmos of the mind. The two powers of the mind act as much in unison as with Bruno's 'cogitiva fantasia', rational imagination.

Hobbes also had one of the most interesting accounts of the irrational to be found in the seventeenth century. In 'Leviathan', he distinguishes two kinds of 'traynes of thought'. The first is

Unguided, without Designe . . . In which case the thoughts are said to wander, and seem impertinent to one another, as in a Dream.[40]

This seeming impertinence, however, is only apparent:

And yet in this wild ranging of the mind, a man may oft-times perceive the way of it, and the dependance of one thought upon another. For in a Discourse of our present civill warre, what could seem more impertinent, than to ask (as one did) what was the value of a Roman Penny? Yet the Cohaerence to me was manifest enough. For the Thought of the warre, introduced the Thought of the delivering up the King to his Enemies; the Thought of that, brought in the Thought of the delivering up of Christ; and that again the Thought of the 30 pence, which was the price of that treason: and thence easily followed that malicious question; and all this in a moment of time; for Thought is quick.[41]

Certain distinctions apparently made in this passage turn out to be only partial. 'Unguided Thought', as the example of the penny makes plain, will only be relatively unguided. Conversely, 'regulated' traynes of ideas are driven by a 'Passionate Thought'. Only mathematics or logic for Hobbes can be entirely independent of passion. So the example of the Roman penny becomes a model for all thought other than scientific reasoning. In this view all non-scientific thought combines wildness and coherence, reason and the irrational, and only the proportions vary. Thus

57

no unassisted human reasoning can be free from the taint of the irrational. Man is not naturally rational, as for Baxter; he can achieve rationality only by artificial means. But more interestingly, Hobbes also sees a principle of coherence in supposedly irrational thought that makes it susceptible to analysis. Dreams become something of a model for undirected trains of thought, their 'impertinence', or 'wild ranging', being typical of the natural action of the mind.

From this point Hobbes could have gone on to a proto-Freudian kind of analysis of dreams. Instead, his insight into the irrational made him commit himself more totally to scientific thought as the only solution. The result was an equivocal attitude to the original insight, which was shared by some of his disciples. Davenant, for instance, at one point in his preface apologises for straying:

> But I feel (Sir) that I am falling into the dangerous Fit of a hot Writer; for in stead of performing the promise which begins this Preface, and doth oblige me (after I had given you the judgement of some upon others) to present my self to your censure, I am wandering after my thoughts; but I shall ask your pardon, and return to my undertaking.[42]

He parades his irrationality at the same time as he is apologising for it. Obviously he could have rewritten the preface and excluded the wandering; however, he retains it and even draws attention to it, clearly regarding it as a sign of ability in a writer, with its own kind of truth. A similar attitude occurs in a comment on Spenser:

> His allegorical Story (by many held defective in the connexion) resembling (me thinks) a continuance of extraordinarie Dreams; such as excellent Poets, and Painters, by being over-studious, may have in the beginning of Feavers.[43]

Here Spenser's unreal world is the product equally of excellence and disease. The comment itself suggests an interesting kind of response to Spenserian allegory. Davenant is aware that Spenser's story is dictated by the allegory, but he fancifully reacts to it with naturalistic expectations. Spenser's story then seems to follow the logic of a dream, the disturbing kind of dream that accompanies a fever. A similar kind of reaction would have converted Cockson's animal into a 'monstrous horse', and Davenant's strategy recalls Marvell's re-use of emblems. Davenant is only playing with the idea, but even within Hobbist terms he could have gone further. Such allegories could be analysed like the example of the Roman penny to uncover the unstated motives directing the sequence. Alternatively, apparent allegories could be used as a strategy, to create a dream-world embodying the action of various 'passionate Thoughts'.

But Hobbes and his disciples resisted his insight into the nature of the irrational with irrational insistence. Immediately before his description of the rapidity and power of the Fancy already quoted, Hobbes gives it only a minor role in the creation of a poem:

> Memorie begets Judgement, and Fancie; Judgement begets the strength and structure; and Fancie begets the ornaments of a poem.[44]

Davenant reveals the extreme ambivalence even more clearly. His praise of wit commences expansively:

> Wit is not onely the luck and the labour, but also the dexteritie of thought, rounding the world, like the Sun, with unimaginable motion; and bringing swiftly home to the memorie, universal surveys . . .

But within a few sentences it becomes:

> in Divines, Humilitie, Exemplariness, and Moderation; in Statesmen, Gravitie, Vigilance, Benign Complacencie, Secrecie, Patience and Dispatch . . .[45]

For wit to become humility so swiftly is dexterity of thought indeed. The case is argued out in 'Leviathan', in a curious and fallacious passage of reasoning which culminates in the statement that:

> Judgement without Fancy therefore is Wit, but Fancy without Judgement not.[46]

To reach this conclusion, Hobbes divides 'natural wit' into two properties, celerity of imagining and steadiness of direction. Celerity is divided into the perception of likenesses, which is called a good wit or a good fancy, and perception of dissimilarities, which in general cases is called judgement, with discretion an important particular case. He then gives his ruling that Judgement without Fancy is wit but not the reverse. If we set up this argument in the form of a Ramist table which the dichotomous progression invites, we can see exactly how the shift is made:

Fancy could have had claims to half the table, but has to share its half with Judgement, which, however, is much closer to 'steadiness' than to 'celerity'. What Hobbes calls an ability to 'observe their differences and dissimilitudes' is really more of a refusal to observe the similarities, and so steadiness rather than celerity of thought. Steadiness of direction is not

59

called judgement, but is clearly more akin to judgement than to fancy. By this means Judgement has encroached on Fancy to occupy three-quarters of the table. To get here Hobbes has offended so blatantly against the law of justice that the argument must be either a deliberate sophistry or a mark of his unreasoning distrust of the fancy. The effect is to trivialize Fancy so that it is no longer the general power of the mind that can 'fly from one Indies to the other and from Heaven to Earth', but merely the provider of similitudes which can be used for ornament. Correspondingly, qualities of steadiness, judgement and discretion assume a proportion of the mind's faculties commensurate with what is desirable in the interests of peace. The aim of Hobbes' acute analysis of the potentially disruptive forces in the mind and in society was to devise means of coming to terms with them and controlling them, but sometimes he betrayed his insights into these forces by simply supposing them out of existence.

Something like this opposition and this resolution of it arbitrarily in favour of judgment can still be seen in Dryden, though with Hobbes' basic insight considerably reduced in potency. The terms 'wit' and 'judgment' (or 'correctness') dominate his critical writings almost to the exclusion of any other evaluative terms. One of the most extended discussions of wit occurs in the preface to 'Annus Mirabilis':

> Wit writing . . . is no other than the faculty of imagination in the writer which, like a nimble spaniel, beats over and ranges through the field of memory, till it springs the quarry it hunteth after; or, without metaphor, which searches over all the memory for the species or ideas of those things which it designs to represent.[47]

Hobbes also used the metaphor of a spaniel to describe the action of the mind, but for Hobbes this was only one kind of regulated thought, the sort that 'run(s) over the Alphabet, to start a rime'.[48] But Hobbes' more general view of the movement of the Fancy, 'from one Indies to the other, and from Heaven to Earth' suggests an eagle rather than a spaniel. Dryden's imagination is a more servile beast.

Dryden goes on to gloss his metaphor, a revealing procedure which contrasts interestingly with Baxter's use of images. Where Baxter's conventional emblematic images involved him in absurdity at the visual level, Dryden's spaniel behaves as a credible spaniel throughout the sentence. Like the Hind which ate grass, the dog has an autonomous existence, though its activities happen to parallel those of the imagination. Since the connection is not intrinsic it has to be explained. Object and significance exist in separate worlds. Meaning does not affect the representation of the physical image to produce absurdity, as in Baxter; but correspondingly details of the image cannot be relied on to be significant. In the literal description of the activity, the 'species or Ideas' that the imagination searches for closely resemble Baxter's 'Idea's, or

60

shapes of things'. Both are some kind of replica of physical objects, deposited in the mind and retaining there their distinctive identity. But Dryden's aim, to 'represent' them, is different, and his images come from different visual modes, which here interact with forms of the same paradigm to produce different kinds of images. Baxter clings somewhat uneasily to emblematic modes, where object and significance couple in isolated units. For Dryden the physical world as a whole retains an independent existence and is represented for its own sake. He describes wit written as:

> Some lively and apt description, dressed in such colours of speech that it sets before your eyes the absent object as perfectly and more delightfully than nature.[49]

The 'absent object' is not to be affected by anything like the 'reflective fancy' of Bruno. So we see why the Hind was described as feeding on the lawns. The physical hind is not just the creature of the mind, but exists in its own right. There is no feeling aroused by it as an object, nor should its presence be responded to too intently; Dryden's spaniel has merely found a species of deer.

Marvell's connection with Hobbes's theories of the mind is as close as Dryden's, even extending to details of expression. The stanza immediately following the mention of Davenant in 'Appleton House' is reminiscent of Hobbes' discussion of Fancy already quoted. Davenant's name may well have been used to point the reference.

> They seem within the polisht Grass
> A Landskip drawen in Looking-Glass:
> And shrunk in the huge Pastures show
> As Spots, so shap'd, on Faces do.
> Such Fleas, ere they approach the Eye,
> In Multiplying Glasses lye.
> They feed so wide, so slowly move,
> As Constellations do above.   (Stanza LVIII)

Marvell here seems to be deliberately recalling Hobbes' description of the action of the Fancy, and showing how it works. Both use the analogy with a Looking-Glass, and in it represent a world. Within this world Marvell flies, if not from Heaven to Earth, from the large to the small and thence to the Heavens. The images in the rest of the stanza are the creation of the Fancy, and serve to define its nature. As in Hobbes' account, the rapidity of the movement derives from 'copious Imagery discreetly ordered'. The similes are not chosen at random, but are meticulously managed optical illusions, with all the necessary equipment provided and the movement of the eye precisely controlled from couplet to couplet. The first couplet presents the real scene, life-sized cattle in a pasture at some distance. In the second couplet both specks and field remain the same size, or at least subtend the same angle with the eye, but since the field is seen as a looking-glass and therefore close, the specks are interpreted as small, like spots. The third couplet retains the same relative and apparent sizes, with the spots now seen as fleas. But the 'multiplying Glasses' lie to hand, threatening to make the fleas as big as the villagers and cattle they in fact are, like Hooke's louse in the Speaker's chair or the giant Grasshoppers of the Abyss of grass. The fourth couplet, however, exactly reverses the direction, and hurtles off to the immensity of space with dizzying rapidity, where preserving the same scale the leveller-cattle-fleas would be as large as suns. The image in each couplet blurs and shifts into the next, which affects its quality, so that for instance the spots that grow out of the cattle will have repulsive jagged edges; and the transition of 'Spots, so shap'd' to fleas is easily made as the focus sharpens. The eye itself must remain rigidly and centrally fixed within a single cone of vision, altering only its depth of focus. The movement is all achieved by this means within the cone, the direction indicated early by 'shrunk' near the beginning of the second couplet and 'ere they approach the Eye' in the third, so that no impression is static nor so clearly focused as to resist absorption into the next. In the second two couplets the cone itself is implicitly acted on, being flattened by the microscope and then extended towards the heavens. As an illusion the whole experience relies on a highly developed sensitivity for the cues of distance and size that would have made nonsense of Cockson's equestrian plate and of so much else in Elizabethan art.

But Marvell here is drawing on an uncharacteristic aspect of Hobbes. Statements like 'Memorie is the World' are not typical of Hobbes, even with a literalist proviso immediately following. They recall someone more like Bruno. The structure of the stanza, too, follows nothing in Hobbes. The way it moves from public to personal and microcosmic to macrocosmic, and attempts to hold all four in a single image, recalls the simultaneity of the interrelated cosmoi in the Brunesque art of memory.

The relation between microcosm and macrocosm was a commonplace in the age, appearing in many forms. However close the resemblance between Bruno's and Marvell's versions, we could not deduce a direct influence. But a particular kind of relationship between small and great is a shaping principle in the imagery and structure of 'Appleton House'.[50] To describe how the poem works, it is helpful to invoke a position very like Bruno's, irrespective of the question of influence.

Take such characteristic lines from the poem as these:

See how the Flow'rs, as at Parade,
Under their Colours stand displaid:
Each Regiment in order grows,
That of the Tulip Pinke and Rose.

But when the vigilant Patroul
Of Stars walks round about the Pole,
Their Leaves, that to the stalks are curl'd,
Seem to their Staves the Ensigns furl'd.   ('A.H.' lines 309 ff)

The flowers in the garden are referred to in military terms with
obsessive playfulness; and then the eye moving through the stanza is
suddenly confronted with stars, again described in military terms. Four
lines later the relation of the garden to England's political situation is
made explicit, with full seriousness:

Oh thou, that dear and happy Isle,
The Garden of the World ere while   ('A.H.' lines 321–322)

The strategy of the poem is like Dickson's: it takes 'pro occasione' the
house and its estates as the 'locus' for contemplation or reflection, but the
poet is always aware of the 'politeia dimensio' which the house embodies,
and its place in the moral cosmos. Within this 'place' images are animated
with a life and principle of motion that comes from the 'cogitiva fantasia'
of the poet. The traumatic events of the civil war are enacted again and
again, as image after image comes frighteningly to life with an erotic and
aggressive energy and motion derived from feelings predominently of
guilt and fear. The animals and plants on the estate act like Hobbes'
Roman penny in reverse, as the mind moves rapidly from them to
thoughts of the civil war. The poem ostensibly celebrates Fairfax's
retirement, but the celebration is subverted by a mnemonic that instead
of reminding poet and patron of matters they want to remember, gives
images for thoughts they cannot forget. The nightmare quality of the
experience is especially marked when the poet alone retreats to the
meadows and then to the woods. The flux of scenes one into another
exploits the potentially bizarre progression of an allegorical narrative,
and recalls Davenant's reaction to Spenser. Davenant's diagnosis of a
'feaver' could also apply to a poet who tosses:

On Pallets swoln of Velvet Moss.   ('A.H.' line 594)

Marvell finally evaluates the experience similarly and rejects it, but he
first recreates it intensely and sees it as a kind of wisdom. Compared with
Hobbes, he seems to understand more deeply the workings of the
irrational and has more sympathy for that aspect of the self, though
compared to Bruno he is finally sceptical about the visions of his Magus.
A way of putting it is to say that the poem represents a Hobbist critique of
Bruno, or a Brunesque extension of Hobbes, but this is to use the two
thinkers as representatives of two traditions, not as specific presences in
the poem.

Marvell has a more explicit account of the imagination. The sixth stanza of 'The Garden' is that and much more, a theory of the creative processes that climaxes in arguably the most intriguing and memorable image in Marvell's poetry or in the whole of the seventeenth century.

> Meanwhile the Mind, from pleasure less,
> Withdraws into its happiness:
> The Mind, that Ocean where each kind
> Does streight its own resemblance find;
> Yet it creates, transcending these,
> Far other Worlds, and other Seas;
> Annihilating all that's made
> To a green Thought in a green Shade.

Modern accounts of this stanza have brought out the worst in Marvell criticism. Following Empson's brilliant and influential article[51] critics have been happier to find an ambiguity than the meaning. A serious student faced with such interpretations may very properly dismiss the stanza and the poem as the work of a trifler, for the two halves of what Marvell is interpreted as saying are often banal, and no further point would be made by saying two banal things at once. But the ambiguity is never a both-ways bet. The argument itself is far too original and interesting for Marvell to want to turn aside and say something else as well. The first couplet, for instance, was seen as ambiguous by Empson, but to England's shame it was nearly thirty years before a Frenchman pointed out that neither of Empson's meanings was correct, and the couplet had a third and unambiguous significance.[52] Legouis' paraphrase is accurate enough: the mind withdraws ' "from a pleasure that is inferior" . . . viz. sensuous pleasure'. The couplet is puzzling, but only because of Marvell's typically careless inversions. The first task in explication accordingly is to restore the words to their grammatical order. Doing this, there is only one reading that makes sense: 'Meanwhile the Mind withdraws from less pleasure into its happiness'. Empson's two readings of the phrase 'from pleasure less' are:

> Either 'from the lessening of pleasure' . . . or 'made less by pleasure'.[53]

To arrive at either would require considerable rewriting: 'Meanwhile the Mind, from (i.e. through) pleasure (being) less'; or 'Meanwhile the Mind, (being) less(ened) from (i.e. by) pleasure'. That is, (to be only slightly perverse), Pleasure grows less, and the intelligence too diminishes. The proposition may describe the progress of Marvell criticism, but it contradicts what the poem is saying, for it is 'Mean while', in the course of the bodily ecstasy of Stanza V, that the Mind withdraws.

This single meaning is not in itself a novel or exciting perception, but it has an important place in the economy of the argument. Its function is to establish the terms and rhythm for the rest of the stanza. The underlying opposition is between mind and body, in terms of which 'from pleasure less' is crucially placed in the movement of the line. It refers to the pleasures of the body, which are less than those of the mind, but it is juxtaposed against the verb 'withdraws' at the beginning of the next line; so the pleasure increases as the mind withdraws, or contracts into itself. This means that 'pleasure' is not exclusively sensuous pleasure, as in Legouis' paraphrase, for the mind's 'happiness' includes it. The opposition between the attributes of mind and body is already partially resolved by the rhythm of contraction and expansion in which both participate.

The second couplet commences the description of the mind. Its basic terms are highly dualistic, a world of objects exactly parallel to a world of innate ideas. The description is not unlike Hobbes' account of the memory as the world or a mirror image of the world, except that for Marvell these ideas are innate and have a strong attraction for the corresponding objects. The image itself, however, is old-fashioned. It found a place in Sir Thomas Browne's 'Pseudodoxia Epidemica' as a vulgar error.[54] and the picture it conjures up is an ingenious drawing in the emblem mode. Hawkins, for instance, concludes a meditation on the belief with a comforting moral:

> In fine, they are another world in themselves, wherein God hath plunged and drencht the diversities of al earthlie creatures.[55]

The next couplet is startlingly different. The quaint conceit suddenly becomes a vision of an infinite recession of worlds as though seen in a hall of mirrors. Hawkins also has a speculation similar to this:

> The number of the Heavens hath not alwayes been agreed upon; for one while they beleeved, there was but one onlie, wherin the starres did sweetly glide heer and there, and glance along, as in a liquid cristal floud. Sometimes have they allowed of eight, by reason of so manie divers Motions and Agitations very different in them; then nine; then ten, and then eleven; and if perhaps some new Galilaeus should devise and frame us other spectacles or opticons to see with, we are in danger to find out yet some new Starres and Heavens never dreamed of before.[56]

Hawkins assimilates Galileo and the new astronomy into a ptolemaic universe, but finds the Galilean extension slightly disturbing – 'we are in danger to find.' In the rest of his meditation, Hawkins limits himself not simply to the traditional spheres, but among these to the syderean, cristalin and Empyreal spheres, all of which have a purity reminiscent of the Virgin. Marvell's lines, however, imply an infinity of worlds not heavens, an unptolemaic conception more closely associated with Bruno than Galileo for the new science, though it had a source in classical times in the Epicureans, lovers of gardens whose atomistic philosophy appealed to so many of the new scientists.[57]

The last couplet has as many interpretations as commentators. The lines contain an apparent contradiction. 'Annihilate' strictly means to reduce to nothing, yet a green thought in a green shade still survives in the last line. The Oxford editor saves the appearances by tentatively supposing 'to' is an ellipsis for 'compared to'. Marvell is capable of such ellipsis, but he is also capable of paradox. Margoliouth's reading gives a limp conclusion to the stanza, and one which does not connect with the preceding argument. 'Annihilating', however, is so placed as to suggest a contrast with 'creates'. The two couplets are implicitly opposed to each other as contrary or complementary actions of the mind, infinite creativity leading to total annihilation, for there is no intervening 'yet' or 'but' between the creation of these 'far other Worlds, and other Seas', and the unrestricted annihilation. It should not be surprising if an annihilation which is the extension to the infinite of the creative process produces something that is both nothing and everything.

The image in the last line is powerful enough to sustain this kind of degree of significance. As an image it seems strongly and precisely visualized yet it is unimaginable. Marvell clearly started from an exact observation, as the earlier Latin version, 'Hortus', shows, which refers to 'Plantae virides, & concolor Umbra'. (Green plants and shades of the same colour, line 11.) Colours were becoming important to scientists as well as to artists by the mid-century. Newton's 'Opticks' at the end of the century definitively established that white light is composed of primary colours, only one of which is green,[58] but Hooke's 'Micrographia' of 1665 includes some extremely interesting speculations on colour which derive all colours from two, yellow and blue, in different intensities:

> Whence I experimentally found what I had before imagin'd, that all the varieties of colours imaginable are produc'd from several degrees of these two colours, namely, Yellow and Blue, or the mixture of them with light and darkness.[59]

But Hooke does not apply this generalization to painters' colours:

> Painters colours therefore consisting most of them of solid particles, so small that they cannot be either re-united into thicker particles by any Art yet knowne, and consequently cannot be deepned; or divided into particles so small as the flaw'd particles that exhibit that colour, much less into smaller, and consequently cannot be diluted; It is necessary that they which are to imitate all kinds of colours, should have as many degrees of each colour as can be procur'd.[60]

That is, only at the atomic level do yellow and blue generate all other colours. Green for him is therefore a derivative colour, but if he had chosen to assume that only one colour generated all the rest, that colour would have been green. Even as a composite colour he praises 'the ravishing pleasure with which a curious and well-tempered Green affects the eye'.[61] It would be a short and natural step to suppose that atomic or

66

ultimate green generated all other colours, and that all colours finally reduced to green. It would give a precise, even technical meaning to Marvell's words if he was referring to a green of this kind, a green that was all colours yet like no colours that actually exist, perceived by a mind whose vision has contracted in an instant from an infinite universe to the ultimate constituents of matter.

But green does not do the main work in the image, whose twin poles are 'Thought' and 'Shade'. The phrase 'green Thought' fuses abstract and physical as is generally recognized, but the union of abstract and physical is both more complex and more explicit than this. The 'green Shade' is not simply the physical shadow it was in 'Hortus', it also represents the other pole of the dualism that has run through the stanza. 'Umbra' meant 'image' for Dickson and Bruno, the form that embodied the ideas. In his Latin poetry Marvell uses the word several times in this sense, and even with magical overtones such as lurked behind the Brunesque use of the word, for 'umbra' also could mean 'ghost'. In one of his epigrams on a portrait of Cromwell he wrote:

Haec est quae toties Inimicos Umbra fugavit,   ('In Effigiem' line 18)
(This is an image which puts enemies to flight)

and he uses the same word in his other epigram on the subject.[62] In his long Latin poem to the Queen of Sweden he writes:

Ipsa licet redeat (nostri decus orbis) Eliza,
    Qualis nostra tamen quantaque Eliza fuit.
Vidimus Effigiem, mistasque Coloribus Umbras.
                                ('Letter to Dr. Ingelo' lines 23–25)
Though Eliza herself (the glory of our world) should return,
Yet our Eliza was just such as she and as great.
We have seen her picture, shadows mixed with colours.

The phrase translated here by Rockwell and McQueen as 'shadows mixed with colours' makes sense if 'umbra' means image or ghost, which in Christina is mixed with colours, or embodied in them. On this interpretation the lines come close to the image in 'The Garden', whose 'Shade' is the ultimate embodiment, the ghost of the Universe, as well as the shade of the actual garden.

This must give the primary meaning of the line. The conclusion of the mind's activity is the creation of an all-subsuming idea in an all-subsuming Image, or the annihilation of the universes of matter and mind to that single image and idea. The stanza as a whole is crucial for an understanding of Marvell, embodying his deepest commitments and modes of thought in both doctrine and image. It is a paradigmatic achievement, and generations of readers are right to have established its final couplet as Marvell's best-remembered image.

Chapter 3

RATIONAL MAGIC

The seventeenth century was crucial for the development of modern science. Some of the particular discoveries were important enough, but even more important for the history of thought were the method and assumptions that allowed these discoveries, and received such powerful validation from them. Some of the general implications of the scientific method were recognized early, and have been a central concern of major philosophers in the Western tradition starting from Hobbes and Locke, but the process can also be studied profitably at the level of leading principles, both the emergence of science out of more widely prevailing habits of thought, and its creative and destructive interaction with alternative modes of thought.

A context of this kind is urgently needed, by literary students at least. Too many of them see the period through a myth that damagingly misrepresents the rise of science and its relation with other areas of thought. Out of this comes not only an impoverished view of the century but also an impoverished response to qualities of style in a poet such as Marvell, and with this a distorted account of his significance. According to this myth Science and Poetry are irreconcilably opposed, and have been since 1660. The rise of science required the death of poetry, the myth runs. The Elizabethan world was a magical, poetic world ruled by the imagination; the world of science is a prose world ruled by reason. So our world is incapable of poetry, but the Elizabethans were incapable of science. The precondition for the rise of science in the seventeenth century was rationality, a demystifying, desacralizing, demythologizing clarity of thought which swept away the cobwebs of superstition or shattered the fragile magic shell of the Elizabethan world.

> We think of our universe in similes. Our Elizabethan ancestors thought of their world in metaphors. The world was not *like* an animal; it *was* animate,

writes Marjory Nicolson, no denizen of the literary backwoods but a scholar with an impressive grasp of both the science and literature of the period. Marvell is usually located with the primitives in this scheme, his poems given early dates in the interests of a closer fit.[1]

Historians of science, however, are acutely aware of at least one inaccuracy in the myth. Most of the great figures of the age of science were as 'superstitious' as any of their contemporaries. Even this is an understatement. In fact many of these great ones were more intensely and systematically superstitious than most of their contemporaries. More awkward still, such beliefs seem inseparable from their scientific achievement. L. Thorndike, in his monumental 8-volume *History of Magic and Experimental Science* generalizes from the case of Fracastoro, whose theories on the spread of disease impress modern biologists but must, Thorndike insists, be understood as coming from magically-based ideas of sympathy and antipathy. Thorndike concludes:

> This order . . . holds true in general for the history of ideas, where magic almost always precedes and lays the foundations for science . . . True it is that Fracastoro attempts a physical and natural rather than magical explanation of the phenomena . . . But this does not alter the fact that the conception of such relationships was magical in origin and essence.[2]

Fracastoro died in 1553; but Sir Isaac Newton, the supreme scientist of the seventeenth century synthesis, can still be regarded as 'the last of the magicians' by Thorndike and Sir Geoffrey Keynes.[3] This magical streak must be acknowledged in any full account of major figures like Copernicus and Kepler, Gilbert and Newton, but historians of science normally regard science itself as completely different from magic. The magical beliefs are tacitly distinguished from truly scientific ones, the assumption being that in spite of such beliefs, which were shared with contemporaries like styles in periwigs, the major scientist qua scientist was less superstitious than either his contemporaries or his ordinary self. The assumption shows in Thorndike's distinction between a 'physical and natural explanation', and a 'magical' one, which implies that a magical explanation is neither physical nor natural. Thorndike goes so far as to define magic as among other things 'a consistent body of error' in his attempt to distinguish it totally from science, but as he especially must have known it is far from consistent and by no means entirely erroneous.[4]

Thorndike's aim was to show the emergence of science, not its continuing affinities with magic. In some more recent work there has perhaps been some shift of orientation. For instance M. Boas in *The Scientific Renaissance* has a sympathetic treatment of Gilbert's interest in magic, in a chapter entitled 'Ravished by magic', though she still takes for granted the fundamental difference between science and magic[5]. Frances Yates, (who is not a professional historian of science) has enthusiastically urged the importance of the connection[6]. But however they are interpreted, the facts are hardly in dispute. Magic was an inseparable companion of science throughout the period of the rise of science.

In Kuhnian terms, the phenomenon is puzzling. Magic and science ought to be successive stages of science, or successive paradigms, incompatible with each other. It is surprising to find such radically different paradigms co-existing for more than a century, particularly in the minds of the leaders of the scientific community. But Thorndike seems to be suggesting something even stronger than co-existence. If Fracastoro and other important scientists had a concept of relations 'magical in origin and essence', then principles akin to the magical were among the guiding principles of the founding fathers of science.

We are here in an area which Kuhn's account leaves vague. For Kuhn, revolutionary science occurs outside the processes of normal science, outside any particular paradigm, and seems merely the product of individual genius. But during this decisive period in the history of science, we seem to have something less idiosyncratic than this. The architects of the revolution were clearly members of the normal scientific community, yet they had crucial leading principles in common which many of their normal colleagues would have felt uneasy about. This is a conflict which we would expect if Kuhn is right about the conservative tendencies of normal science. Normal science re-writes history in its own image, suppressing the achievements of former paradigms. Naturally it would also want to suppress the radically critical and innovatory modes of thought characteristic of revolutionary science, in case another revolution occurred to challenge its own supremacy.

It is easier to focus on a phenomenon if it has a name, so I tentatively offer 'metaparadigm' to describe this distinctive set of leading principles.[7] The science of the metaparadigm has far less definite and exclusive boundaries around it. The great scientists were not simply more speculative and critical than ordinary scientists. Their achievement seems to have rested on a shared set of beliefs, assumptions about nature, language and mind which seem actually 'unscientific'. The scientists of the metaparadigm tolerated imagination, and along with that a kind of magic and a kind of poetry.

(i) 'Science' and Magic

Francis Bacon is a key figure for understanding the myth of science in the seventeenth century. He contains within himself all its main contradictions. He was accepted by his contemporaries as a prophet of the new science. The Royal Society established him as one of their founding fathers. Yet this prophet was notoriously unable to appreciate the really creative work being done by the great scientists of his age. The centre-piece of his programme was the Inductive Method, but no major scientist followed this method, and if they had followed it to the letter they would never have made any significant discoveries. However, in spite of his

70

commitment to empiricism, he was also a dabbler in alchemical and magical works. These paradoxes are commonplaces of the history of science, but I suspect they do not figure as large as they deserve to in the minds of students of literature. Even for historians of science the paradoxes are a problem not a solution. How could Bacon be so irrelevant yet so important?

Part of the answer lies in his relationship to Ramism. His theory of Induction is a fairly direct extension of simple Ramism into the sphere of science. Consider the table which can be used to summarize the contents of *Advancement of Learning*,[8] his most influential pronouncement on science (fig. iii). This table represented his view of the scope of human learning largely unchanged for more than two decades. It is built up essentially by the application of the three basic rules of Ramism, the laws of justice, wisdom and truth, as he explicitly acknowledged.[9] Bacon does criticize Ramus, objecting to the tyranny of the 'one method' with its endless dichotomies. As a result he often distributes into three parts instead of two, and his scheme is full of corrective mechanisms designed to overcome the law of justice's tendency to over-rigid distinctions. 'Philosophia prima', for instance, has exactly this function. Over his career he became increasingly aware of the need for such correctives, as we shall see, and he embodied these in 'de Augmentis', the later version of 'Advancement of Learning'. Obviously a full account of Bacon must take these developments into account. However, the simpler formulations inevitably had a wider influence. If Bacon had not been a simple Ramist, his simple Ramist readers would have turned him into one. To understand Bacon's importance for his age, we have to be unfair to him.

His summary of existing knowledge is arranged in terms of the powers of the mind, memory, imagination and reason. The disciplines of Baconian science are rearranged so that they reflect the nature of things. Bacon like Richardson believed that 'the art is the thing'. But inevitably his method is not neutral about either nature or the mind. These are cut up, compartmentalized, and this affected his conception of both, much more than he realized.

His basic strategy for science required the scientist to dispense with general theories or models of the reality he was studying. The Baconian scientist was to move methodically from 'history' to 'physics' to 'metaphysics', starting with collections of particular instances, going on to study material and efficient causes, and finishing with 'formal' and final causes. This order is the inverse of the Ramist Law of Wisdom, that the more general should be prior. But though the method seems to dispense with all models, in practice it favours one kind of model at the expense of others. In Bacon's implicit model Nature is seen as an assemblage of units of cause-and-effect, not as a field of forces. It is a low-force model,

71

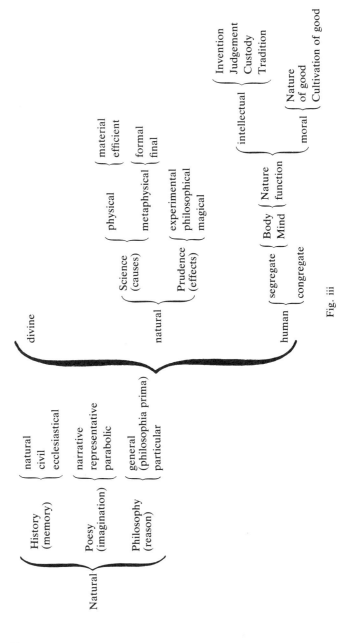

Fig. iii

72

positing a passive, compartmentalized nature, which could be easily controlled by a scientist who knew where the essential lines of division were.

Bacon's strictures on Imagination and poetry are well known.[10] It is worth pointing out, however, that his rejection of these is based on a subtle understanding of both. Ramism for him as for Hobbes provided an illuminating definition of the irrational, as the obverse of its limited account of reason. He used Ramism normatively, to prescribe how the mind ought to work, but his famous account of what he called the 'Idols' of the mind, the tendencies that lead men's thought astray, shows how aware he was of the un-Ramist mingling of the mind and the senses, language and thought, in actual thinking:

> The mind, when it receives impressions of objects through the sense, cannot be trusted to report them truly, but in forming its notions mixes up its own nature with the nature of things.[11]

So intrinsic is the process that he adds 'Idols of this . . . kind cannot be eradicated at all'.[12] Words are equally treacherous.

> For men believe that their reason governs words; but it is also true that words react on the understanding.[13]

In the striking image he uses in 'Advancement':

> words, as a Tartar's bow, do shoot back upon the understanding of the wisest, and mightily entangle and pervert the judgment.[14]

Definitions helped to counter the distortions of words, but in the 'Novum Organum' even this is not an entirely sufficient solution:

> Yet even definitions cannot cure this evil in dealing with natural and material things; since definitions themselves consist of words, and those words beget others.[15]

But Bacon's reaction to his subtle and accurate account of the deceptions of language and the mind was typically to try to slacken the bow of language and the mind.

> For my way of discovering sciences goes far to level men's wits, and leaves but little to individual excellence.[16]

For Bacon as for Hobbes, the Reason was a machine by which the essentially chaotic and irrational processes of the mind could arrive at certainty. Hobbes' machine was only a more sophisticated model. Bacon explicitly uses the mechanistic analogy:

> There remains but one course for the recovery of a sound and healthy condition, – namely, that the entire work of the understanding be commenced afresh, and the mind itself be from the very outset not left to take its course, but guided at every step; and the business done as if by machinery.[17]

So the complex interaction of language, nature and mind is resolved by a machine that deprives all three of most of their intrinsic powers. Out of this programme could come only the science of a reduced world described in reduced words by reduced minds. Rationalism of this kind makes no gains for science to compensate for the elimination of poetry. The opposite is more nearly true, as we can see vividly by juxtaposing Bacon's method of induction with William Gilbert's 'de Magnete' of 1600. This was the greatest scientific work written by an Englishman during the first two decades of the seventeenth century, when Bacon was working out his ideas on method, but he used 'Gilbertus our countryman' mainly as an example of what not to do in science. This judgment was not merely the product of envy that grudged another man's achievements; it was inevitable in terms of the paradigm underlying his inductive method. The clash defines the difference between the two paradigms, one of which is an early and even exemplary form of the scientific metaparadigm. Gilbert should be added to Bacon as required reading for students of literature wanting to know what science then was really like.

A method is central to any paradigm. Gilbert was conscious that he was advocating a 'new style of philosophizing'[18] and briefly described it in his preface, though the method was more convincingly embodied in the achievement of the work itself. Gilbert does not, as Bacon would recommend, avoid hypotheses; instead he starts from a model that represents his conception in a precise visual form. Though loadstones are of all shapes, he commences, he will use a spherical one, which is

> the most perfect, (and) agrees best with the earth, which is a globe, and also is the form best suited for experimental uses . . . The stone thus prepared is a true homogeneous offspring of the earth and is of the same shape, having got from art the orbicular form that nature in the beginning gave to the earth, the common mother.[19]

The word he uses for the Earth here is the poetic 'tellus'. Bacon, like G.P., normally used the prose 'terra', in keeping with his theories of language. But Gilbert uses the aura of nobility suggested by such words as an analogue for degrees of power, and builds this into his model. He calls his loadstone a *terrella* or *mikrogé*, a coinage from the prosaic word for the earth that suggests the superior status, and consequently determining force, of the earth. Moreover, he supports the basic analogy between the earth and the loadstone by a mineralogical account of the earth, showing the widespread occurrence of iron. From this he derives the important conclusion that a loadstone is simply iron ore, and not a different substance as had previously been supposed.

The conception underlying his model is the microcosmic-macrocosmic relationship. This conception is usually regarded as magical rather than

74

scientific, and associated particularly with Paracelsus. Bacon may even have been thinking of Gilbert's use of the concept when he praises the assistance that can be gained from 'matters mechanical':

So it cometh often to pass, that mean and small things discover great, better than great can discover the small: and therefore Aristotle noteth well, 'That the nature of everything is best seen in its smallest portions' . . . So we see how that secret of nature, of the turning of iron touched with the loadstone towards the north, was found out in needles of iron, not in bars of iron.[20]

But the relation of small to great for Bacon is a needle to a bar; for Gilbert it is a needle to the world.

But Gilbert is no more the slave of a common-place analogy than Bacon. Instead of reducing the force of the analogy, however, he tests it experimentally. To do so he leaves it hypothetical and open-ended. Having ground his loadstone into its orbicular shape he experimentally finds the poles. He then shows with little indicator-needles that such a globe will have lines like those of latitude and longitude, including an equator, which correspond to real lines of force, and are not simply fictions imposed to fulfil the analogy. The model can now be tested to prove the analogy. In addition to this it points the way to the discovery of new phenomena. For instance he shows that a magnet aligned with the earth's poles attracts more strongly than one aligned in opposition to them; that is, that south poles attract more strongly when pointing south than when pointing north.[21] The effect is duplicated on his model, where he finds that a small spherical magnet on a large one attracts more strongly when the poles are properly aligned, i.e. with opposite poles together. Again the model has validated itself, pointed the way to the discovery of new facts, and defined the complex relationships with more precision than a description in words could afford, or normal observation might suggest.

If the model seems to come from the magical tradition, Gilbert's conception of the forces concerned seems even more thoroughly 'magical in origin and essence', to use Thorndike's words. Gilbert attributes magnetic effects to 'formales efficientes', a notion that activates the latent animism in Aristotle's concept of a formal cause. Gilbert ascribes this force to

the primary, radical, and astral form; not Aristotle's prime form, but that unique form which keeps and orders its own globe.[22]

Descriptions that refer to 'astral forms' would seem clearly magical. This one, however, had considerable heuristic value. Gilbert can observe, for instance, that iron beaten or heated and cooled in a north-south position acquires a weak polarity.[23] Moreover, he sets up experiments to demonstrate the inadequacy of the alternative materialistic explanation, that attraction was due to an efflux of tiny particles. Magnetized bodies attract across a flame, but when heated lose their potency.[24] And his term 'formales efficientes' describes the phenomena far more adequately than Bacon could. Formal and efficient causes occupied different levels in Bacon's scheme, but in Gilbert's concept the two unite to describe a force that acts on bodies but at a distance, and depends on and determines relationships. Gilbert's account provides a consistent explanation of both polarity and attraction. Action at a distance and the force of a relationship were essential to this explanation, so the magical tradition was the only possible contemporary source for adequate models, in Gilbert's time and for the next hundred years.

In spite of these superstitious premises, his actual method as described above is an exemplary performance in the new scientific mode, and nowhere more so than where Bacon criticized it. Like Bacon Gilbert asserted his independence from the thinkers of the past. But unlike Bacon, Gilbert claimed the right to 'philosophize freely' as his predecessors had done.[25] His reason for doing so was that

> as our sciolists still take their stand on those foundations, they continue to stray about, so to speak, in perpetual darkness.[26]

General notions, that is, affect particular notions, which depend on them as foundations. Useful thought is only possible in terms of a logically dependent system, the outlines and basic principles of which must be to some degree articulated and seen as a whole:

> nor will one reach anything like certitude in the magnetic philosophy, unless all, or at all events most, of its principles are known to him.[27]

Geometry with its powerfully deductive procedure provides him with a model for thought, like most of the major scientists but unlike Bacon. But Gilbert's wide ranging speculations had a firm experimental base, and his investigation started from and continued to return to its source in precise observation and experiment.

Seemingly inconsistently, Bacon chiefly criticized Gilbert for working too long on one area, and for extrapolating too wildly. Gilbert is the archetype of the Ants, those who 'spend their labour in working out some one experiment, as Gilbert with the magnet';[28] but he 'proceeded at once to construct an entire system in accordance with his favorite subject'.[29] Both criticisms are just in terms of the theory of induction. Individual instances have a lowly status at the bottom of the table, and the Inductive version (or inversion) of the Ramist law of wisdom resists huge leaps up the ladder. The theory of induction implies a universe that needs to be understood part by part, in spite of Bacon's mechanisms to correct this tendency. Gilbert's theory and practice assume that its parts cannot be understood at all in isolation from a view of the whole. His theory of the magnet would have been inconceivable if he had considered loadstones in isolation from that 'great loadstone, the earth'. But even more fruitful for science was his ant-like persistence with 'one experiment', which implies the complementary view that as the part cannot be understood in isolation from the whole, the whole is implicit in some of its parts.

In his preface Gilbert states the relation of his method to Geometry.

> And even as geometry rises from certain slight and readily understood foundations to the highest and most difficult demonstrations, whereby the ingenious mind ascends above the aether: so does our magnetic doctrine and science in due order first show forth certain facts of less rare occurrence; from these proceed facts of a more extraordinary kind; at length, in a sort of series, are revealed things most secret and privy in the earth, and the causes are recognized of things that, in the ignorance of those of old or through the heedlessness of the moderns, were unnoticed or disregarded.[30]

Mathematics is as dangerous as Bacon feared; Gilbert has reached the aether before the sentence is half completed. However, the actual method educes physical facts, 'experiments and discoveries' as he calls them elsewhere, and these are not peripheral but an intrinsic and continuous part of the activity. The interaction of mind and senses which Bacon wished to root out as an 'idol' of the mind, Gilbert sees can be used creatively to refine perception, so that things can be observed and understood that had been 'unnoticed or disregarded'.

Gilbert's achievement is generally attributed to his method, the magical beliefs seen as at best a psychological stimulus, at worst fundamentally misleading and unscientific, but this mistakes the contribution of those beliefs and the grounds of the method. Only the magical world-view could provide adequate models to describe forces and relationships. And the method itself was also intrinsically related to some features of a magical world-view. Gilbert's experimental method is distinguished from Baconian induction by its infinitely patient concentration on small-scale phenomena, confident that they contain hints of the nature of the universe and embody its laws. Galileo generalized freely because he believed similarly that

> the knowledge of a single fact acquired through a discovery of its causes prepares the mind to understand and ascertain other facts without need of recourse to experiment.[31]

Newton used the Second Rule of Reasoning in Philosophy, that

> To the same natural effects we must, as far as possible, assign the same causes,[32]

to unite physics and astronomy, the world and the heavens, in the Newtonian synthesis. Both the terms and the method of the synthesis ultimately imply something of a microcosmic-macrocosmic relationship.

Newton, however, distinguishes his views carefully from magic in a formulation that Gilbert also might have used:

> These Principles I consider, not as Occult Qualities, supposed to result from
> the specifick Forms of Things, but as general Laws of Nature, by which the
> Things themselves are form'd; their Truth appearing to us by Phaenomena,
> though their Causes be not yet discover'd. For these are manifest Qualities,
> and their Causes only are occult.[33]

The traditional magical disciplines were a repository of specific effects,
isolated from each other and from a systematically magical view. Porta,
for instance, in his 'Natural Magick' of 1550, insists that

> the knowledge of secrecies dependeth upon the survey and viewing of the
> whole World,[34]

a statement which sounds reminiscent of Gilbert's procedure. But in his
section on sympathies and antipathies he reveals the unsystematic nature
of much actual magical procedure.

> Ivy, as it is the bane of all Trees, so it is most hurtful, and the greatest enemy
> to the Vine; and therefore Ivy also is good against drunkennesses.

And a few sentences later:

> The Ape of all other things cannot abide a Snail: now the Ape is a drunken
> beast, for they are wont to take an Ape by making him drunk; and a Snail
> well washt is a remedy against drunkennesse.[35]

But Porta sees no reason to connect the two cures for drunkenness to each
other or to more general principles. His reactions to the 'specifick Forms'
of things seem remote from any systematic explanation, magical or other.
He has not even taken his examples seriously enough to test them in
'Phaenomena', unless he observed that the thought of well-washed snails
has a sobering effect. Otherwise his examples are like Instances which a
Baconian might test for inclusion in a table of Induction. Both Newton
and Gilbert would be severe on 'magical' beliefs of this kind, but from a
stance that is in some respects more seriously and systematically magical.
Both look through 'Phaenomena' to a geometry of forces that goes
'beyond the aether'.

But the crucial point of difference between the Newtonian universe and
beliefs from traditional magic lay in the conversion of *anima* to *vis*, souls or
spirits to physical forces. The transition is almost visible in one eloquent
passage from Gilbert:

> Wonderful is the loadstone shown in many experiments to be, and, as it were,
> animate . . . In the bodies of the several stars the inborn energy works in ways
> other than in that divine essence which presides over nature; and in the stars,
> the sources of all things, in other ways than in animals; finally, in animals in
> other ways than in plants. Pitiable is the state of the stars, abject the lot of
> earth, if this high dignity of soul is denied them, while it is granted to the
> worm, the ant, the roach, to plants and morels.[36]

There are differences in the way the force acts, but it is the one force. Elsewhere he talks of *vis vegetiva*, the vegetive force, in a way analogous to magnetic forces.[37] But the loadstone is only 'veluti animatus', as though animate, because the capricious and personal 'anima' is now the scientific 'Insita Vis', an inborn energy obeying impersonal laws that are subject to Mathematics. Newton used the same term in the opening of his 'Principia', to refer to the force of inertia.[38] Gilbert's style, too, has a momentum the lack of which makes Bacon's more self-contained style feel finally unsatisfying. The idea of the universe as a diverse but single system of forces itself acts as a source of energy, providing the impulse for five books of careful description and accumulation of evidence before it breaks to the surface: 'Misera conditio astrorum, abjecta sors telluris . . .' (Pitiable is the state of the stars, abject the lot of the earth . . .) the phrases roll on in a way Bacon would have distrusted, though he had his vision too.

Gilbert could use a grand manner like this to convey his vision of the macrocosm, but descriptions of seemingly mundane topics can come to sudden life through his sense of the presence of the forces of the macrocosm.

Neque solum ferri venae a metallicis expetitae, sed etiam terrae ferruginea substantia tantum imbutae, & saxa nonnulla modo eodem in has coeli, seu verius terrae positiones incumbunt, labunturque, si fuerint artificiose collocatae, donec ad quaesitum locum perveniant, in quo avide requiescunt.[39]

(and not only such ores as miners seek, but even earths simply impregnated with ferruginous matter, and many kinds of rocks, do in like manner (provided they be skilfully placed) tend and glide towards those positions of the heavens, or rather of the earth, until they reach the point they are seeking: there they eagerly rest).

The movement of the sentence responds sensitively to the energies being described. The verbs *incumbunt, labunturque*, lean and glide, come like a sudden surprising release from the passivity and inertness of the 'ferruginea substantia', ferrous substance, and the sentence centres on its exact target like a compass needle correcting itself. The sentence pauses for a finer adjustment to be made, then the metal reaches its goal. In the final image, 'avide requiescunt', eagerly rest, the iron's stillness expresses not inertness, but an alignment with the forces of the globe. The fine image so perfectly placed is not an accidental felicity. The sentence in the original is the last in its chapter, typographically narrowing down in a triangular shape whose apex is the final two words. The power and artfulness of the image witness to Gilbert's total trust in language and imagination. The idols Bacon wished to rase from the mind are central to Gilbert's paradigm, or metaparadigm as it may conveniently be called, for in it the fragmenting knowledge of the former tradition could find a more significant place, and out of it grew method and models for the new science, almost fully formed.

(ii) From Ramism to Science

Bacon's thought as a whole should not be reduced to the 'Baconian' or Ramist strand. The distinction between Bacon and Baconianism can be used to help us understand the precise nature of his influence. Works by other authors that seem 'Baconian' might turn out to have been hardly influenced by Bacon's actual works, for Ramism can sometimes be distinguished only with difficulty from 'Baconianism'. An example of this blend that is especially close to Marvell is a work by James Primrose, 'de Vulgi . . . Erroribus', the English translation of which included two prefatory poems by Marvell.[40] Primrose seems a humble worker in the Baconian vineyard. His work tested items in the contemporary pharmacopia in order to eliminate those that were unsound, the essential first stage in the inductive method. However, his habits of thought were those of simple Ramism, which made it difficult for him to entertain certain sorts of ideas irrespective of their truth or falsity; ideas of a kind that could be importantly true as well as absurdly false. His work shows especially clearly the strengths and limitations of the new Rationalism in its assault on superstition and magic.

As his test-case for magical cures Primrose took the 'Weapon Salve', an ointment that was supposed to cure a wound by being applied to the weapon that caused it. He devoted 34 pages of argument and citation to his refutation, though confessing he had never tried it. Admittedly some of the ingredients were difficult or unpleasant to obtain, such as dried Egyptian mummy or moss from the skull of a gallows-knave, but though the cure would have done little good it could have done no positive harm, unlike many of the conventional remedies that Primrose might have prescribed instead. But Primrose relies like a Ramist on the self-evidence of his reason, and this reason is Ramist logic. In the Chapter on the Weapon-Salve, there are 11 disjunctive syllogisms and 21 hypothetical syllogisms, with no Aristotelian forms. A typical passage of reasoning runs as follows:

> Therefore the cure shall result either from the similitude of the weapon to the wound, but that cannot be; for in relations there is no power of acting, but there should rather be antipathy betwixt the weapon and the person wounded: Or else some vertue flowes from the ointment to the wound: (for according to *Crollius* the ointment is of a conglutinating and drawing nature) but they do not touch one another.[41]

The basic argument is a disjunctive syllogism, with both halves of the either-or denied. But this initial disjunction proceeds from some assumptions that his supposed Paracelsan opponents would strongly deny. Implicitly Primrose has assumed a dualism between corporeal and non-corporeal, so that the relationship, a non-corporeal quality, could

80

have no power of acting, such 'power of acting' being understood as bodily action on the physical wound. Conversely, 'vertue flowing' is assumed to be solely corporeal in its action, so that unless the wound and the ointment are in physical contact there could be no physical effect. If this dualism is denied, both halves of Primrose's disjunction can be affirmed: the relationship has power of action and can act at a distance, but it needs a physical medium to act through. One of the essential features of the magical world-view he was combatting was its denial of a spirit-matter dualism in favour of a psycho-physical unity, where non-material qualities, like relationships or symbols, have physical power, but need a physical medium. Crollius is sufficiently explicit:

> The four Astra's of the said Elements are the Seeds in the four matrices or wombs and always two are together and in one, to wit, the Body and Astrum, the invisible and visible: The Bodily growes out of the Spirituall, and abideth in it, and so the invisible vertues, Seeds and Astra's are propagated into many Millions through the corporeall Visible body . . . Angels cannot increase themselves, because they want a body, but Man may because he hath a one . . . (for the Seed or Astrum can doe nothing without the body)[42]

The way dualisms multiply and dissolve into each other here is characteristic of Crollius, who can sustain this sort of thing for pages on end. Gilbert's form of 'magic' is more symmetrically anti-dualist, for though he conceives of Spirit/force acting on bodies, he constantly tests hypotheses derived from these conceptions in actual bodies. In Crollius' form of magic the spirit has absorbed the body almost entirely, allowing it to exist only like some favoured concubine whose sole business is to breed, not correct its master. But Gilbert could formulate, test and refute hypotheses of the Crollius kind. Primrose could not even understand the nature of the ideas concerned. This is not so obvious to us in the case of the Weapon-Salve because there his conclusion happened to be right. But the same reasoning applied without modification to Gilbert's theory of the magnet would similarly have had to deny all power to relationships, all action at a distance, and all concentration of such power on particularly significant objects. Primrose was aware that defenders of magical cures often invoked magnetism, so he first distinguished the two kinds of phenomena, and then described magnetism in entirely corporeal terms. The influence of the salve is different from

> the sympathy of other things, which do insensibly diffuse their virtue into the aire, and need not the spirit of the world to carry them, and do never work unless the object be present, and are terminated and limited within a certain space. But that there are cessations and fallings off from this sympathy the Loadstone shewes, which being rubbed over with Garlick, doth not draw iron, which manifests, that there is not an efflux and wasting of the qualitie only, but of some thinne substance also.[43]

The 'spirit of the world' is physicalized with the faintly ludicrous verb 'carry' but then dismissed, though it is difficult to explain polarity and dip in magnets without some reference to the Earth as a whole. But Primrose's model is formed by analogy with the diffusion of odours, as his revealing repetition of the garlic superstition shows. Again he could not have tried an experiment. Nor has he read Gilbert or Bacon on the subject, both of whom reject the myth.[44] Even the Natural Magician Porta tested and disproved it.[45] Garlic was a sovereign remedy against diabolical influences, but the new scepticism of Primrose can accept it if the action can be conceived entirely in corporeal terms. If the attraction of a magnet is regarded as due to an efflux, the insidious smell of garlic could quite credibly overwhelm the unsmellable smell of a magnet.

Bacon himself is often much less 'Baconian' than Primrose. He had a genuine if intermittent awareness of the limitations of simple Ramism, and a deep though ambivalent interest in the magical tradition. Rossi, who has tracked down much of Bacon's reading in the magical sciences, sub-titled his work 'from Magic to Science'.[46] Bacon's intermittent attempts to go in the opposite direction, from 'Baconianism' to magic, paradoxically brought him as close as he ever got to science.

Though characteristically fond of the neat distribution, Bacon also insisted on the dangers of the law of justice. In the relatively early 'Advancement' he wrote:

And generally let this be a rule, that all partitions of knowledges be accepted; rather for lines and veins than for sections and separations; and that the continuance and entireness of knowledge be preserved.[47]

The statement is general, but it applies especially to the subject Bacon is introducing at that point, 'knowledge of ourselves'. Accordingly, immediately after he has distinguished between knowledges of the body and the mind he set up a third category for the combined faculties. The sciences of the 'league' as he calls it are all magical, but Bacon thinks they can be 'purged and restored to their true state'.[48]

The later Latin version, 'de Augmentis', extends the argument of this section in a number of interesting ways, which derive from a new distribution of the soul. In 'Advancement' Bacon seemed to suppose a two-term entity consisting of mind or soul and body. In 'de Augmentis' the soul is distinguished into 'Spiraculum', the religious soul, knowledge of which can come only from God, and 'Anima sensibilis' or the Irrational Soul, which is a 'corporeal substance', but is invisible, and is the 'Source of Motion'.[49] This soul is then partially distinguished from the animal soul, for it is 'more fitly termed not soul but spirit'.[50] As a result of these distinctions he has a notion of a soul which is a proper subject for scientific study, so that invisible forces become important and legitimate objects of a scientist's attention. Out of this grows an interesting

82

distinction between the perceptible and the sensible. All bodies, he argues, have a power of perception *(vis percipiendi)*.[51] Examples of perception in this sense are the attraction of iron to magnets, and naphtha to flame. 'No body when placed near another either changes it or is changed by it, unless a reciprocal *perception* precede the operation. A body . . . perceives the force of another body to which it yields . . . in short there is Perception everywhere.'[52] Animism, as in Gilbert, is being used as an image for the action of forces at a distance. Bacon's 'Anima' is turning in to the scientific 'Vis'.

Such a conception had valuable consequences for his ideas on Experimental Method. Bacon claimed with justice to be a 'true priest of sense'.[53] For too many men he objects, 'speculation commonly ceases where sight ceases',[54] but he does not seek to reduce the senses as he reduced language and the mind. His aim on the contrary is to extend them greatly in power and subtlety, to go beyond the sensible to the realm of the perceptible. The sensible is merely the somewhat arbitrary area of the perceptible that the sensory organs are equipped to receive. The conception gives a strong impetus to the study of these other invisible forces. Accordingly Bacon seeks to supplement the senses with instruments and even more with 'experiments'. It is here that his advice comes closest to the methods that were to be most fruitful in the advance of Seventeenth Century Science. 'Experiment' meant little more than experience for the Inductive Bacon. 'Experimental Philosophy' was the lowest category of 'natural Prudence', corresponding to natural history. It utilized memory rather than understanding, and could be left to the Ants. Experiments in the context of Bacon's theory of the invisibly perceptible, however, would be a more important and directed kind of activity, designed to detect underlying structures and the action of forces. The division in Bacon's thought points even more clearly than Primrose's example to the difference between the simple Ramist kind of empiricism and the Experimental Method. Induction, like Ramism, did not attach sufficient attention to particulars to justify the kind or degree of attention Gilbert gave his magnets. But a Ramist who queried the law of justice could arrive at a much more interesting position, one not unlike Gilbert's.

The great scientists of the Royal Society had to resist 'Baconianism' much as Bacon himself did. Robert Hooke, arguably England's greatest scientist of the period after Newton, certainly one of the most fertile, paid lip-service to the ideals of the Royal Society in his early 'Micrographia' of 1665. His opening address to that august body began:

> The Rules YOU have prescrib'd YOUR selves in YOUR Philosophical Progress do seem the best that have ever yet been practis'd. And particularly that of avoiding Dogmatizing, and the espousal of any Hypothesis not sufficiently grounded and confirm'd by Experiments . . .

But then he continued:

> Saying which, I may seem to condemn my own Course in this Treatise; in which there may perhaps be some Expressions, which may seem more positive than YOUR Prescriptions will permit:[55]

At no time in his scientific career did he really share the Royal Society's 'Baconian' distrust of the mind or its strictures on hypothesising.

But Hooke also genuinely admired Bacon, and wrote an account of his own method that follows Bacon's work in many respects. He was apparently particularly impressed by Bacon's discussion of the assistance to the senses, which he elaborated with considerable ingenuity and power. Like Bacon, he saw instruments and experiments as 'the adding of artificial organs to the natural.'[56] Each sense is considered in terms of the kind of information it naturally conveys, and assistance can be either direct or indirect, or 'primary' and 'secondary'. For example, smell is concerned with the effluvia of bodies, i.e. the movements of gases, so he gives as an example of 'secondary' smell a barometer with a pointer that magnified the slightest movements of the mercury. The senses can also be more directly assisted

> by making the sensible Qualities of the object more powerful than naturally they are of themselves for affecting the Sense.[57]

As an example he suggests that Motions can be accelerated:

> Thus supposing the Experiment were true that some Authors have delivered us concerning the Acceleration of Sallets, we might possibly see the Motion of Vegetation, as we might also, if that story be true which Clusius tells us, of the strangely growing and rising Tree.[58]

The description suggests that the visual is the primary sense for Hooke, and it is true that his technique for enlarging the power of the other senses is characteristically to translate them into visual equivalents, but the original conceptions are basically kinaesthetic, and even his description of the visual sense suggests a strongly kinaesthetic quality.

> For the Eye is the most Spiritual and most capacious Sense we are endowed with, it affords us the most sudden, most distinct and instructive Information of all; with this we expatiate through the Universe, and pass from one end to the other in the twinkling of an Eye, by this we compare the Magnitude and Measure, the Distances, Motions, and the Velocities of all those vast Bodies which are disseminated up and down through it, and none of the other Senses tend so much to perfect the Imagination as this.[59]

As the sentence progresses the Eye, the 'most spiritual sense', becomes one with the spirit. The eye 'perfect(s) the Imagination' and sweeps through the heavens with the freedom of the spirit. It is like Hobbes' description of the movement of the Fancy in the world of the Mind,[60] except that Hooke's eye has this freedom and rapidity in the macrocosm itself. But his description has even more affinities with Marvell's stanza in 'Appleton House' already discussed. For both men the macroscopic and microscopic extension of the power of the visual sense becomes an image for the action of the perfected or enlarged imagination. Marvell's account is even more strongly kinaesthetic than Hooke's; the experience is almost felt in the eyeballs as the focus shortens and lengthens with a giddying rapidity. But though Marvell is less celebratory than Hooke, his lines give us not a different experience but a more intense and sombre record of a common vision.

(iii) Science and Poetry

Marvell, like Gilbert and Hooke, had his 'superstitious' side, which critics have similarly ignored, prevented by preconceptions from assimilating the phenomenon. His work abounds in the sort of 'Vulgar Errors' that Primrose attacked. The Oxford edition of his works uses Gerard's 'Herball' or Browne's 'Pseudodoxia Epidemica' (of 1646) to annotate some of the most extraordinary examples,[61] but there are many more. Even as a literary quality this is worthy of comment. Donne had created images from the relation of the microcosm to the macrocosm, but the habit of raiding herbals and bestiaries goes further back in the English literary tradition, to the Euphuism of Lyly, a style that was already unfashionable when Donne started to write. Rather than back-date Marvell even further, critics have more wisely chosen not to discuss the quality. But Marvell's use of Pliny and the Herbalists, of course, is not like Lyly's, and the necessary critical discriminations lead into crucial distinctions between modes of thought. In a history of science that has Gilbert and Hooke as exemplars, rather than Bacon, Marvell here is near the intellectual centre of the age. His 'vulgar errors' are not just curious anachronisms, they connect below the level of the factual with the sources of the new science.

Take for instance this example from an early poem:

> The Phlegmatick and Slowe prolongs his day,
> And on Times Wheel sticks like a Remora.
>
> ('Death of Hastings' line 11–12)

Pliny was the major source for stories of this mythical fish, alternatively called Remora or Echeneis. His account typically combines the moral with the magical. After describing how a Remora stopped Caligula's galley dead in its course he exclaims:

> See the vanity of man! alas, how foolish are we to make all this adoe? when one little fish, not above halfe a foot long, is able to arrest and stay perforce, yea and hold as prisoners our goodly tall and proud ships . . .[62]

But being nonexistent the Remora was hard to catch, so the error could not be disproved by experiment. Scientists of the seventeenth century quite properly gave the stories serious attention before dismissing them. Kirchner, for instance, in 1659, rejected the myth on these grounds:

> If then the Echeneis has this retentive power in itself, then clearly it follows that the less powerful would be overcoming the more powerful; but this is impossible . . . for everything that retards something else must overcome the thing retarded by weight or resistance.[63]

Kirchner does not 'See the Vanity of man! alas' because he is more interested in the forces operating between the fish and the boat, and he rejects the story because of the disparity in the forces involved. Pliny of course was aware of the disparity too – it was the point of the story – but he does not try to recreate the forces involved in a force-model. As Kirchner translates the moral 'anima' into the scientific 'vis' the story loses all credibility and all reason for its existence, and becomes inevitably a vulgar error.

Marvell is a poet not a scientist, and his subject is a quality of human life, not the status of a superstition, but his use of the image relies on a precise evocation of the forces involved. The absence of movement of the 'Phlegmatic and Slowe' becomes by extension a force with a powerful negative velocity, which exerts a disproportionate effect on Time's wheel. The rhythm of the line registers the force with the bunched stresses, 'Ón Tímes Wheel sticks', before the line goes suddenly slack with 'like a Remora'. The disproportion may seem even more incredible in this case than in Pliny's, for the 'Phlegmatick and Slowe' is opposing Time's Wheel, which cannot be stopped. But of course, it does not stop. Instead of Pliny's unimagined miraculous effect of the ship stopping instantaneously, there is the vividly realized sensation of a dead weight dragging back against the onward motion of the wheel (and the verse) before the momentum finally proves too strong. Pliny accepts an incredible account of forces for the sake of the moral. Kirchner translates the story into terms of 'vis', and rejects it as physically incredible. Marvell has an equally clear sense of the forces that could be involved, which could have been used similarly to reject the tale, but instead he creates out of the story a poetic image of unnatural forces. 'Vis' becomes an image for 'Anima', with the violation of the laws of physics part of its meaning, just as he used the deviations of emblems from normal scale to suggest a vividly possibly bizarre. The resistance of the Phlegmatick to Time is to be reversed, with a more explicit sense of its physical impossibility, in the last couplet of 'To His Coy Mistress':

> Thus, though we cannot make our Sun
> Stand still, yet we will make him run.

But animated vegetables are even more distinctive of Marvell than remarkable little fish, and here his 'errors' do not have such obvious vulgar sources. Such lines as these could be found in no other seventeenth century poet:

> Bind me ye Woodbines in your 'twines,
> Curle me about ye gadding Vines,
> And Oh so close your Circles lace,
> That I may never leave this Place:
> But, lest your Fetters prove too weak,
> Ere I your Silken Bondage break,
> Do you, O Brambles, chain me too,
> And courteous Briars nail me through.
>
>   ('A.H.' Stanza LXXVII)

The quality must be distinguished from personification, as in Milton's lines, for instance, which may have suggested one of Marvell's images:

> Thee, Shepherd, thee the woods and desert caves,
> With wild thyme and the gadding vine o'er grown,
> And all their echoes mourn.
> The willows and the hazel copses green
> Shall now no more be seen
> Fanning their joyous leaves to thy soft lays.
>
>   ('Lycidas' lines 39–44)

Milton perfunctorily assigns the woods some elemementary and entirely human tasks, but the point of the lines is for him to hear himself saying them. The real source of motion in the willows is the wind; the pretended source is located in the human as reflected on to the plants. 'Gadding' in Milton works as an adjective that describes the straggly form a vine normally assumes in the natural state, but Marvell conveys a sense of the vine in the very process of assuming this characteristic shape. The activity is not imposed from outside by the human or caused by a wind, but represents an intensified sense of the vine's actual processes of growth speeded up immensely, the 'vis vegetiva' made visible. Animation like this is different from personification. It is a transaction, not a convention, achieved through total passivity in the observer, whose 'working and reflective fancy' has made his energies available to the plants, the total energy remaining constant.

Similar comments could be made about the famous stanza V of 'The Garden':

> The Luscious Clusters of the Vine
> Upon my Mouth do crush their Wine;
> The Nectaren, and curious Peach,
> Into my hands themselves do reach;
> Stumbling on Melons, as I pass,
> Insnar'd with Flow'rs, I fall on Grass.

The lines can again be compared with a probable literary source, Jonson's lines in 'To Penshurst':

> The blushing apricot, and wooly peach
> Hang on thy walls, that every child may reach.   (lines 43–44)

Jonson's natural world here is Baconianly inert, and his use of words shows how totally absent their animistic implications are for him. 'Blushing' refers only to the colour, since the apricots have no reason to be embarrassed. His use of the word, confident that he can rely on it remain inert, shows just how far from animism he is. The peach similarly is imprecisely taken for granted; it is merely 'wooly'. Man is so in control that even a child can reach the fruit. Marvell's peach, however, is 'curious'. The word, as elsewhere in his poetry, is ambiguously both active and passive.[64] The peach is elaborately and intricately made, the description implying an intensity of attention on Marvell's part which in general distinguishes his treatment of natural objects from Jonson's, whose world commonly is solidly but negligently present. But the active sense of 'curious' must also apply to these peaches which put themselves into his hands. The two meanings are reciprocal; the fascinated attention causes and is demanded by the movement and the beauty of the fruit. The ambiguity conveys the indeterminate location of the movement, of fruit to hands and lips or of lips and hands to fruit. The illusion of movement is achieved this time by eliminating the point of reference, as when the station seems to leave a train. The result is again to transfer energies to the plants, till the enervated body falls.

The movement of the plants is completed by the energies of the mind, but like the scientific 'vis' it follows its own laws, which do not simply reflect human moods or the dictates of conventional morality. Where this is not true in Marvell the quality of the poetry is very different. The fruit seems similarly co-operative in 'Bermudas':

> He makes the Figs our mouths to meet;
> And throws the Melons at our feet.   (lines 21–22)

The difference that makes the Bermudas a paradise and the Garden faintly disturbing is that the cause of the movement in the Bermudas is 'He', God. So the fecundity is directly subservient to a benevolent and moral God, and the source of the movement is comfortingly understood. Thus it involves no loss of energy for the briskly rowing Puritans. This is a different kind of world to that of 'The Garden'. It would not be out of keeping with its laws for the Puritans to have instant brakes like Remorae, for as in Pliny's world, forces have no independent reality to resist the dominance of the moral. The stanza in the 'Garden' enacts a version of the Fall, but the energies derive from levels of nature and mind below the conscious control of the poet, and the process subtly but radically distorts the reflected moral archetype. The source of movement is not fully understood, and is not unequivocally moral or benevolent. Neither poem of course aspires to literal truth, but 'Bermudas' is finally a fantasy, self-indulgently dispensing with the laws that generate Marvell's real and imagined universes. This makes it a more superficial, a less significant and fully imagined achievement than 'The Garden'. This judgment, of course, corresponds to common evaluations of the two poems, merely making some of the grounds of the judgment more explicit.

We still need to be precise about the kind of connection that exists between Marvell's animated vegetables and contemporary science. Of course Marvell's images are not botanically sound. Their truth is poetic, not scientific. But this distinction is not absolute, and since the differences are so obvious it is more necessary to stress the real affinities. Hooke as we have been was keenly interested in the 'Acceleration of Sallets' and the story of 'that strangely growing and rising Tree'.[65] In 'Micrographia' he described observations and dissections made on the 'sensitive Plant',[66] a plant which also figures in Marvell's poetry.[67] Hooke's interest led to no great advances in plant physiology, but was fulfilled half-a century later in the work of Stephan Hales, the father of plant Physiology.

The starting point for Hales was his conviction that there is a 'great analogy between plants and animals'.[68] He developed the analogy in mechanistic terms, and his success came partly through his novel application of 'staticks' to problems of sap velocity and pressure, but other less simply mechanistic considerations continued to influence his thinking. For instance he writes:

> Tho' vegetables (which are inanimate) have not an engine, which, by its alternate dilations and contractions, does in animals forcibly drive the blood through the arteries and veins; yet has nature wonderfully contrived other means, most powerfully to raise and keep in motion the sap.[69]

As the sentence opens life seems to mean no more than the possession of an engine, but as the sentence continues the interest shifts to the forces involved, and to how 'powerfully' they work. His experiments made force and motion visible by means of columns of mercury and tables of figures. These are experiments used as 'secondary organs of perception' as Hooke called it; they translate forces into visual terms, and allow secondary perception of the 'Motion of Vegetation'. The forces at work in the thrust of sap and the self-directed movement of plants are made to seem far more powerful and 'wonderful' than normally supposed, and these forces are directly associated with a universal source. The emotive words, as with Gilbert, are not hindrances to thought but act as part of the force-model. 'Wonderfully' is partly glossed by 'most powerfully'. The word directs attention and indicates the site of energies. As with Marvell's 'curious' the power of arousing the attention of the mind implies a principle of motion in the thing itself, which Hales proceeds to test.

One place where Marvell plays most explicitly with magical notions is in his poems for Witty's translation of Primrose. The Latin poem indicates the large differences that we would expect between Marvell and Primrose on 'Popular Errors'. At one point he pretends to have burnt the book and exclaims in a subversive parody of a magical cure:

> Naribus O doctis quam pretiosus odor!   (line 12)
> (Oh, to learned nostrils what a precious odour!)

The English poem, after praising Witty's translation, concludes more interestingly:

> And (if I judgment have) I censure right;
> For something guides my hand that I must write.   (lines 37–38)

The first line seemed to indicate his possession of the soberly rational quality of judgment, engaged in its proper task of censuring vulgar errors. The second relates this judgment to an irrational force, as he seems to have become possessed by something like the 'spirit of the world' that Primrose mocked. But this, far from opposing judgment, is its cause.

A similar idea occurs in a poem that contains a more direct response to magical ideas. Joseph de Maniban had apparently analyzed a piece of Marvell's handwriting impressively, so Marvell wrote him in return a bantering but complimentary verse epistle. The form of words is as revealing as their meaning, he commences:

> Flexibus in calami tamen omnia sponte leguntur
> Quod non significant Verba, Figura notat . . .
> Ignaramque Manum Spiritus intus agit.
>
> (Nevertheless, in the turnings of the reed-pen all things are read spontaneously.
> What the words do not signify, the shape makes known . . .
> And a spirit within drives the unknowing hand.)
>
> ('To a Gentleman' lines 5–8)

Again a 'spirit of the world' takes control of his pen. Here it directs both 'verba' and 'figura'. The distinction mirrors the relation of soul and body. So the 'spirit within' is contained within the 'body' of the word as well as in its soul or meaning. This brings out the potential ambiguity in 'figura', which could mean 'shade' or 'phantom' as well as shape; and the use of the singular reinforces the suggestion. Thus the shape or form of the words is as it were animated, both containing and reflecting the 'spiritus intus'.

The framework for this is the magical model of the microcosm–macrocosm:

Usque adeo caeli respondat pagina nostrae,
Astrorum & nexus syllaba scripta refert.   (lines 29–30)

(So much does the page of the heavens correspond to ours,
And the written syllable refer to the patterns of the stars.)

The key word here is 'nexus', which can be translated as 'patterns'. However, the word means more than patterns. Literally it is their 'bindings', and refers simultaneously to their structure and to their effect on the written page. The forces of the macrocosm act on the microcosm to determine its specific form, acting at a distance through the 'nexus', the binding of the common form.

The tone of Marvell's poem, of course, implies some distance from de Maniban's particular art of 'Grammatomancy'. The phrase 'Spiritus intus agit' (a spirit within drives) must recall the famous Vergilian phrase 'Spiritus intus alit' (the spirit within nourishes) but there is a hint of the mock-heroic in the echo.[70] Later on he writes 'Astrologus certior Astronomo', (line 26), the Astrologer is more reliable than the Astronomer, clearly a paradox since the specific predictions of the Astrologer relied on general laws found out by Astronomers. There is no naive commitment to Astrology: de Maniban's claims are only hypothetically entertained and explored.

Like most magical arts, however, Grammatomancy was capable of a rational form. De Maniban interpreted 'vitae casus, animique recessus', the second of these, the recesses of the mind, certainly a worthy object of scientific study. Bacon was interested in a development of this kind, parallel to the reformed science of 'Physiognomy'. He distinguished Grammar into 'popular' and 'philosophical', the aim of the latter being to examine 'the power and nature of words, as they are the footsteps and prints of reason'.[71] In 'de Augmentis' he gives further hints of what he had in mind. This science would seek

signs . . . concerning the dispositions and manners of peoples and nations, drawn from their languages.[72]

He supplements this with some scattered observations on certain features of vocabulary and syntax in Greek and Latin. 'Grammatomancy' could similarly become the study of how words and their 'nexus', their patterns or structures rather than their shape on the page, reveal the 'recesses of the mind' of their author far more fully than he intended.

A macrocosmic–microcosmic model of this kind is also a frequent structural principle in Marvell's poetry, transmuting otherwise conventional tropes. Take Celia in 'The Match', for instance. She is 'one perfect

Beauty', (line 16) and in this seems only like countless other Celia's, who are presented as ideals, and so can be loosely categorized as 'platonic'. Marvell's Celia is similarly perfection, but she is not a preordained exemplar from another and higher mode of existence. Nature forms her by affinities:

> But likeness soon together drew
> What she did separate lay; (lines 13–14)

Celia is the concentration of physical delights, not a pattern from above. She is a Paracelsan kind of microcosm, including the world through the possession of common elements, so that she represents active power:

> For, with one grain of them diffus'd
> She (i.e. Nature) could the World repair (lines 11–12)

The Paracelsen source is more prominent in the second half of the poem, where Love's 'Magazine', or store of forces, is stocked with alchemical substances. The quality of the forces is created with typical vividness:

> The Naphta's and the Sulphurs heat,
> And all that burns the Mind (lines 23–24)

The image is active and destructive, the chemicals unpleasantly present. The quality seems to contradict the last stanza:

> So we alone the happy rest,
> Whilst all the world is poor (lines 37–38)

How can a mind be happy when it is burning with sulphur? How could such forces be said to rest? This is not simply inattention on the part of the poet, for the title itself punningly includes forces of destruction and unity. Their 'Match' is both union and a spark to inflame the world. But the beauty is a kind of power with nothing exemplary or moral about it, so it can coexist uneasily with the more destructive elements of the poet's love in a single complex emotion.

Marvell's poem is trying to do something interesting and unusual, but finally it is a failure, and its failure can be described in terms of the forces involved. The forces do not bind together in a satisfactory 'nexus', with the negative locked against the positive. Instead they act separately, and their antagonism disintegrates the poem. Equally damaging is the inattention to the magnitude of the forces. The concentration of energies and essences in the two lovers deprives the world of all force and beauty, so the macrocosm is left with no power to resist the lovers. But as a result the concentration of everything in the lovers feels unreal, and the poem floats away into vacuity. Marvell has not fully understood the disturbing emotions he is dealing with, and this failure is embodied in confused and contradictory forces, wilfully detached from any intelligible cosmos.

Donne also draws images from a microcosmic–macrocosmic model, but his different conception of its nature leads to a very different kind of imagery. For Donne as for Marvell the macrocosm was commonly the world of public affairs, the 'dimensio politeia' to use Dickson's term, but for Donne the spheres are related by similarity, and do not affect each other. Thus he characteristically tries to include images from public life in his microcosm, to make 'one little roome, an every where'. Sometimes he denies any power to this microcosm, in spite of the implications of the imagery:

> Alas, alas, who's injur'd by my love?
> What merchants ships have my sighs drown'd?

Sometimes the absorption into the microcosm appears total:

> She is all States, and all Princes, I,
>   Nothing else is.[73]

but the macrocosm still exists independently in the penumbra outside his assertion. The model is a strategy to include potent and desirable objects from the public world along with his love. It is poetry of inclusion and exclusion, possession and loss, its images typically a clutter of objects collected by the jackdaw poet.

Such a model cannot easily represent or explore man's relation to society, or conceive man as participating in a set of dynamic relationships. Marvell's kind of model, however, is not limited in this way. The estate at Appleton House is 'Paradices only Map' (line 768) but the poem uses it to comprehend the forces of the macrocosm in order in some measure to control them. The twin macrocosms of public life and the physical universe both act through things that can be found in the microcosm, and public significance is felt as forces of macrocosmic magnitude. So it is not the presence of particular things that surprises, as so often with Donne, but the extraordinary forces latent in them. Many of the resulting images are less visual than kinaesthetic, creations so unusual and so unprepared for by any critical theories of the time that it is easy to mistake their quality. Take the great image of the Halcyon near the climax of the poem:

> The modest Halcyon comes in sight,
> Flying betwixt the Day and Night;
> And such an horror calm and dumb,
> Admiring Nature does benum.
> The viscous Air, wheres 'ere She fly,
> Follows and sucks her Azure dy:
> The gellying Stream compacts below,
> If it might fix her shadow so;
> The stupid Fishes hang, as plain
> As Flies in Chrystal overt' ane.   (lines 669–678)

93

Pliny, needless to say, mentions the Halcyon and its traditional association with calm weather.[74] He considers two explanations: either it actually affects the weather, or it knows when the weather will be calm enough for it to build its nest on the waves. The second is the more rational alternative, but Marvell typically takes the more magical explanation, and then recreates the mythical property in terms of forces sufficiently powerful to make the story scientifically possible. Though 'modest', the Halcyon exerts a powerful paralysing effect on Nature, which responds with an equally invisible and powerful attack on the bird. The conception of the forces involved is highly magical. The air has the properties of a liquid, an analogy which Torricelli, Boyle and Hooke used so effectively,[75] but it is also active as it 'follows and sucks her Azure dy'. The 'Shadow' that the water attempts to catch must refer to the bird's image reflected in the water. As with the Latin 'umbra',[76] this is an image embodying the essence of the bird. But the Halcyon uses even greater powers to resist such attacks. She stupifies the fish, vitrifies the water, and resists the air's assault on her by continuing her flight; even to continue it being a difficult and dangerous achievement. The bird is associated in the poem with Maria, young Mary Fairfax, daughter of the house, but this passage is not a simple celebration of her tranquillity, youth and innocence. The bird's traditional tranquillity becomes not an easy absence of the disturbing but a triumphantly achieved equilibrium between immensely powerful opposing forces, the eager immobility of Gilbert's ferrugineous substance. Maria's modesty and innocence must exist in a field of hostile forces, but is itself a powerful and potentially destructive force. She is no static exemplar which the world if it were ideal would follow. Maria and the bird act as the focus of forces as cosmic as the 'spirit of the world'. By a conventional hyperbole she is seen as the tutelary deity of the estate, but the forces that would be involved in this condition are fully and vividly rendered, to give new and disturbing life to the stock image.

The connections I have been trying to make in this chapter have necessarily been tentative and indirect, a matter of deep-seated affinities rather than overt influences. Outside the poems the evidence for Marvell's interest in science is slight. He was never a member of the Royal Society like Dryden, and unlike Cowley he wrote no panegyrics to it. John Pell, one of the leading mathematicians of the day, was one of his closest friends according to Aubrey, but not much can be built on that.

But affinities do not have to be direct and overt to be important. In stressing these affinities my aim has been a re-orientation rather than a demonstration, a new way of seeing, not a fresh body of facts. Some of Marvell's best-known images gained an extra dimension of significance for me, when looked at in this context. I also hope that in the process literary students will see that there is no essential antagonism between science and poetry. Both are supreme products of the human mind, requiring similar qualities: intelligence, imagination, insight and precision. It is no accident that great ages of science have been great ages of poetry. Galileo, Kepler and Gilbert were contemporaries of Shakespeare, Marlowe and Donne, as Marvell was contemporary with Newton and Hooke.

Chapter 4

THOROUGH HIS OWN SIDE

Some time between 1650 and 1655 Marvell changed his allegiance, from being a Royalist to supporting Cromwell. What his reasons were we can only guess, since he left no records at the time, apart from some of the greatest but most difficult political poems in the language. Here more than anywhere else in Marvell, an explication of a text is inseparable from an account of the age. Marvell's change of allegiance can be interpreted in different ways, which must affect our judgment of the poems concerned. Qualities like courage, honesty and integrity matter in poetry as well as in life. If Marvell had effectively capitulated to the fact of power, I for one could not wholly admire poems which dignified such bad faith, and disguised it as something more complex, poised and controlled. But Marvell did not renounce his new allegiance when the Restoration came. For instance, he seems to have worked strenuously on Milton's behalf to save the blind regicide from execution. He was a conscientious MP for Hull, a consistent opponent of the King's party. Another explanation for his change of allegiance is possible. Marvell, bourgeois and puritan, finally and belatedly discovered which side he really belonged to, and renounced, with profound regret, the political order he had believed in and the illusions that had supported it. The cost of self-knowledge was the renunciation of his own youth, his own past. The famous 'poise' is not open mindedness nor neutrality but a sense of this cost coexisting with recognition of its necessity.

(i) The Grounds of Change

In this chapter I want to trace this complex process of decision, as far as can be done. This means looking again at the poems, especially those enigmatic masterpieces, his two major poems about Cromwell. The 'Horatian Ode' is the more famous, notoriously complex and opaque. The 'First Anniversary' is less often looked at but is no less difficult, worth understanding in its own right. But before we turn to the poems we need a context, a gloss to bring out the issues in contemporary terms, and see the ramifications of their significance as political acts.

Here again the notion of paradigms is helpful. Paradigms allow us to go behind particular arguments to the way those arguments would have been understood. They help us to distinguish kinds of argument which might otherwise seem much the same, and trace their roots in profoundly different modes of thought, different political communities. Particular controversies can gain a new dimension of significance if they are seen as instances of paradigm conflict.

One controversy that throws light on Marvell is the debate about the Engagement Oath in early 1650. J. M. Wallace has focused on this as the most relevant and manageable context in which to situate Marvell's political thinking at this crucial period of his life.[1] The Engagement Oath was designed for people in Marvell's position, former Royalists who might be persuaded to acquiesce in the new regime. The Rump parliament, uneasy at the dubious legality of its status, required that from 2nd January 1650, all male citizens over the age of 18 should take an oath to be 'true and faithful to the Commonwealth of England, as it is now established, without a King, or House of Lords'.[2] The form of the oath was deliberately innocuous but with a sting in its tail. It appealed to patriotism, loyalty to the Commonwealth, by which it meant some kind of acquiescence in the legality of the Rump. The absence of King and Lords tags on the end like a minor oversight, whereas it was of course the main point at issue. The oath was asking for acceptance, passive if not active, of the fact of revolution.

Persons who took this oath might have interpreted it very differently. Important differences in paradigms could lie behind seemingly similar decisions, and vice versa. Some of the qualities of Ramism are relevant in understanding this kind of deep antagonism or alignment. Simple Ramism, with its liking for simplistic certainties, for black-and-white choices, would be unable to deal with the ambiguities of the Engagement Oath and the political situation. Simple Ramists would tend to polarize into those who would not dream of taking the oath and those who could have taken it in a much stronger form. Reluctant takers of the oath might have formulated their decision through either a modified form of Ramism or a form of traditional logic.

Contemporaries saw this decision as a case of conscience, to be resolved by casuistry. Ten of the pamphlets listed by Wallace actually include 'case' or 'conscience' in their title. What I have called a difference of paradigms would have been regarded by contemporaries as different kinds of casuistry. Ramist casuistry, commonly found amongst Presbyterian divines, was different from scholastic casuistry. But when kinds of casuistry collided with events, with the realities of political crisis and social revolution, they were liable to develop rapidly or be discarded. Paradigms survive only as long as they help to explain.

This particular debate gains representative importance because one of the participants was Bishop Sanderson, author of the standard scholastic logic of the century. Sanderson wrote two versions of his ruling on the oath, both of them models of scholastic casuistry.[3] A study of them helps us feel the very texture of his paradigm. He establishes the relevant general premises, and proceeds scrupulously by careful steps to set out the range of positions a conscientious man might take. The conclusion is not a single ruling but a description of the circumstances in which it would be either wrong or permissible for a Royalist to take the oath. The argument is lucid and logical yet flexible. Sanderson himself apparently did not take the oath but he does not condemn those who can in conscience do so.

In the case of the Engagement Oath he considers the nature of language and political allegiance in general, and subordinate to this the nature of oaths. Then he takes the actual words of the oath, scrupulously determining the range of interpretations the words could legitimately bear. In terms of this framework he is able to define conditions under which particular laws can rightly be disobeyed. Laws must be understood in terms of the intention of the law-giver, he commences; but this intention can be distinguished into a specific intention and the more general intention which is directed towards the public good.

> The former intention binds, when it is subservient to the latter, or is consistent with it, and consequently bindeth in ordinary cases, and in orderly times, or else the Law is not a wholesome Law. But when the observation of the Law, by reason of the conjuncture of circumstances, or the iniquity of the times (contingencies which no Law-giver could either certainly foresee, or if foreseen, sufficiently provide against) would rather be prejudicial than advantageous to the Publick; or is manifestly attended with such inconveniences and sad consequents to the Observers, as all the imaginable good that can redound to the Publick thereby, cannot in any reasonable measure countervail: in such case the Law obligeth not, but according to the latter and more general intention only; even as in the operations of nature, particular Agents do ordinarily move according to their proper and particular inclinations; yet upon some occasions, and to serve the ends and intentions of universal nature (for the avoiding of some things which nature abhors) they are sometimes carried with motions quite contrary to their particular natures; as the Air to descend, and the Water to ascend for the avoiding of vacuity &c.[4]

The movement of the passage here is characteristic of Sanderson. He commences with the more general pösition, where general and specific intentions are at one, before proceeding to the rare occasions when this unity does not apply. An important assumption underlies the assonance in the phrase 'in ordinary cases, and in orderly times'. The form of the words seems to connect them intrinsically, so that ordinary times will be orderly times, and ordinary cases will reflect this order. The argument contains many either-or statements, but these are not Ramist disjunctive syllogisms. Typically they are hierarchically arranged and are not exclusive. In the first sentence, for instance, 'consistent' is weaker than 'subservient', but all laws subservient to the general intention presumably will also be consistent with it. The two clauses indicate the limits of the normal. They are not separate alternatives. But though the argument proceeds in this careful fashion from the certain and generally true to the less certain and more aberrant, the argument returns finally to a higher order of generality, the laws of the universe, just as in conditions of uncertainty recourse is made to the more general and public intention behind the law. There would be nothing surprising to a reader of Hooker in any of these general propositions about the system of laws common to nature and society. Sanderson's response to the moral dilemma posed by the event of the civil war is a clear and orderly restatement of the great commonplaces of the scholastic paradigm.

But Sanderson was a Bishop of the established church, committed to the old order. He would have had good reason to see the revolution as only a minor aberration, the political equivalent of a water spout. His importance is representative, but he probably did not represent Marvell very closely, even though he obliquely legitimated the decision Marvell took. Wallace saw much greater affinities between Marvell and Anthony Ascham, whose 'Of the Confusions' was the most original pamphlet directly concerned with the engagement oath.[5] This in fact was the only other writer Sanderson chose to mention and refute. The choice showed sound judgment. Ascham's argument seemed similar in effect to Sanderson's, but Ascham had been a Parliament man throughout the war, and the real basis of his argument was a version of Ramism. The very similarity made Ascham's argument more dangerously subversive of the grounds of traditional casuistry, as Sanderson was aware.

In traditional or scholastic casuistry circumstances altered cases, and casuists established the range of permissible actions within an overall framework of general laws. Simple Ramist religious casuistry as exemplified in the influential works of Ames and Baxter was less flexible,[6] as would be expected from the principles of the logic. Such works essentially consisted of a set of clear directions for particular situations. Ascham's mode of arguing, however, developed Ramism into a kind of unscrupulous scepticism. He divided his work into three parts, each subdivided in chapters, but though the first part argues in more general terms than the second, there is not an orderly progression from first principles to particular probable conclusions as with Sanderson. In fact Ascham's central point is to deny that any such descent is normally possible. A strict dualism between the ideal and the real allows him to talk piously of how things ought to be, but argue that no inferences can be made certainly from such knowledge. This releases him from the obligation to consider any such inferences at all. The law of justice acts as rigorously as in simple Ramism, but in the interests of scepticism not of certainty.

When he deals with the problem of allegiance his scepticism is nearly total. Here he argues that we can have no certain knowledge of the past, either of fact or right.

> As for the point of Right, it is a thing alwayes doubtfull . . . (and) the point of Fact on which we would ground matter of right, or a justifiable cause . . . ever is perplext and difficult to have perfect Intelligence of [7]

Anything short of perfect intelligence is no intelligence at all, by the application of an implicit disjunctive syllogism. However, the present possessors of power can be known 'perfectly', which gives them the only possible claim to allegiance. This last assumption is somewhat arbitrary, and since Ascham had supported Parliament before they were undoubted possessors of present power, the argument may have been disingenuous, which shows the dangers of his kind of scepticism. It effectively undermined the very bases of conscientiousness, and tended 'to the bringing in of Atheism, with the contempt of God and all religion', as the normally mild and pacific Sanderson put it. [8]

Ascham's form of scepticism could not be arrived at by pushing the flexibility of scholastic casuistry to the limit. Behind a scholastic casuist's flexibility was an over-riding belief in general laws, so that oaths could on occasion be interpreted with latitude but they never lost all their obligatory force. For Ascham the bond of an oath can only hold or break. There is no middle course between a morality interpreted with Ramist absoluteness and an amoral and incomprehensible flux, where reason can apprehend only a single connex syllogism: swords kill, exacting submission, 'the naked sword permitting no nicenesse of obedience'. [9]

But Ascham was not a consistent sceptic, and did not need to be. His world was not completely overturned by the events of the war. The right side, his own side, had won, and was ready to employ him. In his work scepticism jostles with an incipiently mechanistic account of reality that at some points comes close to Hobbes's, two incompatible but equally natural developments of the paradigm. Something of this conflict affects his brief references to physical nature. Where Sanderson could argue from general truths about the physical universe to the nature of law, relying on a conviction that the whole of nature ultimately formed a single coherent whole governed by a single system of laws, Ascham typically distinguishes.

> Plain reason shewes us, that Naturall and Mathematicall causes have more certitude than Civill, [10]

he writes, using an argument that Bishop Bramhall was to use only six years later against Hobbes.[11]

> For Nature is alwaies uniforme, and alike, in its operations. Hence fire alwaies burnes and never wets; a stone in the aire naturally tends downwards, and never stayes in the middle.[12]

The simple Ramist in him invokes 'plain reason'; Sanderson usually talks only of 'reason' or the reasonable. Ascham seems here to have acknowledged the same commonplace as Sanderson used of the regularity of nature, but then denied the analogy with the laws of human society. But Ascham illustrates the commonplace from a different kind of physics. Sanderson used the behaviour of air and water in his example. These were basic elements, whose tendency to rise or fall to find their proper place in the hierarchy of the elements was a basic principle of motion for scholastic physics. Even the exactly contrary motion can be explained in terms of a more fundamental law. But the fact that fire burns was used by Ramus as an example of a simple axiom.[13] It is the kind of isolated property that could be received into a Baconian table of Induction. This property of fire has no connection with Ascham's other example, the falling stone, except for the regularity they have in common. This second example comes even closer to Sanderson's, and points the contrast more clearly. Ascham has curiously limited his statement to the situation when stones are 'in the aire', as though when they are on the ground the rule may not apply. So Ascham uses examples that would be appropriate to the old commonplace, but they have changed subtly to imply a physical universe no longer to be comprehended as a coherent system, though this was the original point of the commonplace. But the advantage is not all with Sanderson. His last vague '&c.' hints at his lack of interest in the independent reality of the physical universe. Asham's simple Ramism could at least be seriously believed in 1650.

It is interesting that Asham should have used the same argument as Bishop Bramhall used against Hobbes, since elsewhere he shows many signs of Hobbes' influence. The relationship between the two thinkers, however, is as equivocal as we would expect. Hobbist doctrines attracted him but he had a simpler version of the Ramist paradigm. For instance, Ascham postulates an original state of nature, a concept he probably took over from Hobbes or Grotius, both of whom he used frequently.[14] From this he justifies his doctrine that possession constitutes the only legitimate claim to power.

> Where as 'par in parem non habuit potestatem', so I conceive that inequality perfectly bred dominion, and that Property; It being but naturall, and no injury, that in a state where there is no mutuall obligation, the inferiour in force should give way to him that is so much superiour. This necessarily

breeding feare in many, could not but breed generall compact or conditions for secure neighbour-hood, and for holding what was first laid hand on, though in unequall parts. Probably hee who by power overawed other mens persons, assign'd them their portions; yet this followes not, but he the first possessour or distributer had what he had, first by Occupation.[15]

Though this is not quite Hobbes's opinion the argument superficially seems to come from a Hobbist cast of mind. Ascham appears to be arguing consequentially: inequality causes dominion, dominion causes property, and property gives rise to a general compact. But given this causal mode of arguing, the verb he favours for the process becomes significant. 'To breed' implies an organic model of causation, the model so important in Aristotelian political thought, but for Ascham the metaphor is so dead that he does not bother even to provide two parents.

On closer inspection, the resemblance to Hobbist rigour appears less close. He starts from a Latin tag, an implicit appeal to authority such as Hobbes would never have made. He then argues not from the tag but from its negation. In strictly logical terms this involves the fallacy of denying the antecedent, so that what looks like a deduction is really an assertion made by way of contrast. The remainder of the argument is similarly loose. Ascham has a symptomatic fondness for the participial construction, which indicates a relationship, but leaves the nature and terms of this relationship ill-defined. For instance, in the passage of argument 'This necessarily breeding feare . . . could not but breed general compact' the reference of 'This' is left vague, so a reader is not sure precisely where this particular sequence comes in the chain of argument. The participle 'breeding' obscures the causal sequence within the sentence itself, so that fear could have given rise to the compact, as would seem a natural interpretation, or both fear and the compact could have arisen at much the same time as a result of 'This'.

A more serious obscurity is involved in the last sentence. Till this point Ascham had seemed to be arguing that property followed from dominion. The last clause suggests the exact opposite, that property somehow may have bred dominion. But these two incompatible propositions are simply stated within the one sentence, linked by an obscurely worded logical connection 'yet this followes not, but . . .', which is the negation of a negation and still does not suggest how the two could both be true.

So even when Ascham is at his most rational his arguments tend to wander about, making only erratic and tangential contact with their fellows. Society as he conceives it is made in the image of his logic. Society consists of the free play of market forces:

. . . if one had neede of another, then he who were most prest, would come to the price of the other, and therefore want or plenty is the measure of estimating things, and is the bond of society, whereby also one man shewes

> he is or may be usefull to another; & nature hath so ordered it, that no man is so rich, who hath not some neede of the poore, and no man is so meane and abject, but he may bee some wayes usefull to the rich[16]

Economic necessity is the only 'bond' between men in this society, and their various relationships can all be expressed in terms of money. Apart from this economic flux the structure of society is necessarily simple. There are essentially two classes, rich and poor, though most of the advantage is with the rich, who need the poor but only to do things for them, whereas the poor are lucky that they can be 'usefull' to the rich. Society accordingly has no value of itself, and it could be difficult to justify a society with any degree of structural complexity in such terms. Ascham thus justifies society by the benefit it confers on every individual member:

> Few wild men live so well as our beggars, which even makes most inferiour people in a state, feare confusion

he writes,[17] probably without asking the opinion of too many of 'our beggars'. But his argument that the rich gain no more advantage from society than the poor do is even harder to take seriously:

> By this argument there is no quarrell to be made with those who live softlyer than others, as doing them injury thereby; for their natures receive no advantage by it; nay they are unhappier than the poore, because they cannot want so many things as the other can, & are more sharply punisht for their delicatenesse; Plowmen being rarely rack't with gouts, tormented with petulant consumptions, the stone, or the like.[18]

The traditional view of the nature of society provides the first premise in Sanderson's discussion of the principles at issue in the Engagement controversy:

> First, then, it is to be considered, that Allegiance is a Duty that every subject, under what form of Government soever, by the Law of Nature, oweth to his Country, and consequently to the Sovereign Power thereof. For the very same law (which we may call the Law of Nature, at least in a large acceptation) which inclineth particular men to grow into one civil Body of a Common-wealth, must necessarily withal, imprint a sense, and a tacite acknowledgment of such a duty of Allegiance in every inferiour member of the Body, unto the Caput Communitatis, or Sovereign Power, by which that Commonwealth is Governed, as is necessary for the preservation of the whole Body. So that the bond of Allegiance doth not arise originally from the Oath of Allegiance; as if those that had not taken the Oath, had a greater liberty to act contrary to the Allegiance specified in the Oath, than those that have taken it, have: or as if, in case the Oath should be quite laid aside, there should be no Allegiance due. But it is so intrinsecal, proper, and essential a duty, and (as it were) fundamental, to the relation of a Subject, qua talis, as that the very name of a Subject doth, after a sort, import it . . . (so) that the Bond of Allegiance, (whether sworn or not sworn) is in the nature of it perpetual and indispensable[19]

For Sanderson the basic unit is not the individual but society, whose complex but harmoniously organized structure is conveyed through the metaphor of the body politic. Organic metaphors are integral to the whole conception; so the verb 'grow into' is not a dead metaphor like Ascham's 'breeds', but recalls an analogy that is an intrinsic part of the argument. The bond also is closer and more 'intrinsecal', part of the nature of man, not the external kind of bondage of Ascham's cash nexus. But where the looseness of the relationships in Ascham's view of society allowed a kind of freedom, in Sanderson's account the 'naturalness' of the organism which is the state entails the total absorption of the individual into the state. The subordination is to the state in the first place, but the sovereign is so closely identified with the body as a whole that patriotism is barely distinguishable from loyalty to the sovereign, and both are as natural as the obedience of hand to brain. So Sanderson would not need to pretend an unconvincing sympathy for the discomforts of affluence in order to justify society to beggars. On the other hand his model would be quite incapable of accounting for the Civil War, or giving guidance in the crisis of allegiance which the Engagement Oath raised. The Commonwealth had proved disturbingly able to carry on with its head cut off.

In spite of the differences, Ascham clearly brings us closer to the problematic figure of Hobbes. Hobbes in turn brings us closer to Marvell. We saw the affinities between Hobbist and Marvellian logic, and their accounts of the irrational.[20] There are also common factors in their social situation and political allegiance. Both were tutors in aristocratic households, and both were Royalists during the Civil War. Hobbes did not take office under Cromwell, but 'Leviathan', published in 1651, would have justified his doing so, if Cromwell had been willing to employ the notorious atheist and defender of absolutism. Wallace sees it as an indirect contribution to the Engagement controversy.[21] So both Hobbes and Marvell occupied an equivocal position, combining commitment to the old social order with a radical form of the new modes of thought. Not surprisingly, Hobbes made his Royalist associates feel uncomfortable.

Part of the disturbing effect of Hobbes's political thought came from his basic premises about society. He confronts a Sandersonian belief in man's social proclivities with a stark version of Ascham's view. Hobbist man is a supreme egoist, with violent, self-seeking urges that are more likely to destroy society than bond it. Hobbes gives us the classic statement of the theory of possessive individualism, to use MacPherson's influential formulation.[22] Interestingly, it is because of Hobbes' royalist commitments that he presents this view so clearly. Ascham takes his view of society for granted, but Hobbes focuses sharply on it, as the supreme problem which his political philosphy must solve. His commitment to the older order also leads to an equivocal attitude to the

104

commonplaces Sanderson relied on. He attacks these premises fiercely, but he would have liked them to be true. For instance, he takes one important traditional image for society, the commonwealth of bees, and gives six reasons why the analogy does not apply. One is that

> amongst these creatures, the Common good differeth not from the Private; and being by nature enclined to their private, they procure thereby the common benefit. But man, whose Joy consisteth in comparing himselfe with other men, can relish nothing but what is eminent.

Another reason is that

> the agreement of these creatures is Naturall; that of men, is by covenant only, which is Artificiall: and therefore it is no wonder if there be somewhat else required (besides Covenant) to make their Agreement constant and lasting; which is a Common Power, to keep them in awe, and to direct their actions to the Common Benefit.[23]

But Hobbes is only denying the analogy, not the values it represented. He accepts that the society of bees is naturally harmonious, and would be an ideal pattern for human society. In fact he is using the trope in the conventional manner, to indicate the imperfections of human society. The differences he points out between men and bees are precisely the undesirable qualities his system is designed to eliminate or circumvent. Here and elsewhere, he accepts the traditional images of society as ideals, but cannot believe that men left to themselves will 'grow into' such a society. So Hobbes's society must be tied together by the bonds of 'Reward and Punishment', and by the weight of the Common Power. A Sandersonian belief in man's natural social propensities must have seemed implausible to men who had experienced the civil war. The chaos and dangerous confusion of a time of war was, however, central to Hobbes's reasoning. He adapts to his vision another commonplace image for a harmonious and comprehensive structure, the comparison of the state to a building:

> For men, as they become at last weary of irregular justling, and hewing one another, and desire with all their hearts, to conforme themselves into one firme and lasting edifice; so for want, both of the art of making fit Lawes, to square their actions by, and also of humility, and patience, to suffer the rude and combersome points of their present greatness to be taken off, they cannot without the help of a very able Architect, be compiled, into any other than a crasie building, such as hardly lasting out their own time, must assuredly fall upon the heads of their posterity.[24]

The sentence itself is built like a 'crasie building'. Segments of sentences lean against each other in an extended but asymmetrical system of stress and counterstress. 'As' is balanced by 'so', but within the first branch of the construction 'weary' is opposed to 'desire', and after the division the counterstressing elements proliferate. But in spite of these oppositional devices, which normally give a static effect to a construction, the sentence progresses linearly, following the causal and temporal sequence of the events it describes. The weariness is followed by the desire for peace, the desire by the incapacity to achieve it unaided and this by the need for external help, the incapacity by instability, and the instability by the final collapse of the building on the heads of posterity. The two principles of construction co-exist in a state of tension, resulting in the energetic but jerky and self-checking movement of the sentence, which continually throws up the beginnings of a stable symmetrical structure only to subvert it by a further restless progress.

There is another source of tension in Hobbes's version of this commonplace. Men are both the makers and the matter of the commonwealth, so its stones behave with confusing wilfulness, hewing their fellows as though each was the mason and the rest all stones. For Ascham society was a loose aggregate of individuals, acting only intermittently on each other. For Sanderson the desire for society was an innate teleological principle which directed the actions of men sufficiently powerfully and independently to be the basis of a complex social order. For Hobbes this motive occurs naturally too, but it is not innate, independent or reliable. It arises at one stage in a sequence, which he presents in terms of a vigorously mechanistic causality, but this wish for a stable society is a transient stage in the inexorable progression. If the sequence is not stopped by a sufficiently powerful force, it will finally end in consequences which no one willed.

Hobbes essentially has taken Ascham's image of society to an extreme, and deduced the repressive apparatus that would be needed to control society so conceived. But this mode of reasoning did not come from Sanderson's paradigm, and the resemblance between a Hobbist and a Sandersonian sovereign would have been only superficial. Sanderson's sovereign was not deduced, he grew, and his repressive powers would merge into the eager loyalty of his subjects. Hobbes ruthlessly cut away the ideology that had softened the fact of Tudor and Stuart power. His commonwealth was a metallic simulacrum of the Sandersonian view. 'Leviathan' was a strategy against revolutions, but also a strategy for accepting successful ones. Hobbes could have taken the Engagement Oath in support of a Commonwealth without King or Lords, so long as it had a 'Common Power', with total military control to keep the people in awe.

(ii) 'The First Anniversary'

Marvell also used the commonplace comparison of a state to a building, in his poem on the 'First Anniversary' of Cromwell's Protectorate. We have briefly looked at the image already, in contrast to Milton's use of it;[25] now we are in a position to set the image in its context, in the poem and in the political thought of the time.

The poem as a whole is a curious and difficult work to interpret. It is addressed to Cromwell at a time when the former Royalist apparently had come to accept the rightness and necessity of Cromwell's rule. It commences like a typical panegyric with a comparison of Cromwell to the Sun, but the focus of attention quickly turns in line 15 to an attack on 'heavy Monarchs', who, however, make a very 'wide Return' by line 117, to become 'Unhappy Princes, ignorantly bred'. In the passage that follows, the poet seems to see his task as to wake these slumbering kings. 'Angelique Cromwell' commands the Horn of Marvell's Muse only as a temporary substitute, who is performing the proper task of kings. Cromwell's sun which shone so strongly and evidently at first is now obscured with unpanegyric clouds of doubt: 'If these the Times, then this must be the Man'. (line 144)

The image of the state as a building contains similar difficulties, as we shall see. In both form and content it recalls Hobbes's use of the same kind of image. The passage as a whole is 50 lines long, longer than many whole poems, and it pursues the comparison over this length with a rigour Hobbes shared with Marvell despite his distrust of his Fancy, and which few of their contemporaries could sustain. The section from line 75 to line 98 recalls Hobbes in content as well, and the affinities go deep. Both exploit the bizarre effects that arise if stones are animated to act like men. For Marvell even more than for Hobbes this leads to a subversive parody of the harmonious and organic state of the scholastic paradigm. The conflict between the paradigms is first embodied in the transient ambiguity on 'willing' in line 76. Initially the 'frame' seems 'willing', meaning co-operative, properly subordinated like the body to the sovereign reason in the traditional view. Instead, we learn several lines later, the frame of the commonwealth is actively willing, wilful, capricious and hard to manage, like Hobbes's stones that jostle and hew one another.

Like Hobbes, Marvell does not share Sanderson's belief that men will 'grow into one civil Body of a Common-wealth' naturally in the beneficent course of time. They are driven more by a 'perpetuall and restlesse desire of Power after power', and Marvell's sense of the energies involved is typically even more acute than Hobbes'. For Sanderson the particular inclinations are harmoniously related to the whole in both the physical and the social order. Apparent deviations merely obey a higher order. Marvell's image seems closer to Hooker's earlier and more authoritative formulation than to Sanderson's. In a famous passage Hooker invoked a general over-riding law in things, which bindeth them each to serve unto other's good, and all to prefer the good of the whole before whatsoever their own particular; as we plainly see they do, when things natural in that regard forget their ordinary natural wont; that which is heavy mounting sometime upward of its own accord, and forsaking the centre of the earth which to itself is most natural, even as if it did hear itself commanded to let go the good it privately wisheth, and to relieve the present distress of nature in common.[26]

The scholastic paradigm allowed Hooker and Sanderson to move easily like this from descriptions of the social order to analogous phenomena in nature. Marvell follows the same procedure, but the result of translating normal political reality as described by Hobbes, or as exemplified by the civil war, into physical terms is something like a self-generating and continuous explosion, which fulfils Hooker's grim warning of what would happen 'if nature should intermit her course'.[27] So the wayward stones represent no normal physical reality, but are a reductio ad absurdum of this central analogy. The passage implies a critique of the scholastic paradigm similar to Hobbes's more explicit rejection of the analogy between human society and the commonwealth of the bees.

Marvell's solution is as Hobbist as his analysis. The Commonwealth is a mathematician like Hobbes. Men are as susceptible to mathematics as are stones, and are subject to equally amoral and asocial forces, their 'anima' transformed to 'vis'. Men like stones must be placed so that the weight of the commonwealth acts on them in a line directly through their centres of gravity to the centre of the earth. So a stable society can be built only by someone who understands and can direct the potentially anarchic and destructive forces it contains. Innate social tendencies may exist but are no sound basis for a stable state. The bonding force is the force of political gravity acting downwards through individuals to the centre of the earth. Cromwell's 'Protecting weight' also acts downwards, much more like Hobbes's 'Common power, to keep them in awe' than the head that directs Sanderson's Body. The parallel between the laws of physics and of politics has been restored, but it is a new kind of physics and therefore a new kind of politics.

But this is only half the image. As a whole the passage falls into two sections, lines 49–64 and 73–98, with a link passage in between, and the principle of the division is the contrast between the ideal and the actual. In the couplet that introduces the whole image Marvell says that Cromwell is learning 'To tune this lower to that higher Sphere'. The first Amphion accordingly is ideal. His hand is 'gentle' on the lute as the stones move responsively into position. Matter is more amenable to the persuasions of the music because of the presence of spirit in it. So Amphion can build an entire and perfect city with effortless ease.

Line 73, however, introduces 'our Amphion', whose reappearance for a repeat performance would be redundant unless he were being distinguished from the first, the ideal Amphion. The quality of the act of creation is now very different. This Amphion cannot merely stroke the strings; he has to strike them 'once . . . and twice'. What follows then is something like an explosion, as we have seen, where both spirit and matter resist the architect, who now has to put aside his lute and thrust the recalcitrant stones into place by the direct force of his physical hand. The solution must be imposed and maintained by force, though it must be force exerted with understanding. Both sections divide into two. In the first section, the world of the ideal Amphion, the stones immediately begin to respond in the first paragraph, foreshadowing the order more fully realized in the second paragraph. The second section divides exactly into two, natural anarchy and a rigid, artificial or imposed order.

'Our Amphion' is clearly Cromwell. The connection is re-inforced by frequent puns, the 'Instrument' of line 68 referring to the Instrument of Government that established the Protectorate, 'Order' and 'Consent' in the previous line also being Parliamentary terms. The description of the state created by this Amphion similarly corresponds to the form of the Protectorate. The most obvious hint is the final reference to the 'Roofs Protecting weight', but the rest of the description applies closely to the constitution established by the Instrument of Government. Lines 89–92 refer to the elected Commons, the 'crossest Spirits' and those whose Nature 'leads them to divide'. The equivocal relation of the Elected Council is nicely caught by the Orwellian joke of calling them the 'most Equal'.

The first section also has one or perhaps two parliamentary puns, 'Measures' in line 51 and 'order' (less certainly) in the next line. But if these lines too refer to some political reality their implications are surprising, for they could only be an idealized account of the constitution of pre-war England. The second paragraph, for instance, seems unmistakeably to describe an upper house. But not till two and a half years later, in 1657 when Cromwell was also empowered to name his successor, was an 'Other House' set up under Cromwell's rule. The three couplets from lines 59–64 correspond to the three traditional modes of Greek music, but they also describe some people who were not at that particular stage serving under Cromwell. The 'Martial rage', of course, could equally well refer to the Army on whose support Cromwell relied, or to persons knighted on the field of battle. The image of the 'flocking Marbles', however, is not an obvious image for the enervating Lydian mode, and makes no sense unless it refers to courtiers. If they refer to courtiers, however, the lines have characteristic Marvellian wit and point. The hint of the ludicrous in the image of courtiers 'flocking', and the requirement that the touch should be 'more sweet', would embody a wit as courtly as its object; the intelligence that so urbanely but accurately mocked their too ready pursuit of place and their affected aestheticism would be perfectly at home in such company. The third couplet concludes with the 'graver Notes' and the Temples they create. Cromwell's piety is praised elsewhere in the poem, so the lines could refer to his preference for men of similar piety, but the only form of government under Cromwell which specifically included such persons was Harrison's Rule of the Saints. But Cromwell had come to dislike their rule and had dissolved their Parliament. In any case, they had had no 'flocking Marbles' to adulterate their sanctity. The Temples look much more like the Lords Spiritual in the former House of Lords.

The preceding paragraph likewise is more pointed and witty if it refers to an aspect of the pre-war constitution. 'Rougher Stones' already implies the existence of others less rough. It also makes a contrast across the line with Amphion's 'gentle' hand. If these 'rougher Stones' refer to the common folk, the opposition suggests the easy relationship of gentlemen and commoners in this ideal state. 'Quarreys rude' on this interpretation would be a witty way of referring to the constituencies from which they 'danced', the humour being courtly and not without a hint of aristocratic superiority. This is only a more good-humoured form of his attitude, expressed in the bitter pun in 'crossest Spirits', to the corresponding level in the actuality of Cromwell's government.

On this interpretation the passage makes continuous sense at both levels, and displays Marvell's characteristic wit and allusiveness. If there were no reference of this kind the lines would be mere amplification, a repetitious and pointless elaboration of the original comparison which would be entirely uncharacteristic of Marvell. So unless Marvell here had fallen far short of his normal level of intelligence, it would seem that his ideal form of government even in 1655 was derived from the pattern of pre-war Royalist England. His description of the Protectorate is slanted to emphasize its similarity to this form.

But Marvell is not a surreptitious Royalist. The genesis of Cromwell's government is described so as to bring out its Hobbist foundations, and Cromwell is shown as a more complete political mathematician than in fact he was. Marvell has accepted the change of sovereignty and its most revolutionary implications. There is no continuity with the past. Between the two Amphions stand the 'tedious Statesmen', the lawyers of the Parliamentary side, who resisted the rule of Cromwell as much as Charles by their appeals to precedents. The world of the first Amphion is as remote as a Golden Age, although it mirrors the form of Roaylist England of Marvell's youth. As an ideal it exerts a powerful emotional pull on the poet, and it provides a model for the new commonwealth to aspire to, but the Royal Martyr was no Amphion, and his government fell like any other actual government through faults in its architecture. The first Amphion is separated from the second by the gap between the ideal and the real, not just by the ten years of the war. But this gap is not so absolute as for Ascham. So Marvell can accept Cromwell without a scepticism that regards the ideal as unknowable or irrelevant in the world of affairs.

There are tensions and even contradictions in such a position. The theme of time, for instance, recurs throughout the poem, after its initial statement in the opening section. 'Heavy' Kings tell a 'useless Time', but still leave kingdoms to their sons. A radically new government can end as violently as it began. So Cromwell's government must break with the past but not the future, and a proof of the soundness of its architecture is its ability to last.

> There is no perfect form of government, where the disposing of the Succession is not in the present Soveraign,

wrote Hobbes.[28] Marvell is similarly anxious about the consequences of Cromwell's death. So the poem must be, as Wallace argues, concerned with the Kingship question,[29] though not in a simple-mindedly polemic way, for the issue aroused deeply conflicting emotions in Marvell, more powerful than he could control or organize in a single poem. For the more Cromwell's rule extends into the future, the more it participates in normal time, and only the coming of the Millennium can save it from reaching back into the trauma of the past as well.[30]

So in lines 173–220 of this 402 line poem, at its numerical centre and in the same position as the more famous description of Charles's death in the 'Horatian Ode', is the most curious and disturbed piece of writing in the whole poem, a vision of Cromwell's death and its consequences. It was an extraordinary tactic to put an elegy for the subject of a panegyric at the poem's centre: it cannot be paralleled in any other seventeenth century poet. Even the polemical wish to remind Cromwell that he too was mortal and should provide himself with a successor could not explain the strength of feeling in this description, which generates a greater intensity of grief than the poem Marvell wrote for Cromwell's actual death.

Not only is the predominant feeling in this section excessive and out of keeping with its subject, it also sees Cromwell in terms which contradict much of the rest of the poem. For the death is described in terms reminiscent of the death of Duncan in 'Macbeth', and Duncan there is one of Shakespeare's fullest embodiments of the ideal king of the traditional order. Duncan's horses

> Turn'd wild in nature, broke their stalls, flung out.   ('Macbeth' II.iv.16)

Cromwell's horses

> The green Grass, and their known Mangers hate.   (line 196)

The sympathy between man and nature which the second Amphion passage seemed to deny acts with full strength:

> Thou Cromwell falling, not a stupid Tree,
> Or Rock so savage, but it mourn'd for thee:
> And all about was heard a Panique groan,
> As if that Natures self were overthrown.
> It seem'd the Earth did from the Center tear;
> It seem'd the Sun was faln out of the Sphere   (lines 201–206)

The lines are notable for weight rather than subtle intelligence or originality. Cromwell is implicitly likened to Christ through the reference to a 'Panique groan' but Marvell is more concerned with the scale of the catastrophe than with its precise form. Something of the direction of this feeling is then revealed in his attempt to relate the passage to the fact of Cromwell's continued existence:

> We only mourn'd our selves, in thine Ascent,
> Whom thou hadst left behind with Mantle rent.
>   For all delight of Life thou then didst lose,
> When to Command, thou didst thy self depose.   (lines 219–222)

Through the notion of ascent Marvell moves from Cromwell's imagined ascent to heaven to his actual ascent to power, so that in this ascent to power he had to depose his 'self' as well as the King. So the elegy is partly called forth by the terms under which Cromwell came to power. Its vision recalls what Hooker warned would happen 'if nature should intermit her course'; and the strength of the feeling is appropriate to an event on that scale, the death of a paradigm. Cromwell is celebrated at last as a traditional king, but this is only possible when he is imagined dead and has become the king he deposed, and he and his destructive achievement can be lamented in the same terms.

So the poem as a whole does not hang together. Only in relatively short passages, pre-eminently the Amphion section, is Marvell fully in control, able to master and order the contradictory elements of his response. He is committed to Cromwell, but is still reluctant to acknowledge what that commitment entails. The result is an over-all uncertainty of tone and direction, and the poem fails in the terms it sets itself, for the Amphion-image is an image for Marvell's art as well as for Cromwell's politics, and the poet whose poem comes to pieces has failed like the architect whose building collapses, or the leader whose political settlement suffers a reversion 20 months after his death. But some men's failures are more interesting than others' successes. Confusion can sometimes be a more honest and intelligent response than lucidity and control. Cromwell at

112

this stage in his career was caught in an insoluble dilemma, a revolutionary leader who was the main bulwark of conservatives against political and social radicalism. The merit of Marvell's poem is to reflect these contradictions, which were more than personal, and more than he could resolve.

(iii) The Royalist Roots

Most accounts of Marvell's political development naturally focus on the 'Horatian Ode' of 1650. The poem is variously interpreted as a balanced or ambivalent view of Cromwell, or as a more conventional panegyric whose intention was to praise the new ruler. The interpretations are contradictory but both agree in locating the change of allegiance around 1650. This agreement establishes a context in which disputes about the Ode can take place, but it gives a most misleading account of the course of Marvell's development, as far as we can glean this from other poems and from such isolated facts as we have. Worse, it can lead to distortion or suppression of much of this evidence, which includes poems which are interesting in their own right. For instance, if the Ode was written close to this turning point, then 'First Anniversary', over four years later, should be a poem of confident commitment, and is usually taken as such. But if, as I have argued, deep confusion co-existed with Marvell's admiration and loyalty towards Cromwell even in the later poem, then his change would seem to have been far more protracted and painful than is usually thought. If Marvell had this kind of ambivalence and uncertainty even in 1655, we needn't impose consistency on the progress of his political thinking, or minimize or ignore apparent contradictions between and within poems.

The evidence for Marvell's Cromwellian phase is relatively full and consistent, though much of it is superficial in character. Milton's letter to Bradshaw recommending that Marvell he appointed his assistant is dated 21st February 1653. The post was largely concerned with foreign affairs. Margoliouth's reasons for dating 'The Character of Holland' between November 1652 and June 1653 seem conclusive.[31] This confidently and amusingly anti-Dutch poem praises 'Our sore new-Circumcised Common Wealth', and refers to Cromwell as 'Our Neptune'. Marvell did not get the post under Milton but became tutor to Cromwell's protege and son-in-law elect William Dutton, the son of a Royalist who had died in the Civil Wars. Marvell wrote to Cromwell himself about the job in a letter dated July 23 1653, addressing him, naturally, with due respect and deference. Shortly afterwards, between November 1653 and April 1654, Marvell wrote his longest extant Latin poem, ostensibly a private letter to

Dr Ingelo but really intended for Scandinavian eyes.[32] In this letter he sees 'Victor Oliverus' as the leader of a new protestant crusade.

So from the beginning of 1653 at least, Marvell clearly felt he could actively support Cromwell and his regime. 'First Anniversary' reaffirms that support. But apart from the Dutton tutorship Marvell's political activity is restricted to foreign affairs, where it is England whose interests he urges against those of other European powers. In these poems written before 'First Anniversary' Cromwell is mentioned only briefly, even perfunctorily for poems of such a genre, though he is unmistakably identified with the interests of the country. Much is left unsaid in them. The tone is carefully public and impersonal even in the letter to Ingelo.

Marvell's royalist sympathies are similarly consistent before 1650, and are part of the normal account of Marvell. However, their intensity and the depth of their roots have not received a proper emphasis. The elegy he wrote for Francis Villiers is militantly Royalist, its attitude to Cromwell unequivocal. Fame would have been disappointed at the heroic Villiers' death:

> Much rather thou I know expectst to tell
> How heavy Cromwell gnasht the earth and fell.   (lines 13–14)

Villiers died on 7th July 1648 after taking part in the abortive rising of that year. Marvell's elegy for another hopeful Royalist youth, Lord Hastings, was written at some time after Hastings' death from small-pox on June 24th 1649. There was no occasion for reference to Cromwell in such a poem, but Marvell alludes contemptuously to 'Democratick Stars'.

But the best and most revealing of these early Royalist poems is his poem to Lovelace, probably written some time not long before February 1648. Lovelace's significance for Marvell is stated in the opening couplet:

> Our times are much degenerate from those
> Which your sweet Muse which your fair Fortune chose.

Lovelace is a representative of 'that Candid Age' and embodies its values. His poetry is therefore a political act, as is Marvell's praise of it. The terms in which it will be censured by others are religious and political in essence: its imagined critics will

> cast a reforming eye,
> Severer then the yong Presbytery.   (lines 23–24)

However, they will be reduced to making legalistic charges on political grounds, with equal absurdity Marvell implies, for Lovelace unites the heroic with the courtly:

> Whose hand so rudely grasps the steely brand,
> Whose hand so gently melts the Ladies hand.   (lines 37–38)

114

The poem gives an early sketch of the world of the first Amphion. Our 'degenerate' times contrast with the golden world associated with the perfect Cavalier, and the poem itself combines the grace and masculine force it celebrates in Lovelace. There is no hint of the nostalgic in his evocation of this world, since it is fully embodied in Lovelace, nor is there any uncertainty in Marvell's commitment to it.

The roots of this Royalist feeling go deep into Marvell's past. His first Horatian Ode, the 'Parodia' of 1637, expressed loyalty and respect towards the King, though this is hardly significant given the occasion. But a year previously Marvell's father had given unforced and unmistakeable proof of where his own allegiance lay. In 1636 he preached to the Aldermen of Hull on the occasion of the swearing in of a new mayor, exhorting them to

> suffer not to let slip or to be shaken out, the commandement mouthword, countenance or pleasure of ye KING of Kings God, or rather of his viceregent the king on earth . . . because it is back'd with an Oath wch you should not violate; wth ye Oath of God in regard of attestation, by whome you have sworne, or observation who is privy to your oath & behaviour afterward or obligation, by wch you are tyed to him who is a god by title, & by resemblance of authority likewise[33]

This is not the language of flattery or platitude but direct and even contentious admonition, addressed to a group of men not all of whom were to support the king in the coming civil war. The King is not merely God's 'viceregent', he is himself a 'god by title'. The oath of office is represented as an oath of allegiance to the King. Magistrates are subordinate to the King as a King is to God, and as citizens are to magistrates, as he makes explicit elsewhere.[34] The view of society implicit in this argument is hierarchically organized like Sanderson's, but the levels are more tightly and rigidly bonded, with powerful sanctions reinforced by the will of God rather than with natural bonds of allegiance. It is a Ramist kind of royalism but only the more unequivocal for that. A father's views need not be the same as his son's, but this evidence, added to the later poems, extends the poet's contact with royalist feeling right back into his formative years. A man who was the son of a vehement supporter of the king and was himself a royalist till the age of 29 would not find such beliefs easy to repudiate.

The neatness of the picture before 1650 requires some slight modifications. Marvell apparently did not fight in the civil war, and was probably touring the continent in the mid-forties.[35] The poem to Lovelace has a curious line suggesting that even then there were those who doubted his loyalty. A lady assails him 'Thinking that I too of the rout had been' (line 42). He gallantly but firmly denies the accusation, but the exchange implies that some might make it, with what justice we cannot tell.

But this hint of irregularity is as nothing compared to the confusing sequence of the poems between 1650 and 1652. In this period he wrote four political poems, 'Horatian Ode', 'Tom May's Death', 'On the Legation of O. St. John', and 'Appleton House'. Both 'Horatian Ode', written between 26th June and 17th August 1650, and 'St. John', written between February and June 1651, could be interpreted as supporting Cromwell's rule.[36] So despite his Royalist background Marvell could have decided to accept the result of the Civil War at about the time he took employment in the house of Fairfax, the former leader of the Parliamentary forces. The crucial difficulty arises with the poem on Tom May's death. Tom May died on 13th November 1650, therefore after Marvell must have composed the Ode. May, a minor poet and playwright in the Caroline court, had gone over to Parliament. Marvell shows unmistakeably his contempt for the turncoat. Moreover the poem comes very close to the famous Ode at many points. Both poems are concerned with the role of the poet in these difficult times, and with the conflict between 'Ancient rights' and 'successful crimes'; and they both even echo Lucan in May's translation. Cleanth Brooks is clearly right that the poems 'are closely related and come out of the same general state of mind',[37] but the points of contact only make the contrast between the two poems seem more total. The ominous but heroic figure in the Ode becomes 'Spartacus' in 'Tom May', and his victim is 'great Charles'. But more important is the difference in tone. For the achievement of 'Tom May' is its confident and witty contempt for the 'most servil' wit, and Mercenary Pen', tightening to a fierce indignation and sense of total commitment to the rightness of his cause:

> When the Sword glitters ore the Judges head,
> And fear has Coward Churchmen silenced,
> Then is the Poets time, 'tis then he drawes,
> And single fights forsaken Vertues cause.
> He, when the wheel of Empire, whirleth back,
> And though the World's disjointed Axel crack,
> Sings still of ancient Rights and better Times,
> Seeks wretched good, arraigns successful Crimes.   (lines 63–70)

There is no possibility of irony here. The movement of the verse carries complete conviction. The poem to Lovelace had its own integrity but did not aspire to a statement as weighty as this. Alongside it, the heroics of the Villiers elegy feel merely contrived. This is his strongest, most confident Royalist statement. But if the same poet had set his pen to praise Spartacus-Cromwell less than six months previously he is as much a 'servil' wit' as May himself, and his wit at May's expense becomes cheap and his heroics the most contemptible posturing. Either that, or we must look more closely at the Ode again.

116

(iv) 'The Horatian Ode'

The recent critical history of the 'Horatian Ode' is another illustration that progress is not invariable even in a science like literary criticism. The accretion of articles around the poem has tended rather to obscure than develop insights that were available to Cleanth Brooks in his fine early article. The problems arise from uncertainty about Marvell's political stance as this affects a reading of the poem. Clearly it matters a great deal whether Marvell supposed that the ode was pro-Cromwell or not. For instance, if Marvell was firmly for Cromwell then the ambivalence many critics have seen must be due to lack of control by the poet, or lack of judgment by these critics. But if he was hostile to Cromwell then some of the apparent praise for him might really be crude irony. In fact I believe that generations of readers have been essentially right to see the poem as ambivalent. Cromwell emerges from it an impressive but disturbing figure, but Charles also arouses intense compassion. The poem does not need a new interpretation so much as a new context, or a renewed sense of it as a political poem growing out of Marvell's deep involvement with issues of the age. This need not be a substitute for close reading: it can go very well with a sharper sense of nuance and implication in the language of the poem itself.

'Tom May' alone is sufficient to show that Marvell at least did not think of himself as a turncoat at the end of 1650. So the Ode could not be pro-Cromwell, except in ways that Marvell himself was not fully conscious of – and he was a great deal more intelligent and self-aware than most of his modern critics. This sense of the poem's basic orientation is confirmed if we ask ourselves what kind of audience it seems to assume. Cromwell for instance would hardly have responded to the poem with offers of political office. In spite of the form of address it could not have been meant for his eyes. The poem was not published at the time, so presumably it was not intended as a public tract. No manuscript copies survive, so the circle of its intended readers may have been small, and we do not know certainly who any of them were. But two indirect pieces of evidence survive, both mentioned by Brooks but neglected by subsequent critics. One is a poem by Robert Wild, a Presbyterian-Royalist, for the death of another Royalist, Christopher Love, in 1652. One couplet comes particularly close to Marvell's words:

> His keener words did their sharp Axe exceed;
> That made his head, but he their hearts to bleed.[38]

Wild seems to echo Marvell at other points too.[39] He was strongly puritan but equally staunchly Royalist, with all the unyielding certainty of a simple Ramist. The similarity of his poem to Marvell's is no key to Marvell's far more complex and earlier work, but it does suggest that

Wild had probably read Marvell's poem in manuscript, and felt he could draw on its picture of Charles's death for his own entirely loyal poem. This perhaps recovers one of the poem's earliest readers: and we discover that he was a committed Royalist, who apparently did not find the whole of Marvell's poem alien to his convictions, or stained by apostasy.

Another contemporary poem that has similarities to Marvell's is far more directly relevant to understanding the Ode. Fanshawe's translation of Horace's Odes of 1652 contains the only other near-contemporary use so far found of the metre Marvell used for his own ode.[40] Since this occurs in a work translating Horace the connection becomes significant. Fanshawe translated five poems into this metre, but only one of these had a political subject: Ode IV.iv, to Drusus Nero. The significance of 'Horatian' in the title of Marvell's poem has previously perplexed critics, who usually take it generically, supposing that it implies something akin to Horace in the attitude, perhaps the 'Horatian art of time-serving' to use the words of one critic.[41] But Marvell characteristically focused on particular poems, and his own normally grew out of a critical and evaluative reaction to these specific and recognizable poems. In his first Horatian Ode, the 'Parodia', the relevant poem was obvious from the closeness of the parody. In the great Ode, the clue in the title is apparently not sufficient, or critics who have looked for the relevant poem among Horace's 'Odes' would have found it. A second clue is necessary. The metre and the subject, together with Fanshawe's translation, narrow the choice down to the single poem, which has a parodic relationship to Marvell's poem, and is as important to its understanding as its presence in the title suggests.

The proof of the relationship must wait a detailed comparison but if we anticipate this for the moment, some interesting inferences suggest themselves concerning the original audience for the Ode. Fanshawe, a zealous Royalist, had started to translate Horace by 1648, when he published a few translations as tracts for the times, with a strong Royalist bias evident.[42] This small edition did not include the Drusus Ode nor any other poem in the same metre. The Drusus Ode was not actually published until 1652 but could easily have been written before 1650, so that Marvell could have seen it, but only in manuscript. A detailed comparison makes a relationship the other way unlikely. Given Marvell's reputation as a Latinist, his opinion could well have been asked on a translation before it was published. There is another connection between the two men, intriguing though indirect. Fanshawe was a close friend of Mildmay Fane, Fairfax's brother-in-law. Marvell probably used an image from Fane's book of poems, 'Otia Sacra' in 'Appleton House'.[43] Fanshawe and Fane may have been members of a group of poets and litterateurs, of a predominantly Royalist but unseditious cast of mind, to whom Marvell showed his works. Fairfax himself could conceivably have been part of this group during his retirement. But whatever the size and precise membership of the group for whom Marvell wrote the poem, it does seem that it was written for a group of this kind, probably including Fanshawe and perhaps Wild as well. Fanshawe's version with its stanza form acts as something of a code for Marvell's Horatian allusions. The poem therefore is highly esoteric, which partly accounts for some of the difficulties it now presents. It may have needed the protection of this obliquity. Wild's poem ends:

> But stay, my Muse grows fearful too, and must
> Beg that these Lines be buried with thy Dust . . .
>   The Author begs this, lest, if it be known,
>   Whilst he bewailes thy Head, he lose his own.[44]

Marvell might have had similar anxieties about his own poem.

The Drusus Ode does not celebrate either of the two Caesars who dominate discussions of Marvell's Ode. Augustus is praised in passing, but the main subject of the ode is Drusus Nero, a young relative and protege of Augustus, whose promising career ended before he could succeed to the imperial throne that was to be occupied at a later date by his less promising descendant. Horace first praises the amoral force Drusus displayed in his youth:

> Youth whilom and his native courage
> Drew from his nest ere he could forage;
> And now soft winds (being fair)
> Teach him to form ith'air
>   Unwonted steps: Anon more bold
> With hostile force assaults a fold;
> Resisting snakes anon
> For fight and prey sets on.   (Ode IV.iv. 5–12)

Drusus is presented as a wilfully predatory animal, a force of nature like Cromwell in Marvell's ode, but Horace implies no hostility to this quality. Natural force of this kind was necessary for Nero to defeat the Vindelices, enemies of Rome; and he had had the discipline of an education under Augustus's own roof. Drusus's victory then recalls the even more notable victory of his ancestor, Claudius, who had helped to overcome Hannibal, and Horace devotes most of the second part of his poem to praise of this Claudius, and the family of Nero in general:

> What unto Nero's, Rome thou ow'st,
> Speak Alpes, and Asdrubal's red ghost.   (Ode IV,iv, lines 37–38)

The lines read ominously to ears conditioned to associate Nero with Tyranny and wilful cruelty, especially after Horace's images for Drusus's predatory youth. Horace did not live to see the Emperor Nero, and there is no reason to see his praise as ironic. But Marvell knew his Roman history, and Lucan's 'Pharsalia', which was in his mind when he wrote his poem, would inevitably have recalled this particular emperor. Fanshawe's phrasing almost seems to echo May's Lucan:

> But if no other way to Neroes reigne
> The Fates could find . . .
> Let dire Pharsalia grone with armed Hoasts,
> And glut with bloud the Carthigian Ghosts; . . .
> Yet much owes Rome to civill enmity
> For making thee our Prince[45]

So Marvell's two literary sources come together in the ambiguous figure of Nero. In spite of Lucan's fulsome praise of Nero his patron, he had plotted, unsuccessfully, against the tyrant before his poem could even be finished, and this fact totally subverts his hyperboles. Fate's end was as bad as its means. Caesar and civil war lead to Nero and tyranny. Horace did not know where his Drusus led, but it was to the same Nero. Both poems must have been present to Marvell when he wrote his own ode, and the effect of the conjunction of the two must have been to make out of Lucan a Horace with hindsight.

Horace's poem ends with a speech by the defeated Carthaginian Hannibal, who praises not Nero but the regenerative powers of the nation itself, which

> Like a dark Oak on the rich top
> Of Algidum, which hatchets lop;
> Growes by its loss, and takes
> Strength from the very Axe . . .
> Plunge them ith' Sea; they swim (fresh) out;
> Foyle them, with doubled force they'l rout
> The Conquerour   (Ode IV.iv. 57–60, 65–67)

These lines come closer to the foreign princes' praise of England in the 'First Anniversary' than to anything in the Ode. Roman history did not subvert Horace's sentiment here as it did the praise of the Neros, and Marvell's use of a similar image in the later poem suggests how positively he must have responded to this part of Horace's poem. Just before these lines Hannibal had imaged his troops scuttling before the victorious Romans:

> Poor Sheep (of Wolves the prey)
> We worry, whom to fly
> Is a great Victory.   (Ode IV.iv. lines 51–53)

Fanshawe's translation at this point is ambiguous, and might suggest that the Romans are ravening sheep, but Horace's Latin makes it clear that it is Hannibal's troops who are 'cervi', sheep, or more accurately and as in

Marvell, deer. In Marvell's poem it is the Scots who are hoping for a similarly minimal kind of victory:

> Happy if in the tufted brake
> The English Hunter him mistake;
> Nor lay his Hounds in near
> The Caledonian Deer.   ('H.O.' lines 109–112)

Marvell's lines suggest no sympathy for the hapless Scots who have so unwisely provoked the 'English Hunter'.

Horace concludes his poem with praise of the Neroes, which again echoes ambiguously against Lucan and history:

> What is't but Neros can effect
> Whom Heav'ns with prosperous Stars protect,
> And their own prudent care
> Clews through the maze of War.   (Ode IV.iv. lines 73–76)

On this occasion Marvell is closer to Fanshawe than to the Latin, which has 'Nil Claudiae non efficient manus'. He writes:

> What may not then our Isle presume
> While Victory his Crest does plume!   ('H.O.' lines 97–98)

'Can effect' confidently asserts a power equal to aspiration, and the support of heaven is unqualified, when backed by 'prudent care'. Marvell's 'Presume', however, is double-edged. 'May' leaves the presumption dangerously open, and 'while' makes it conditional on continued success.

The vaunts about the hopes of England and the fears of her enemies are followed immediately by reference to two campaigns, Caesar's against the Gauls, and Hannibal's in Italy. Hannibal and Caesar were both great generals, as was Cromwell, but there was an important difference between their two campaigns, unnoticed by modern commentators, but immediately obvious to anyone coming to the poem from the Drusus Ode. Caesar's campaign against the Gauls was successful, as even Lucan grudgingly admitted, but in spite of his courage and military prowess Hannibal was defeated, one of the victorious Roman generals being Claudius Nero. Again the two sources oppose each other to give sharper definition to the terms of the ambiguity that readers generally see in the figure of Cromwell in the poem. Marvell's ambiguity is not the vague oscillation of moral indecision. He is not having it both ways, nor is he balancing Cromwell's good and bad points with liberal fair-mindedness. The poem presents the terms of the disjunctive axioms that contain the phenomenon of Cromwell. Saviour or tyrant, victorious or defeated; the alternatives harshly exclude each other but are equal potentialities of the kind of natural force that is Cromwell and Caesar, the Neroes and

121

Hannibal. At that moment in history all four possibilities intersect in Cromwell, waiting for history to complete its disjunctive syllogisms.

So as is characteristic of Marvellian logic the alternatives are distinct to the intellect but inextricably combined in actual phenomena. The eight lines that open the poem make clearcut oppositions impossible in practice. These lines recall Lucan, and particularly two passages from Lucan's poem.[46] But Lucan is used only as the basis for a more complex kind of statement, his poem helping to give the precise connotation of words and phrases. Marvell does not simply transpose Lucan's narrative to fit English circumstances, exactly the fault he criticized in May.

Marvell's ode apparently starts not with Cromwell but with a 'forward youth', who seems to be the poet, since he must 'forsake his Muses dear'. The description of this youth is strongly reminiscent of Lucan's youths of Ariminum, who also attended to their rusty weapons on the approach of Caesar.[47] But these youths were not poets, and their only 'action' in Lucan's poem was to lament the unfortunate geographical position of Ariminum. Marvell's 'forward youth' is a poet and lover of the Muses, but he is not ineffectual, and he seems to merge into the figure of Cromwell/Caesar. The connection partly works through allusion. May refers to Caesar's 'forward Sword' in a passage which as a whole has many other echoes in Marvell's poem.[48] But the syntax also brings out the connection. 'So restless Cromwel' makes the description of Cromwell follow directly on from the previous section. Syntax and allusion concur to make Cromwell also a youth of Ariminum. So in terms of Lucan's history Cromwell is both ambitious adventurer and the resister of such ambition, though unlike the youths of Ariminum Cromwell's resistance was to be entirely effective, and his lightning was to blast through Caesar's laurel crown. And the 'forward youth' – who perhaps also recalls the youth of Drusus Nero as well – is as much Cromwell as the poet, and the two cannot be distinguished. So the rhetorical denunciation of Caesar indulged in by Lucan, 'malicious Poet' as Marvell calls him in 'Tom May', is already inapplicable, for Caesar and his opponent meet in the single figure of Cromwell, and the poet is united to the soldier by his awareness of the same oppositions within himself.

In the lines following line 29 Cromwell too leaves, if not his 'Muses dear', at least an equivalently private and meditative kind of existence. His garden recalls the Garden of Epicurus rather than the elemental simplicity of a Stoic farm, a surprising context for Cromwell, so that his austerity there already strikes a slightly jarring note. But as Marvell develops the image of Cromwell as gardener, it more importantly recalls the traditional view of the organic state, and the description of Cromwell's career in these terms has even more subversive implications. Through the pun on 'plot', the activity of the gardener presiding over and

122

assisting natural processes becomes the machinations of a Machiavel, its end rapid destruction not gradual growth. The kingdom itself is described in the metallic imagery of the Hobbist paradigm. 'Cast' initially seems the natural and human though destructive act of throwing, but 'mold' in the next line gives it a more restricted meaning that refers to the artificial processes by which things like cannons are made. The analogy is prefaced by 'As if'; the similarity is consciously contrived, connived at by Cromwell himself. So as in 'First Anniversary', the events of the civil war are described through a trope central to the older paradigm, which is transposed into the mechanistic terms and causal system of the supplanting paradigm. But where in 'First Anniversary' civil conflict is resolved by this mechanistic simulacrum of the older order, in 'Horatian Ode' the apparent similarity masks something wholly alien and destructive.

Marvell immediately goes on to articulate the underlying doctrine. Justice and the 'Ancient Rights' have no intrinsic power of themselves to bond men in society, he says. The strength of the bonds is the strength of men who are strong enough to impose them on others. So Justice and these ancient Rights have power only as words to 'complain' and 'plead'. The position is akin to Hobbes's. In his 'Leviathan' of the next year Hobbes was to write that words and acts declaring allegiance to a sovereign

> are the BONDS, by which men are bound and obliged: Bonds, that have their strength, not from their own Nature, (for nothing is more easily broken than a mans word,) but from Feare of some evill consequence upon the rupture.[49]

Marvell then states the basic axioms on which his political reasoning is based. These axioms are drawn from physics, and applied to politics, preserving that unity of the two sciences which Ascham and Hobbes' opponents denied. Unlike Hobbes Marvell takes his axioms from Aristotelian physics, not from the new mechanics of Galileo, but he uses them to arrive at a similarly un-Aristotelian political theory. As Brooks perceptively noted, it is 'amusing' that Marvell has applied a law about physical bodies to the action of 'Spirits'.[50] Part of the point of the wit is the suggestion that Cromwell's 'spirit' is thoroughly corporeal in its action, a Hobbes-like cynicism about the 'workings of the Spirit' in the Puritan general and his independent supporters. But such a transformation of 'anima' to 'vis' was also a serious and even definitive step for the new science. It was a radically new way to unite physics and politics. In the analogy that opened the 'Leviathan' the Sovereign is likened to an artificial soul, 'as giving life and motion to the whole body'. The foreign princes at the end of 'First Anniversary' repeat a similar notion:

> The Nation had been ours, but his one Soul
> Moves the great Bulk, and animates the whole.   (lines 379–380)

Sovereignty is the concentration of the force, not the reason, of the body politic; so the science of politics must be concerned with the action of these forces, that is, with the physics of sovereignty.

Marvell then relates Cromwell's career to this axiom of power:

> What field of all the civil wars
> Where his were not the deepest scars?

The Cromwell of these lines is an ambivalent figure, however. His greatness seems to be measured in scar tissue, his penetration of the sovereignty by the penetration of his sword. But these could also be his own scars, another hint at the real cost of apparently remorseless victories. In either case the line reverberates against Lucan:

> Nor the Punicke bands
> This waste had made; no sword could reach so far;
> Deepe pierce the wounds receivd in civill warre. (May's Lucan, lines 31–32)

So far a Royalist like Fanshawe or Wild might have found much in the poem that disturbed him, but nothing treasonable. The political situation is seen in Hobbist terms but Fanshawe had drawn similar lessons from his reading of Roman history. In 'A Short discourse of the Civil Wars', published in 1648 as a tract for the times, he wrote of the period after the end of the Republic:

> This was the beginning of Civill Warre, and impunity of Swords in the City of Rome, thenceforth Might overcame Right, and the most powerfull was held the best man.[51]

And the death of Charles is the emotional centre of the poem, framed by the Royalist propaganda that Cromwell connived at Charles' escape to Carisbrook. It is not surprising that Wild drew on this section for his own loyal poem. The scene is profoundly moving. The picture of Charles as graceful, dignified and serene in the face of death exerts an unequivocal appeal. There is no self-indulgence or meretricious sentimentality. The description is as elegant and controlled yet totally serious as Charles himself, and the words simultaneously evoke the poignancy of the fact and the ambiguity of its significance.

The death is described as though it were a play. The metaphor itself is ambiguous. For Wild it gave universality and dignity to the death of Christopher Love.[52] Milton however made play with Salmasius' use of the word persona for the person of the king, twisting it to mean an actor or impersonator, a player king, so that the role and the man were split with Ramist absoluteness.[53] Marvell seems to recall the Miltonic pun, calling Charles the 'Royal Actor', but resolves the split, for Charles was born a king, and the man and his role are one.

But the death of Charles is not an isolated effect. He is linked by a

124

complex set of relationships to the figure of his conqueror, and his death gains meaning from its part in the dialectic of the poem. The reference to the keenness of Charles's eye implicitly contrasts his kind of wisdom with Cromwell's. Charles's eye tests the axe. The axe will test his neck with the wisdom of Cromwell, but his eye is keener, more penetrating than the axe.[54] So Cromwell penetrated to the Sovereignty with his sword, but Charles penetrates and goes beyond Cromwell's wisdom with his own greater wisdom, his insight into the nature of death.

But the two men cannot be simply opposed like this. Caesar and the youth of Ariminum meet in the figure of Cromwell, and conversely Charles 'himself does chase'. He too is a divided self, one part an ineffective Machiavel who has been outreached by his more cunning opponent to become his own worst enemy. The poem is organized by a rhythm of expansion and contraction which locks the two men against each other. The stanza form enacts this rhythm, with the expansive movement of the longer couplet commonly checked or undercut by the chop of the shorter one following. So Cromwell explodes from the confines of his private garden to his present power, from contemplation to action, while Charles contracts from supreme power to this isolation on the scaffold, confronting death with the prepared heart of the adept in the arts of meditation. Yet at this moment he ironically approximates to the ideal, with an illusory Amphion-like power over the hearts of his subjects. The Parliamentary troops assist the scene in spite of the real intention of their actions, and they are transformed to spectators of the triumphant royal performance, though the savage irony of this parody of obedience really emphasizes the isolation of the king, and the antithesis between the ideal and the actual.

So the poem does not present the conflict between Cromwell and Charles, Parliamentarians and Royalists, as a simple opposition between might and right, or ruthless ambition and Ancient Rights. The political activity of both Parliamentarians and Royalists is seen in Hobbist terms. The Royalist armies fought for the reality of Charles's power, and Charles can fully represent the ideal only at the extremity of his career, the point at which Cromwell, too, in the 'First Anniversary' could transform into the ideal. As in the later poem, the ideal takes a Royalist form, and is concentrated in the person of the king, but Marvell does not suppose that the reality of Royalist England ever corresponded to this ideal. In the 'First Anniversary' the ideal exists outside time, but still provides a model on which the resolution must be based. In the Ode the opposition between ideal and actual is more acute. The perfection of the ideal is the political impotence of a noble death, its values fixed in contemplation of the other world.

This great section has an almost cathartic effect. As Brooks recognized, the poem turns around it as a fulcrum. The change in Cromwell's status is signalled in the couplet:

> This was that memorable Hour
> Which first assur'd the forced Pow'r . . .   ('H.O.' lines 65–66)

The memory of the previous scene still acts through the repetition of 'memorable', and the word has a bitter tone that prevents what follows being a celebration. Marvell may be alluding here to a Royalist tradition about the King's death, which Milton reacts to more sceptically in his Second Defence against More: ' "The King was heard' you say 'on the scaffold repeating to the Bishop of London Remember, Remember".'[55] The difficult phrase 'forced Power', however, contains the germs of a resolution. The Power assured by the execution of Charles is described as 'forced', so it must refer here not to Cromwell but to the office of sovereignty which Cromwell has taken by force. 'Power' is also used in this sense in line 119. So it is the sovereignty of the state that has been assured by the death of Charles, not specifically Cromwell. Cromwell is assured only insofar as he is identified with the sovereignty.

This potential distinction is made more starkly by the incident of the bleeding head which immediately follows. A reader will naturally find something sinister in this omen, until comforted by commentators who usually annotate it from Pliny. However, the doubts of readers are well-founded, and there is a good case for exhumation. The common story exists in a number of versions. Pliny gives the story as an example of a good omen that was fulfilled, but in his version of the story the head was not bleeding.[56] But historians also mention the story, and these are obviously more relevant sources for a poem that takes Roman history so seriously. And it is the historians who mention details such as the blood on the head. They also invariably mention who found it – Tarquin the Proud, the last tyrant before the great days of the Republic. Livy, for instance, saw it as a good omen 'portending the greatnesse also of the empire', but the goodness of the omen did not extend to the current ruler. Livy goes on immediately after this to tell the story of a serpent that appeared at a banquet held by Tarquin. This serpent,

> having put the beholders in great fright and caused them to flie into the kings pallace, did not so much amaze the kings heart with suddaine and momentanie feare for the present, as fill his head with perplexed cares what the thing might portend.[57]

He was right to worry, of course; the omen portended his downfall. Marvell's addition of the frightened architects (a detail that does not occur in any version of the story of the Bleeding Head) looks like a conflation of this adjacent omen. A reader's natural sense of the

126

ambiguity of the omen is only confirmed and clarified by a knowledge of the source.

The first fruits of the prophecy are the Irish. They have given nearly as much trouble to commentators on the poem as to Cromwell. Their praise of Cromwell seems incredible even to those who can read the poem as a eulogy to Cromwell, but the lines resist a reading that inverts their sense and makes them wholly ironic. The difficulties arise because Irish praise of Cromwell is very hard to find, and must have been equally rare at the time. But paradoxically the passage presents far less of a problem if Marvell was a Royalist writing for Royalists. The lines are troublesome if we suppose that Marvell wishes to praise Cromwell and to do so has renounced his critical powers, accepting the blatantly false propaganda of his new party; or even worse, if he is a cynical rhetorician manipulating his former colleagues, a 'most servil' Wit, and Mercenary Pen' who on this occasion has failed to earn his pay, lapsing into a glaringly specious argument. But if neither Marvell nor his readers relish the thought of Cromwell's virtue, his acceptance of the Irish testimony becomes not a sign of wishful thinking or moral slackness, but an over-readiness to accept unpalatable truths, a far less reprehensible error of judgment.

Since Marvell made this mistake of fact about the sentiments of the Irish we need to look more closely at the passage to see what he really intended by it.

> They can affirm his Praises best,
> And have, though overcome, confest
>   How good he is, how just,
>   And fit for highest Trust:
> Nor yet grown stiffer with Command,
> But still in the Republick's hand:
>   How fit he is to sway
>   That can so well obey. ('H.O.' lines 77–84)

As the lines progress we can see the Irish being forgotten. The praise is Royalist praise. The Irish, for instance, would not be greatly concerned at what his position is in relation to the 'Republick's' hand. They are merely the mask for others who have been overcome, to whom the words are increasingly relevant. The Royalists knew that the discipline of Cromwell's troops had been exemplary, while the licentiousness of Cavalier generals like Goring had alienated the uncommitted wherever they went. Clarendon saw Cromwell as a 'bold, bad man', but commended his sense of justice:

> In all other matters, which did not concern the life of his jurisdiction, he seemed to have a great reverence for the law, and rarely interposed between party and party. And as he proceeded with this kind of indignation and haughtiness with those who were refractory, and dared to contend with his greatness, so towards all who complied with his pleasure, and courted his protection, he used a wonderful civility, generosity, and bounty.[58]

The admission did not make Clarendon change his allegiance. However, such a recognition as this would give the testimony of the Irish a more subtle kind of irony than comes from a simple inversion. Cromwell's very virtues, his scrupulousness and restraint, were shaming to the Royalists. The irony is even more complex than this, for Cromwell's new humility is excessive, and in terms of the logic of power as dangerous as his assault on the kingdom. The repetition of his fitness to rule comes like an urgent chant:

> How good he is, how just
> And fit for highest trust . . .
> How fit he is to sway
> That can so well obey

The lines embody the very rhythms of the king-making impulse, but Cromwell has stopped short of assuming sovereignty, and the energy of the lines comes up against the contrary hyperbole of Cromwell's offer to the Commons. Captain Thompson, Marvell's highly unreliable eighteenth century editor, has unfortunately introduced an emendation here that obscures Marvell's point. He reduced the subversive impact of the lines by adding an 's' to 'Common', an addition perpetuated by the Oxford edition. However, the lines should read as in the folio:

> He to the Common Feet presents
> A Kingdom, for his first years rents;   ('H.O.' lines 85–86)

The 'Common Feet' are of course the Commons, but the image implies that this is an inappropriate place to deposit kingdoms, whether Irish or English. Charles' perfection on the scaffold was defined by his avoidance of everything 'common'. In the 'First Anniversary' Marvell reveals his contempt for the commons at far greater length. So Cromwell's selflessness, however admirable it may appear, runs the risk of making the kingdom a football for the populace, and could be more damaging than the original recasting of the kingdom.

The falcon image that immediately follows acts as a warning of the dangers to Cromwell himself of this new virtuous self-abnegation. Now that he has killed he can be 'lured', and he merely 'pearches'. He no longer 'does both act and know', but is now as vulnerable to the waiting 'Falckner' as was Charles to Cromwell's former self. The very sound of the name is ominous, enacting the sudden grasp of the hand that slips the hood over the eyes of the sated bird. The term 'to hoodwink' comes from the sport of falconry. Cromwell has come close to Charles, threatened by someone or something even more cunning than himself. The rhythm of the poem now has Cromwell's potency contracting after his moment of greatest power, but in the dialectic of politics it can only contract to the scaffold or expand in further wars. So on the one side Cromwell faces the

128

fate of Charles, on the other the way divides between Caesar and Hannibal, victory or defeat.

The final sixteen lines divide into two exactly equal parts to present the dichotomous terms of Cromwell's present position. In the first eight lines, Cromwell is a Drusus-figure, the national leader who has Marvell's patriotic support, and the poet's sword-like wit is at his service. The joke against the Scottish 'party colour'd Mind' is neat and chauvinistic, all its edges nipping the Scots, not Cromwell. But opposed to this is Cromwell's 'Valour sad'. It is a mistake to make the adjective unsurprising, to historicize its force away, as Margoliouth does with his gloss of 'steadfast'. The dull clothes of Cromwell's troops, like the drab colour of his mind, are the necessary cost of his valour, and the Scots will find that the jibe is not so funny in the event. But the basic meaning of the word, then as now, was 'unhappy'. Its use here suggests that this grim, all-conquering hero is also an unhappy figure. The 'Industrious Valour' that ruined kingdoms has now become 'this Valour sad' as it marches on yet another kingdom.

This hint is developed in the next section, introduced by 'But', as the poet's attention now turns as though to address the successful leader. After the image of the Scots scampering for cover like deer before his invincible advance, 'But thou' distinguishes him from them, locking him in the imperative of his power: 'March indefatigably on'. He is the son not of a Stuart nor even of any human now, but of 'Wars and Fortune'. His advance is so inexorable that he himself cannot stop it. The image has a pathos that counterbalances that for Charles. It is the restriction of the man compelled to do, whereas Charles transcended the limitations of the scaffold by making it, as a stage, a microcosmic ideal kingdom, in which through death he could 'act' perfectly.

Cromwell has to live, and must live by the sword, held 'erect'.

> Besides the force it has to fright
> The Spirits of the shady Night.   ('H.O.' lines 116–117)

The lines refer to the shape of the hilt, but there is a sardonic joke here, for the sword is not inverted to look like a cross but held erect, ready for battle. The 'Spirits' are thereby corporealised, as the 'greater Spirits' were in line 44. They are frightened by what frightens men. Cromwell cannot rely on religious methods of persuasion in political matters, even with fellow Protestants.

The image of the erect sword makes political morality an exact inversion of normal morality. The war against the Scots becomes something of a Black Crusade, so that Cromwell is condemned by his power to commit an act tinged with blasphemy. Fairfax had resigned rather than lead this army against the Scots. So Cromwell is committed to the arts of war, a tragic position if the humility and desire to kill no more of lines 73–90 were genuine. Cromwell too deserves an elegy, which the later poem to him makes more explicit:

> For all delight of Life thou then didst lose,
> When to Command, thou didst thy self Depose;
> Resigning up thy Privacy so dear,
> To turn the headstrong Peoples Charioteer.

('First Anniversary' lines 221–224)

The assumption of rule, even if a deliberate act of the will, had to be carried through to the limit as an execution of the self.

So there is no simple answer to the question of Marvell's allegiance in the poem. Charles and Cromwell, the apparent political alternatives, are direct antitheses yet also aspects of a single figure, who includes the poet. The form of the dialectic is perhaps even a deliberate strategy to transcend choice or make it meaningless. So the Ode is not a celebration of Cromwell. It is not a Royalist poem either, in any simple sense, but nor is it written from a neutral standpoint. Its 'facts' are derived from Royalist sources, its Charles is a Royalists' King and its Cromwell a Royalists' Cromwell. The Royalist perspective even lends stature to this Cromwell, a stature that has been partly lost in the Cromwell Marvell had known at first hand, complete with the warts of sincere religious feeling and familial affection, when he came to write his elegy for the dead Protector. But the poem provides no comforts for a Royalist. On the contrary, it is created out of the pain of the Royalist experience, written for Royalists by a Royalist who thought too much.

The Ode is unique, but its conflict is not merely idiosyncratic. A traditional Royalist like Sanderson acknowledged allegiance to country as primary, but hardly distinguished this from loyalty to the sovereign. The disastrous events of the 40's set up a contradiction in the Royalist position, which the exclusive and dichotomous terms of a Hobbist or Ramist kind of dialectic could only intensify. The result for Marvell was not a clash between IS and OUGHT[59] but between two aspects of the former unity, patriotism versus loyalty to the rightful king. Many others no doubt saw the issue like this, but Marvell's dialectic carried him further. Unlike Ascham he still tries to sustain moral action in a real world that is inimical to the ideal, while accepting Hobbes' conclusion that power is intrinsic to sovereignty and that such power must be ruthlessly and amorally dedicated to its own preservation if the state is to survive. The result is a moral paradox: amorality in the service of one's country can become a moral imperative.

The political dilemma had a personal dimension as well, which must have affected his political conclusions. Marvell probably saw his problem as a conflict between the claims of the contemplative and active lives.[60] Religious considerations which can only be touched on here must have shaped Marvell's thinking, but the Ode itself makes it clear that for Marvell the active life engaged with the real condition of fallen men, and was necessarily harsh, unattractive, a constriction of the divine essence. The contemplative fixed his gaze on the ideal, cultivating his individual spiritual and moral perfection. The contemplative way of life was attractive, even seductive, but fundamentally immoral for fallen man. This opposition bonds the poem: Charles, Cromwell and Marvell all move between the poles of public and private, contemplation and action. The symmetry of the poem is not static, a matter of divided allegiance, but derives from a set of complementary movements between these poles. Out of the conjunction of the private dialectic and the penetrating political analysis comes a grim conclusion: the life of action in the world as it is must sacrifice not only the Muse but morality as well. It is an extreme, even desperate view, lacking the detachment and sanity so often ascribed to Marvell. The poem was not written from above the political scene. It has only the pose and detachment of a man on a rack. But indifference would hardly have been the best mood out of which to write one of the greatest political poems in the language.

Chapter 5

APPLETON HOUSE

'Upon Appleton House' occupies a special place in the understanding of Marvell's poetry. In the past, when the coherence of its structure was not appreciated, it was regarded as the quarry out of which Marvell drew greater, more finished works. However, some of the best work on Marvell in recent years has been concerned with this poem.[1] We are now in a better position to appreciate its coherence as well as its range. Its apparently episodic manner should no longer mislead critics, for its underlying structure is evident enough once it is pointed out, falling into clear sections, each of which contributes to the dialectic of the poem. 'Appleton House' is Marvell's most sustained and comprehensive exploration of his major themes, undertaken at the height of his powers. Its attempted synthesis is a proper context in which to consider the unity of Marvell's poetic vision. As well as this we have crucial knowledge about the circumstances of this poem which we lack for the other great poems. Wild and Fanshawe serve to give a name and face to the reader that completes the experience of the 'Horatian Ode', but Fairfax's relation to this longer poem is far closer, more certain and more essential. He is both its subject and its object, and we can have a fuller knowledge of him from both inside and outside the poem. He was interesting and important enough for his own sake, yet curiously he has been taken for granted by students of history and by readers of Marvell alike, and such knowledge as we have has never been brought into contact with a reading of the poem. The importance of the poem and the exactness of our knowledge coincide. Such good fortune should obviously be used with gratitude.

(i) The Great Lord Fairfax

The external details of Fairfax's career are readily available, but a quick summary may still be useful.[2] He was born in 1612, the son of a prominent Yorkshire family. His father had married the daughter of the Earl of Mulgrave. His grandfather was created Baronet in 1627, a title Fairfax was to inherit on his father's death in 1648. After three years at

132

Cambridge he served a military apprenticeship fighting for the protestant cause in the Low Countries. In 1632 his father refused to allow him to go to Sweden to enlist there under Gustavus Adolphus, so he spent the next ten years on the family estates. He was thirty years old when war broke out in 1642. Both he and his father took arms on the side of Parliament. For the first two years of the war they met with mixed success, but young Fairfax won some notable victories, often against heavy odds, to become one of the most respected generals on the Parliamentary side. So when Parliament decided to reorganize the structure of command at the end of 1644 owing to dissension involving Cromwell and Manchester, the obvious choice for the supreme command was the able but uncontentious Fairfax, who unlike the other possible candidates was not a member of either House. He was appointed on January 21st 1645, although still recovering from a severe wound. The New Model Army, as it was called, became under his command a well-disciplined and invincible army. The rout he inflicted on the Royalist army at Naseby in June of that year was followed up with a decisiveness and efficiency that both sides had lacked till then, and the complete defeat of the king soon became inevitable. In less than a year after Naseby the King had given himself up, and the civil war was virtually over, militarily at least.

In the new situation Fairfax's reactions quickly isolated him from his former associates. He displayed sympathy and deference to the defeated king, which Royalists duly noted as a hopeful sign. Since he did nothing material to assist the king, however, and his integrity was respected even by Royalists, they supposed that Cromwell must have cast some sort of spell over him:

> Cromwell had the ascendant over him purely by his dissimulation, and pretence of conscience and sincerity. And there is no doubt Fairfax did not then, nor long after, believe that the other had those wicked designs in his heart against the king, or the least imagination of disobeying the parliament

wrote Clarendon,[3] his words echoing Marvell's in his Elegy for Villiers, which refers to 'long-deceived Fairfax'.

But the king proved hard to negotiate with, and when war broke out again in 1648 Fairfax again led the armies of the parliament, prosecuting the war with greater severity than he had previously shown. The uprising was soon suppressed, and events headed irresistibly towards the execution of the king. Fairfax was strongly opposed to this expedient. Though he was appointed to the Commission that tried the king he attended only the preliminary meeting. When his name was read out at the start of the trial proper his wife caused a stir by calling out from the Gallery that neither he nor any other upright man was present in the chamber. He did not resign immediately, however, and did not do so until 1650, when Parliament proposed to invade Scotland and wished him to lead the

English army. Clarendon gives two reasons contemporaries attributed to him:

> The Presbyterians said, it was because he thought the war unlawful, in regard it was against those of the same religion; but his friends would have it believed that he would not fight against the king.[4]

So in 1650 he returned to his Yorkshire estates. The conventional picture of this move represents it as a serene retirement, a fitting reward for a lifetime of virtuous endeavour.

> Lord Fairfax retired to Nunappleton with his wife and daughter, and at length obtained that rest which he so much needed, and had so well earned

writes Markham, his Victorian biographer, perhaps unduly influenced by Marvell's poem. Milton in 'Defensio Secunda' of 1654 has a similar account. But even this work, Parliamentary propaganda that could not afford to acknowledge scruples in Fairfax, hints at hostile speculation: 'But whether it were your [Fairfax's] health, which I principally believe, or any other motive which caused you to retire . . .'[5]

Fairfax was only 38 at this time, younger than Cromwell had been at the start of the war. Only Cromwell's name commanded greater respect as a general, from Royalists and Parliamentarians alike. Fairfax had resigned, not retired. This was a political act. It left Cromwell without a military peer, but set up a potential rallying-point for the disaffected, a new centre for Royalist hopes. So Thurloe, head of Cromwell's intelligence service, received a number of reports of Royalist intrigues involving Fairfax, though none with any substance. When Mary Fairfax married the Duke of Buckingham in 1657, fresh suspicions were aroused, but again Fairfax made no move that was actively disloyal to Cromwell's rule. However, he remained politically active in peaceful ways. He was returned to parliament in 1654, where his reputation gave weight to his rarely-stated views. But he finally fulfilled some of the Royalist hopes in him by taking a decisive role in the Restoration. Before Monck made his move from Scotland he had established contact with Fairfax, who raised a small army in the North to prepare the way. Lambert swept up to meet him with a much larger force, but his troops had deserted en masse to their former general, and Lambert had to flee. The name of Fairfax had been as potent as the Royalists had hoped, and after this bloodless victory Monck met no opposition to his triumphant march on London. Fairfax had insisted that the more pragmatic Monck should declare for a return to full constitutional rule, and appropriately was appointed to head the commission which went to the Hague to discuss terms with the King.

This was the man whom Marvell was to join in the early 1650's when he became tutor in languages to Mary Fairfax. The exact date the appointment commenced cannot be fixed certainly, but the end of 1650 seems likely. The poem to Witty mentions a 'Caelia' who is apparently learning French and Italian with astonishing facility. She is usually identified as Mary Fairfax, plausibly enough. It was unusually enlightened to provide a language tutor for a mere girl.[6] Moreover Witty, a former teacher at Hull Grammar School, knew the Fairfax family well, at least in his later years.[7] He could easily have recommended Marvell for the job. This would at least explain the extraordinary appearance of Caelia in a work about medicine, as an allusive expression of gratitude.

Witty's dedication is dated 30 November 1650. If Caelia is Mary Fairfax, Marvell must have commenced at Appleton House some time before then. Since 'Tom May' must have been written after May's death, on November 13th 1650, this would mean that it was probably composed at Appleton House. Margoliouth resists this conclusion, but only because it is 'not the sort of poem Marvell would have written under Fairfax's roof'.[8] But Fairfax as we shall see would not necessarily have found anything offensive about its celebration of purely virtuous action or its contempt for temporizers and turncoats. Even the Ode, written between 25 June and 14 August 1650, could have been composed there, and must have been written within months of the move. There would have been much in common between the Royalist impelled by patriotism to active service of his country, and the Parliamentary general who had just resigned rather than lead the army against the Scots, moved by regret at the death of the King and distaste for the manner in which public affairs were being conducted. The one choice was the exact obverse of the other, and during the summer of 1650 the curves of the two lives intersected in the trauma of the execution, and the crisis of decision it precipitated in each.

But on the estates of Appleton House Fairfax's political importance resided in potentiality not act, and though distressed by physical pain that was to immobilize him in later life he had time to think. One of his tasks, a commentary on some works of the Hermetic corpus, reveals something of his state of mind at this time. The Hermetic corpus is a vague and inconsistent body of Neoplatonic writings, and the mere fact that Fairfax had read some of them would be unilluminating, perhaps even misleading. It might for instance imply a general interest in neoplatonic ideas,[9] whereas the commentary in fact suggests the opposite. The mysticism of the text clearly attracted him, but he continually transposes its vague descriptions into biblical terms, and illustrates out of the Bible, not from Plato. A Calvinist obsession with sin and depravity recurs, even where it has no basis in the Hermetic text. Fairfax was especially interested in the 'Poemander', which contained an account of the creation of the world and a kind of Fall reminiscent of the book of Genesis.

Fairfax's commentary makes it even more so. For instance, the Hermetic writer has:

> After a little while ther was a darkness made in part, coming downe obliquely fearfull & hidious, wch seemed unto mee to be changed into a certaine moyst nature, unspeakably troubled . . .[10]

The Hermetic polarities are matter and spirit, darkness and light. Fairfax is more concerned with good and evil. His marginal heading for this section is 'Devine Justice is agreable to the good, odious to the wicked', and he interprets the darkness as

> his terable Justice & in part hidious, or odious, & unpleasing, being so from its nature or rather on our part, for in its own nature it is not odious, but in poynt of execution . . .[11]

This concern with the ambiguity of God's justice corresponds to nothing in the Hermetic text. Fairfax's correction of himself 'or rather on our part' revealingly suggests a personal sense of this ambiguity, as though he has caught himself calling this justice 'odious & unpleasing' and realizes that this is to see it from the point of view of 'the wicked'.

Behind Fairfax's religious thinking is evidently the harsh doctrine of Calvinism, which would not have sweetened his retreat. For Calvin, repentance and assurance are marks of God's elect, but the effect of the fall was total depravity, of soul as well as body, a corruption of the will itself from which not even the Elect were exempt in this life. A sign of the damned was their sense of their depravity, but the struggle with temptation and doubt for the Elect also was 'a continual matter of strife, wherwith they may be exercised'.[12] This left a dangerously fine distinction between the experience of the Elect and the Damned. As Calvin put it

> This therefore is the proper reward and punishment of unbeliefe, so to tremble for feare, that in temptation he turneth himselfe away from God, yet doth not open himselfe the gate by faith. Contrariwise the faithful whom the weighty burden of temptations maketh to stoupe, and in a maner oppresseth, do constantly rise up, although not without trouble and hardinesse.[13]

Calvinism did not make a retreat from the world a pleasant experience, for there was no escaping a sense of sin and the necessity for self-examination, which still had to co-exist with a sufficiently saving assurance. Repentance was a dangerous remedy if taken to excess.

Fairfax's past would hardly bear thinking on for a Calvinist. He valued tradition, and had a strong sense of his own family's roots in the past. He paid a retainer to Dodsworth, the antiquarian, whose genealogies included the Fairfax family tree. The family papers include another suggestive document, a table of 'The Saxon-Monarchs, or ye Kings of England since the Year of Christ 800'.[14] This stops at Henry VII, but its interesting feature is that it goes across the Conquest without a break.

This implies that Charles's right to the throne was based not on conquest but on a hereditary right like Fairfax's own, of far greater antiquity. This would make the execution of the King an attack on the foundations of his own position. A Calvinist accustomed to look earnestly at events to learn God's will must have been deeply disturbed to see that this was the result of his best endeavours over so many years.

We do not know certainly whether he read or endorsed this particular table, but similar doubts are evident in this 'Memorial', a short but revealing attempt to justify his actions during the war. He begins:

> Now when yᵉ Lord is visitinge yᵉ Nation for yᵉ Transgressions of their wayes, as formerly he did itt to one Sort of Men, soe now doth he itt to another, soe that all may see their Errors and his Justice; and as we have Cause to implore his Mercy (Who) have sinned against him, soe must wee still vindicate his Justice, who is alwais cleare when he judgeth. Now, therefore, (by his Grace and Assistance) I shall sett downe truly yᵉ Grounds my Actions moved on duringe this unhappy Warre, and those Actions which seemed (to) yᵉ World most questionable in my stearinge through yᵉ turbulent and perrilous Seas of yᵉ Time.[15]

This is the punitive God of Calvin, and God's justice on a sinful nation is the context for Fairfax's self-examination. The national suffering is a sure sign of God's displeasure, and the two 'sorts' of men are united in being sinners who deserve such chastisement. Fairfax attempts to dissociate himself but can do so only partially, and even then obscures the extent to which this is possible. The structure of the sentence is unable to sustain the weight of so many partial distinctions. 'Now' is interrupted by two balanced structures of the form 'as . . . so', the first of which unites men of the past and of the present (perhaps Royalists then and supporters of Parliament now) in the common category of sinner, the second of which distinguishes these sinners and their need for mercy from God's absolute rectitude. Within the sentence pairs of oppositions are related symmetrically, 'one Sort' balanced against 'another', 'their Errors and his Justice', 'his Mercy' and 'his Justice', but as the sentence progresses it loses its original direction. So Fairfax has to pick up the 'now' of his own attempted justification, separated by a period but part of the original intention of the first sentence. But its disjointed symmetries included the terms of his own position, so that his defence can only at most deplore the consequences of his actions, and must rest on God's mercy not his justice.

Having given the Calvinist terms through which he interpreted history and in which his self-vindication had to be managed, he goes on to consider the nature of the conflict as it had come to seem to him from the perspective of Appleton House:

> The first imbarkinge into the sad Calamity of the Warr was about yᵉ Year 1641, when yᵉ general Distempers of yᵉ three Kingdoms had kindled such a

> Flame even in ye Heart, (I mean the difference between ye Kinge and Parliament) as everyone sought to quench his owne House by ye Authority of both those; but ye different Judgm and Wayes was so contrary, y^t before a Remedy could be found, almost all was consumed to Ashes.[16]

The opening metaphor seems only a cliché, but he soon drops this for the metaphor of disease, which through the comparison of fever to a flame extends to a general image of a conflagration. But though the metaphors in this complex are tangled they still organize the whole sentence, and he has clearly used them as the materials of his thought. So his parenthetical 'I mean' is a necessary attempt to reduce the confusion to some degree of clarity, and is not the self-conscious uncoding of a metaphor to be found in a Ramist like Baxter. The constituents of this metaphoric confusion are the two important commonplaces of society, the image of the body politic and the comparison of it to a building. But where Hobbes and Marvell both exploited the incompatibility of the two kinds of image, Fairfax is unable to resolve the confusion till House and Body arrive at a common fate in 'Ashes'. Public and private are similarly not distinguished, as Fairfax seems to be talking of the heart of the State, but goes on to talk of 'everyone', as though 'heart' might also refer to the individual hearts of men, whose own houses are aflame like the building or body of the state, and who try to quench these flames by a now divided 'authority'. The conflation of individual and state, of the public and the private dilemma, are not accidental excrescences of Fairfax's language but are part of the texture of his thought.

During the war, things had seemed much simpler to the General. For instance he commenced one letter to his father, ten days before Naseby, as follows:

> May it please your Lordship,
>
> I am very sorry we should spend our time unprofitably before a town, whilst the King hath time to strengthen himself, and by terror to force obedience of all places where he comes: the Parliament is sensible of this now, therefore hath sent me directions to raise the siege and march to Buckingham, where, I believe, I shall have orders to advance northwards, on such a course as all our divided parties may join.[17]

The directions with which he begins his message indicates his impatience at the needless inactivity, and the syntax is as vigorous as the action he desires. The closest the language gets to the metaphoric is the image from commerce latent in the formula 'spend time . . . unprofitably'. The King trails no aura of sanctity about him for Fairfax, to arouse loyalty in either Fairfax or anyone else. He forces obedience solely through fear, a fear which the general does not feel.

After the military defeat of the King, however, the right course of action became less obvious, and little more than a year later Fairfax was

138

writing to his father in a different vein:

> My Lord,
>
> I was sorry I could not more fully understand your Lordship's mind, by the messenger you had committed it to; for I should be exceeding glad to receive often such light and help as I might have from your lordship in this troublesome condition I am in; but I trust the Lord will make it some ways comfortable to me, if I have no end to myself in it; nor do I see yet the army hath any, but principally seeks to do that which is for the honour of God, and the good of the kingdom.[18]

In the light of later experience he was unable to retain even this faith in the purity of the motives of others, and he observed in his 'Memorial':

> But this shininge Mercy soone become clouded with ye Mists of abominable Hipocricys and Deceipt, even in those Men who had bene instrumentall in bringing this Warr to a conclusion.[19]

So in his retirement his principal defence endorsed the Royalist jibe against 'long-deceived Fairfax', as he clung to the integrity of his own motives:

> Thus beinge ledd on by good Success and cleare Intention of a public Good, some of us could not deserve (discern?) the Serpent, which was hidd under these spredinge leaves of soe good Fortune, or believe ye Fruits of our Hopes would prove as Cockatrice Eggs, from whence soe viperous a Brood, should afterwards springe upp.[20]

The most venomous viper hatched from these hopes was the trial and death of the King, which in his 'Memorial' he referred to with unequivocal regret:

> My afflicted and troubled Minde for itt, and my earnest endeav to prevent itt, will I hope sufficiently testify my dislike and abhorrency of the Fact; and what might they not now doe, havinge thus cutt downe the Cedar to the lower Shrubbs.[21]

His distress at the execution was evidently sincere, and must have preyed deeply on his mind. For instance, there is a book from the Fairfax library on the life of Julius Caesar, which has Fairfax's monogram at the end and a number of corrections to the text in the same pen.[22] Where the book has 'a full Senat cruelly Murdered Him' the words 'cruelly Murdered' have been heavily scored through. 'Murderers' received the same treatment in the sentence 'All his Murderers perished miserably', though the author had not made any explicit or obvious parallels between Caesar and Charles. Fairfax's sensitivity to the charge that he had murdered his lawful king must have intruded obsessively into the rest of his reading in the privacy of his study. But though he denies his own complicity, the figure of the King has by this stage accreted to itself traditional associations working through traditional images. Before the battle of Naseby

Fairfax had known that he was hunting an armed and mobile opponent who could be fought on equal terms, not a static but potently symbolic Tree. And inextricably involved in this traditional imagery is his sense of the equal threat to the foundations of his own position.

So the architect of Parliament's victory had come to see it as an assault on 'Justice', a betrayal of the 'Ancient Rights' that reached their roots back into the past and sustained the family whose name he bore, and whose history he traced so carefully. No-one likes to admit that the result of his life's work has been the destruction of what he values most. For Fairfax this natural reluctance was intensified by his Calvinism, for unless the cause could be totally distinguished from the effect the agent of evil was liable to damnation. So he took a sombre, even anguished view of the turning point in his public career, his elevation to the supreme command of the Parliamentary forces:

> Then was I immediatly voted by ye Parlt. to come to London to take my Charge, though not fully recovered of a dangerous Wound, wch I had received a little before, and wch I verily believe (without the miraculous Hand of God, had proved mortall. But here (alas), when I bringe to minde ye sadd Consequences designinge Men have brought (to) pass since from those inocent undertakings, I am ready to lett goe ye Confidence I once had with Job, to say till I dye, I will not remove my Integrity from mee, nor shall my Heart reproach me so longe as I live. But now more fitt to take upp his Complaint (with a little Alteration), and say, why did I not dye when I had that Hurt. Why did I not give up ye Ghost when my life was on the confines of the Grave. But (God having bene pleased to give me thus my Life for a Prey), I took my Journey Southward . . .[23]

Fairfax is at the limit of despair a Calvinist could tolerate consistent with a saving faith. His recovery that had been seen in providential terms as a miraculous sign of God's favour was, it turned out, an ambiguous gift, and the words of Job allow him to question the divine will in a way that would otherwise have marked him for damnation. God gave him his life only as a prey, and left him amongst scheming men who have turned his 'inocent undertakings' to a sad conclusion. Almost doubting his own integrity and crippled by physical pain he was left to brood on his role in the civil war and to try to define its issues with an energetic but undisciplined mind. The Fairfax whom Marvell joined in 1650 was too radically divided in his soul to be able to fulfil any Royalist hopes that he might still reverse the results of the Revolution.

(ii) The Poem

The structural principle of 'Appleton House' is apparently a stroll around the Fairfax estates. The critical mistake of the past has been to look no further, and simply to enjoy the parts of the poem as separate episodes in

isolation from each other. But just as the seeming negligence of
' "Rehearsal" Transpros'd' masked formidable intellectual powers, the
poem's structure is a remarkable display of architectonic virtuosity,
coherent and tightly controlled yet as complex and intricately formed as
the details themselves. The lives of the poet and patron are the material
of the work, and just as the opposing movements of Cromwell and
Charles provided the structural principle of the Ode, so Fairfax and
Marvell give a similarly symmetrical form to the longer poem. The first
half primarily concerns Fairfax. It has three sections, concluding with
stanza XLVI. The second half signals the switch of attention to the poet
himself:

And now to the Abbyss I pass.   (line 369)

It too contains three sections, occupying 51 stanzas, only five more than
the first half. As in the Ode the opposing figures are as inextricable as
aspects of the same self or of the same problem, although here oppositions are less remorsely symmetrical.

This dialectic gains a further level of complexity by being set in a poetic
world conceived as a set of concentric cosmoi, which find their centre in
Fairfax and the estates of Appleton House. The sense of the interpenetra-
tion of the wider worlds of the nation and the Universe is at its strongest
in the sections on the Garden and the Meadow, which as sections 3 and 4
stand at the centre of the poem, but in spite of this partial symmetry the
relationship of these spheres to each other and to the movement of the
poem is fluid and variable, following an unpredictable logic of its own.
Within such a form the poem's overt linking device, the tour of the estate,
gathers a richer significance. The tour is a journey of discovery for both
Marvell and Fairfax, exploring the implications of their contrary choices,
Fairfax's retreat from public life and Marvell's commitment to action.
This journey moves between Art and Nature, which thus become key
terms in the dialectic of the poem. Art is the ordering power of man,
Nature the organizing principle in natural things. The poem starts with
the house of the present then the house of the past, then moves to the
garden, the meadow, and the woods, in a gradual progression away from
the civilizing power of reason and the distress of public life to the solitude
of the woods, before Maria and the coming of evening recall the poet
back to the house again.

The apparent negligence masks this elaborate form, but it also
corresponds to a genuinely random quality in the poem's progression.
Sometimes the poet's wayward wit captures his delighted participation in
the leisured and civilized way of life to be found at Appleton House: at
other times it can respond to unpremeditated pressures from the
experience itself, as the poet achieves wisdom by resigning his reason to

141

the impulses of Nature and the forces of the irrational. So the seeming casualness is both courtly wit and the art of the irrational, itself a resolution of the opposition between Art and Nature. The result is a poem with a local texture of unparalleled richness. A sense of the abundance of the poet's creativity is as essential in a reader as an awareness of its structure and general argument. So the poem demands a reading that moves through the experience of the poem alert to the underlying structure of its argument, but able to pause to allow something of the inexhaustible riches of the poem's local life to come into focus.

The poem opens with ten stanzas in praise of the actual house. This section has often been isolated from the rest of the poem and compared to other poems praising the houses of noblemen,[24] but Wallace has argued that many of the details of these early stanzas recall Davenant's 'Gondibert'.[25] There is much to support this contention. Davenant can be shown to have been in Marvell's mind during the composition of the poem, since he is mentioned by name; the connection does not rely on a chance phrase but involves whole stanzas, which would be well-chosen to sum up something of the quality of the poem; and the relationship is precise and evaluative, implying a critical response that is highly relevant to the concerns of Marvell's own poem. The most obvious point of contact between Davenant's poem and preface and Marvell's theme is Davenant's discussion of Epic and its connection with the virtues of the active life. Marvell completed the other term of the opposition by connecting the contemplative life with Davenant's Hobbist account of the action of the undirected mind but in this opening section he conceived the opposition in more conventional terms. So his form of the Christian Epic is created out of a Christian resistance to the values of the epic, its distinctive quality a sense of heroic energy and aspiration held in check by the constricting force of morality.

But we can approach the poem by another route, through another kind of comparison. For Marvell does, like Jonson, Carew and Herrick, describe a house so as to imply the style of life of its noble owner. There are no unmistakeable echoes signalling a parodic relationship, but Marvell's opening is like Jonson's in contrasting the extravagance of other men's houses to his patron's less pretentious home. Marvell knew and respected Jonson's poetry, and used him in 'Tom May' as the spokesman for the qualities of severe integrity in terms of which May was condemned. In the same poem Jonson, the former Poet-laureate to the King, speaks with respect of Davenant, his successor to the post. The two poets might very naturally have come together in Marvell's mind. Though Davenant was the starting point, a poem like Jonson's probably served as a model for its final form. This second kind of comparison must be handled tentatively, but a representative poem like Jonson's does at least help to establish initial expectations in a precise form. In this case it allows us to define the relation of poet to patron, by registering the subtle interaction of Marvell's poem with the norms of the convention.

Jonson starts his poem with a series of negatives:

> Thou art not, Penshurst, built to envious show,
> Of touch, or marble; nor canst boast a row
> Of polish'd pillars, or a roofe of gold:
> Thou hast no lantherne, whereof tales are told;
> Or stayre, or courts; but stand'st an ancient pile,
> And these grudg'd at, art reverenc'd the while.   (lines 1–6)

But these negatives do not imply that Penshurst is a poor-house, and Jonson goes on immediately to describe her considerable wealth of natural resources. It is a poem of distinctions not of oppositions, and so wealth is not set against poverty, nature against art, but true nobility is distinguished from vulgar and pretentious forms of it.

Marvell initially might appear to have had a similar aim, but the quality of the language immediately signals a difference in the intention. Though an octosyllabic couplet may seem less heroic and epic than Jonson's pentameter, that metre had not yet acquired its alternative name 'heroic couplet', and as Jonson uses it its affiliations are with the elegy and the verse-epistle rather than with the epic mood. Within this form his sentences have an almost Ramist simplicity. This opening passage consists largely of negatives of simple sentences or of even smaller units, linked by simple copulative connectives, 'of' and 'nor' doing the work of 'and', and the movement within the couplet form is thoroughly relaxed and easy. Marvell's first stanza is, typically, a single sentence, which fits its complex structure into the units of line and couplet with a sense of constraint. The syntax is ambitious as well as complex, and the images strain the understanding as they try to include as much meaning as they can. Behind the description there are already the dualistic terms of Marvell's metaphysic. 'Frame' in the opening line comes to refer to both body and poem.[26] The tortuous comparison of the house to the architect's skull and the arches' effect on the analogously arching brows of onlookers make a similar point.

The criticism implicit in Marvell's images is far more extreme than anything Jonson suggests. Penshurst is not exactly a 'sober Frame', but owners of over-ornate piles are merely vulgar and pretentious, and do not reveal the grotesque and destructive perversity of Marvell's 'Forrain Architect'. The alternative Marvell presents to such buildings is similarly extreme. The example of animals wittily argues against the need for houses at all. Body and house should ideally be as one. Gondibertian man is seen from the perspective of the grave. Davenant had written lines which seem to come close to Marvell's at this point, describing Astragon:

> So vast of heighth, to which such space did fit
> As if it were o're-cyz'd for Modern Men;
> The ancient Giants might inhabit it;
> And there walk free as winds that pass unseen.　　('Gondibert' II.ii.7)

Marvell's lines echo hollowly to Davenant's:

> But He, superfluously spread,
> Demands more room alive then dead.
> And in his hollow Palace goes
> Where Winds as he themselves may lose.　　('A.H.' lines 17–20)

Along with the size of Davenant's ancient giants Marvell's lines recall the fact of their death. All aspiration after earthly greatness is seen as futile, and meets in the vision of the grave and its unanswerable question:

> What need of all this Marble Crust
> T'impark the wanton Mote of Dust?　　('A.H.' lines 21–2)

The values brought to bear against Gondibertian posturing must have appealed strongly to the ascetic in Fairfax. In lines 71–72 Marvell directly recalls Fairfax's own poem on his new house, which begins:

> Thinke not o Man that dwells herein
> This House's a stay but as an Inne[27]

Such a critique is so absolute that it leaves no room for any form of human greatness. Following this logic the life of Penshurst is hardly less futile than Astragon, and since Appleton House is not a hovel, even Fairfax is exceeding his proper limits. But the implications of Marvell's imagery when he turns to the house suggest the exact opposite of this criticism. Where Penshurst is 'reverenc'd' for its virtues, Marvell suggests that 'some will smile' at the smallness of Appleton House. 'Dwarfish confines' suggests a ludicrous disproportion between the greatness of the occupants and the size of their dwelling. Though stanza VI suggests the perfect harmony of this house which 'Humility alone designs', the next stanza commences with a qualifying 'Yet'. This stanza contains an image that has been regarded as an error of taste on Marvell's part:

> Yet thus the laden House does sweat,
> And scarce indures the Master great.　　('A.H.' lines 49–50)

Certainly there is something faintly grotesque about the image, but the images in the rest of the stanza have a similar quality. They convey a tacit criticism of excessive renunciation, which the next stanza makes unobtrusively explicit:

> So Honour better Lowness bears,
> Then That unwonted Greatness wears,
> Height with a certain Grace does bend,
> But low Things clownishly ascend.　　('A.H.' lines 57–60)

144

Honour only bears lowness better than lowness can sustain greatness. The careful qualifications discreetly hint at an inversion of values which is repeated later in the poem, with the image of 'Grasshoppers like men' and the reference to the Levellers. Greatness such as Fairfax's has a duty to assert itself, a moral claim at least as strong as the pious wish to renounce the world and all material power. From this comes a crucial difference in tone with Jonson, who can celebrate wholeheartedly the harmonious way of life of Penshurst since it involves no conflict of choice to either himself or the Sidneys. They could all leave as they liked for London and the world of affairs, but Fairfax's retirement was premature and apparently permanent, a self-willed and total exclusion from high office which left the nation the poorer.

So Marvell's description is no celebration. The extravagance of its praise hints at criticism of Fairfax's decision, though he also gives images that undermine the grounds of all human greatness and enter into the state of mind behind that unfortunate decision. The result is a poem that engages with its patron at a far deeper level than Jonson's or any other poem in the genre, as its images recreate the tensions in Fairfax's position with quiet but disturbing force.

The opening section, then, establishes the terms of the conflict, and even hints at where the poet's allegiance lies, but the poem could not end here, with the conflict neither developed and explored nor resolved. The second section, however, is linked apparently casually to the first. This has probably done more than anything else to conceal the coherence of the argument of the poem, for if this section is taken as a tangentially-related episode the reader has gone one-third of the way through the poem without having followed the underlying argument, nor even realized the need to do so. But the nun's speech and the episode as a whole plays a vital role in continuing the dialectic of the poem. As the stones of the nunnery have become part of the fabric of the physical house, so the conflict is part of the Fairfacian character. It is a Founder's myth for the House of Fairfax, and the arguments used are especially calculated to find a response in Fairfax, who was keenly interested in the history of his own family, and also in monasteries and their sister-institutions.[28] He had the knowledge to evaluate the nun's rhetoric and a side to his nature that would feel its force.

As Marvell tells the story, one of the nuns wins Isabella Thwaites, Fairfax's ancestress, over to the monastic ideal. The elder Fairfax tries to use persuasion unsuccessfully, and finally resorts unromantically to a court-order. Even with this, however, he needs to use force, and carries Isabella off 'weeping'. The nun's speech that works so successfully on Isabella is a magnificently persuasive dramatic creation, presenting both the strength and the nature of the appeal of the celibate life. Fairfax as a good antiquarian would have already known some facts which we need to be told, which provide a standard by which the rhetoric can be evaluated. For instance, the prioress was both relative and guardian to Isabella, so her hold on the girl was a close one sanctioned by the law, but her motives were partly as mercenary as the frustrated wooer suggests. And the nun's tempting suggestion that Isabella would soon succeed the head of the nunnery on the imminent death of the prioress would have proved far out, for Isabella's guardian was still prioress when the nunnery was abolished 24 years later.[29]

But the appeal of the nuns' way of life is strongly present and subtly evaluated in the language itself. The nuns are not mere hypocrites. Some of their lines present an ideal which in itself is thoroughly admirable. For instance their practice of the art of embroidery is represented as inseparable from their way of life, both being equally concerned to express a religious ideal:

> But what the Linnen can't receive
> They in their Lives do interweave.
> This Work the Saints best represents;
> That serves for Altar's Ornaments.　　　　　　('A.H.' lines 125–128)

though they immediately go on blasphemously to suggest that Isabella might stand in for 'our Lady' (line 131). But the vision of Isabella glorified has a sudden beauty that has nothing spurious about it:

> I see the Angels in a Crown
> On you the Lillies show'ring down:
> And round about you Glory breaks,
> That something more then humane speaks.　　　　　　('A.H.' lines 141–144)

But over the length of the speech erotic, sensuous and narcissistic impulses are at work, woven into the texture of their religious protestations to give a powerful sense of the perversion of these admirable ideals even as they are made most winning. No other lyric poet of the century was so aware of the way unconscious motives infuse themselves into the language a man uses. Marvell's insight into these processes is presented with a clarity that comes close to caricature. For instance, towards the end of her speech the nun says:

> What need is here of Man? unless
> These as sweet Sins we should confess.
> Each Night among us to your side
> Appoint a fresh and Virgin Bride;
> Whom if our Lord at midnight find,
> Yet Neither should be left behind.
> Where you may lye as chast in Bed,
> As Pearls together billeted.
> All Night embracing Arm in Arm,
> Like Chrystal pure with Cotton warm.　　　　　　('A.H.' lines 183–192)

The first couplet implies that confession too has its sweetness, which makes sins themselves more sweet, a thoroughly subversive notion which is unobtrusively introduced as though an afterthought by 'unless'. In the next line 'fresh' restores the erotic meaning to the Biblical 'Virgin Bride', and the nightly change of partners seems like an effort to sustain the level of stimulation by constant novelty. In the next couplet the nun reveals her anxiety that the companion, too, should not be left behind; the slight quickening of the pace and drop in tone signal the sudden self-concern, but not crudely. The stress on the chastity with which the nuns lie in bed with each other is not the sort of remark that should occur to a nun describing the sleeping arrangements. The revelation of the self is not blatant but the implications are unmistakeable, underlined with a clarity that stops just short of overt ridicule.

The images that close the stanza are a more total imaginative achievement. Meaning and experience are curiously dissociated in this symbol for the nuns' quality of life. Pearls and crystal as emblems signify purity, but the conjunction with the less obviously emblematic 'cotton warm' brings out their sensuous quality. This sensation, compounded of smooth hard pearls, sharp cool crystal, and warm, soft, opaque cotton, is unusual but not unpleasant. The *brio* of a discreetly deviant eroticism might appeal to a connoisseur of sensations. The admirable ideal has provided images and even sanction for its own perversion.

The clarity with which Marvell understands and can render the processes by which the contemplative ideal is perverted in the lives of the nuns does not come from a disinterested and external power of judgment. Marvell's imagination has been fully engaged in creating the allure of the perversion, and the claims of the ideal itself cannot be simply dismissed. The elder Fairfax also knew that the nuns were poor representatives of the ideal, but still sees the competing claims as inextricable:

What should he do? He would respect
Religion, but not Right neglect:
For first Religion taught him Right,
And dazled not but clear'd his sight.   ('A.H.' lines 225–228)

So the elder Fairfax was no simple man of action either, but was held immobile by the analogous division in himself between the soldier and the judge, the man of action and the man of deliberation. If he had not resolved the conflict the present Lord Fairfax would not have been born, a sufficient argument for just and decisive action. But its claims are embodied in the language, not presented in terms of self-interest:

Is not this he whose Offspring fierce
Shall fight through all the Universe;
And with successive Valour try
France, Poland, either Germany.   ('A.H.' lines 241–244)

After the rapid but facile rhythms of the nun's speech and the clogged, self-checking movement of Fairfax's deliberations the line surges with epic vigour against obstacles worthy of its energy, and the poet's eye sweeps through vast tracts of time and space, across history and 'through all the Universe'. The sense of release from the claustrophobic and cloying sweetness of the nun's world and the constrictions of the moral dilemma validates the decision by its felt superiority as a mode of being. For Fairfax especially it must have recalled the exhilaration of the early days of the civil war, before the 'Mists of abominable Hypocricys and Deceipt' had clouded God's 'shininge Mercy', and perverted Fairfax's 'inocent undertakings'. It is this experience recreated in the verse which shatters the nun's spell, though 'bright and holy' Isabella weeps, the mother of the contemplative tendency in Fairfax, her tears the guarantee of the truth of the ideal.

So the Founder's Myth of the House of Fairfax has a clear commitment to action, in spite of the extent to which Marvell's imagination has registered the attractions of the opposite way of life. But Fairfax has chosen otherwise. The next section, on the Garden, attempts to come to terms with this decision. More than the previous sections it is built out of careful symmetries. Its main body is a block of eight stanzas, four of which talk of the Garden using military metaphors, and four of which talk of England as though it were a Garden. This principle of division is continued in the two stanzas about Fairfax which conclude the section: one describes the process of his religious life in garden imagery, the other as a war. The structure underlying these eighty lines is not usually noticed by critics of the poem, who transform to bees or butterflies when they come to a Marvellian garden, but it is as crucial to Marvell's meaning as the similarly sustained symmetry of 'Drop of Dew' and the less formal balance in the Amphion section of 'First Anniversary'. The ideal world of the garden is penetrated by images from the real world, and the civil war is understood as a fall from the perfection of the Garden.

But since the experience of the Garden is so permeated with images from public life, Fairfax cannot simply choose a serene and peaceful retirement in the perfection of his garden. The use of military metaphors threading through the first description of the garden is a delightful game but is also more than that, just as Fairfax almost compulsively recalled the war in the lay-out of his garden:

> Who, when retired here to peace,
> His warlike Studies could not cease. ('A.H.' lines 283–284)

In fact Fairfax avoided military images in his own poetry,[30] and did not adapt the traditional vocabulary to the technical improvements made in the instruments of war since classical times. Marvell refers to details

148

unknown to the ancients. The innocent war of the flowers is fought with guns and gunpowder which is susceptible to damp. The sentinel Bee, who 'runs you through, or asks the Word', could recall a popular story about Fairfax as general. Once he had returned very tired after an all-night scouting expedition and forgot the pass-word, so his well-disciplined sentry had refused to allow him through. The general had had to stand in the rain till another officer came and identified him. Fairfax had duly rewarded the soldier, and the incident became a symbol of the independence and discipline of the New Model Army.[31] The recollection would not have decreased Fairfax's enjoyment of his garden. Part of the pleasure of the experience is its inclusiveness, as mind and senses become preternaturally alert. The senses which the ascetic Fairfax resists share in a sensuous experience as unusual as any cultivated by the 'curious Taste' of the Nuns. The eye and smell 'hear' the exploding sweetness and beauty of the flowers, but the synaesthesia is an extension of the powers of sense to an exhilarating state of awareness normally impossible to man since the Fall.

But the four stanzas have moved imperceptibly from morning to evening, from the 'drowsie Eylids' of the dew-drenched flowers to the sudden glimpse of the macrocosm of the 'vigilant Patroul of the stars'. The image exemplifies the laws of the Marvellian imagination as it moves from the small to the immense, from innocence to threat; so the movement to the great apostrophe of Stanza XLI has the inevitability of its truth to the nature of the mind, and implies the necessary impermanence of the paradisal state of mind for fallen man:

> Oh Thou, that dear and happy Isle
> The Garden of the World ere while,
> Thou Paradise of four Seas,
> Which Heaven planted us to please,
> But, to exclude the World, did guard
> With watry if not flaming Sword;
> What luckless Apple did we tast,
> To make us mortal, and The Wast?　　　　　　('A.H.' stanza XLV)

The intense patriotism unites with the personal sense of irrecoverably lost innocence, and the ever-widening spheres of significance find their centre in the Garden of Eden and the myth of the Fall. As in the Ode the civil war is described in images taken from natural processes:

> But War doth all this overgrow:
> We Ord'nance Plant, and Powder sow.　　　　　　('A.H.' lines 343–344)

But Marvell is not here trying to generate tension out of the incompatible terms of the images. The garden now can provide images for imperfection as well as perfection. War is seen as a noxious weed, and the proliferation

149

of guns and ammunition as an error of husbandry. The perverse sterility of war is contrasted with the beauty and variety of peace, but the radical and disturbing conflict between the mechanistic and organic principles of causation of the competing paradigms is not forgotten, it is resolved in the context of the garden, which even in its unfallen state had its 'Stoves' and 'Magazeen'.

But the strength of Marvell's feeling for his country's plight comes up against Fairfax's decision to retire:

> And yet their walks one on the Sod
> Who, had it pleased him and God,
> Might once have made our Gardens spring
> Fresh as his own and flourishing.
> But he preferr'd to the Cinque Ports
> These five imaginary Forts:
> And, in those half-dry Trenches, spann'd
> Pow'r, which the Ocean might command.   ('A.H.' stanza XLIV)

There is no mistaking the regret at Fairfax's decision, though the syntax leaves it unclear whether the decision is still open, whether God and Fairfax could still 'please' to do otherwise. But the regret coexists with genuine respect for the grounds of the unfortunate decision. Fairfax's cultivation of the 'Flow'rs eternal' of Conscience recalls the nun's words to Isabella, but this validates the ideal behind those words as much as the nun's example warned of the insidious dangers in the way of such an endeavour. And Fairfax's form of the life of contemplation is a much more strenuous and less indulgent kind of activity:

> And in those half-dry Trenches, spann'd
> Pow'r, which the Ocean might command.

The couplet suggests the triviality, even absurdity of the 'half-dry Trenches' that are the object of these great abilities, but the energy required to contain and concentrate such powers is fully created through the sense of effort at the point of transition between the two lines: 'spann'd/Pow'r'. The inversion of epic values involved in Fairfax's decision has something of the heroic about it, and the conquest of the microcosm is no ignoble aim. So Marvell can accept and even admire Fairfax's decision while the weight of his feeling goes against it.

The conflict in attitude towards Fairfax is apparently left unresolved as Marvell takes leave of his patron:

> And now to the Abbyss I pass   ('A.H.' line 369)

but the two sections that follow remain relevant to Fairfax's own position, for the meadow and the wood correspond to the two terms of his choice, the life of action in the public world and the possibility of a retreat into a private and solitary existence. The description of the meadows seems to

150

consist of a series of allegorical tableaux, but Marvell has dissolved the clarity of their outlines and transfused them with shifting ambiguous emotional values to give them more the character of a dream.

With whistling Sithe, and Elbow strong,
These Massacre the Grass along:
While one, unknowing, carves the Rail,
Whose yet unfeather'd Quils her fail.
The Edge all bloody from its Breast
He draws, and does his stroke detest;
Fearing the Flesh untimely mow'd
To him a Fate as black forbode.   ('A.H.' stanza L)

The simple task of mowing becomes suddenly charged with menace with 'massacre'. Fairfax could have seen his own reactions in the unknowing executioner's disgust and fear for his own safety, though he himself was technically not responsible for the death of the king. But the lines are not an indirect accusation, as they would be if this were an allegory. The victim's name associates it with the king through a devious pun Rail/Royal, but she is a female. The logic of the dream proceeds by displacement as well as by arbitrary associations, and the figures do not have the stable identity of either reality or allegory. 'Bloody Thestylis' in the next stanza has the same sexual ambiguity, a Cromwell or Ireton in skirts. The images of guilt that obsessively re-enact the traumatic events of the war are shadows from Fairfax's past, profoundly affecting the quality of his retreat. Such contemplation is neither a preparation for action nor a rest from it, and the quality of the experience is a compelling argument against such a withdrawal from the world of public life.

Marvell does not insist on his insight into Fairfax's state of mind, which could only have appeared an offensive intrusion, so the vision is presented in personal terms, but through images so vivid as to go beyond the limits of both the personal and the public. The crucial stanza LVIII describes and enacts Marvell's view of the processes of the imagination, an exhilarating yet frighteningly rapid motion of the wit as it ranges through the world of the mind and the natural universe, but this is only a more disturbing and disordered version of the mind's play in the Garden section. The affinity links the Garden and the Meadow, Fairfax and Marvell: moreover it works both ways, so that as the Garden cannot protect the mind from memories of the war and the world outside, conversely there is pleasure in the meadow, and not all its images are the focus of unpleasant emotions:

And now the careless Victors play,
Dancing the Triumphs of the Hay;
Where every Mowers wholesome Heat
Smells like an Alexanders sweat.   ('A.H.' lines 425–428)

151

The rhythm trips along as he celebrates the innocent pastime, and there is no disgust at the 'wholesome Heat' of the sweating Mowers – though the hint of their pretensions to be Alexanders is both ominous and absurd. The rapidity with which a paradisal image can switch to its opposite is a primary characteristic of the experience:

> The World when first created sure
> Was such a Table rase and pure.
> Or rather such is the Toril
> Ere the Bulls enter at Madril.   ('A.H.' lines 445–448)

The volatility, though slightly over-symmetrical and forced in this example, gives the experience its truth to laws of the mind hardly suspected by most of Marvell's contemporaries.

But Marvell retreats from the meadow to the woods, into a more isolated and personal kind of experience. Its significance is given more precise definition by an allusion to a poem by Lovelace, his 'Aramantha'. This long pastoral poem occupied a key place in Lovelace's first book of poems. It opens with the maiden Aramantha in a rural or pastoral setting. She hears the sobbing of a lover in the woods, finds that it is Alexis, her lover, and reveals to him that she is really Lucasta, which identifies Alexis as Lovelace. She explains how she came into the wood in a passage of overt political allegory:

> How chac'd by Hydraphil, and tract,
> The num'rous foe to Philanact,
> Who whilst they for the same things fight,
> As Bards Decrees and Druids rite
> . . . each destroyes
> The glory of this Sicilie.[32]

The allegory has a simple one-to-one correspondence with political reality. Hydraphil is Parliament, the many-headed monster, Philanact the king-loving Cavalier. Lovelace even shares Marvell's regret that the real loser of the war is England.

Immediately after this come the lines which recall Marvell's

> From this sad storm of fire and blood
> She fled to this yet living Wood;
> Where she 'mongst savage beasts doth find
> Her self more safe then humane kind.

Marvell's lines are:

> But I, retiring from the Flood,
> Take Sanctuary in the Wood;
> And, while it lasts, my self imbark
> In this yet green, yet growing Ark.   ('A.H.' lines 481–484)

For both poets the storm or flood is an image for the civil war, though Marvell explores this image at far greater length. But there are some slight but significant changes between the two. Where Lucasta 'fled', Marvell retires and takes sanctuary; he had muted the force of the verb and given it a religious dimension, though significantly the religious and prudential motives are inextricable. Lovelace's phrase, 'yet living wood', is slightly puzzling if one asks what dead wood it is being contrasted to. Marvell's lines answer such a question. His 'yet green, yet growing Ark' is unlike the normal ark, which has to be hewn out of dead wood by the artifice of man. This brings out a pun on 'imbark', which can also mean to become enclosed in bark, to be like a tree. The pun implies that the end of such a flight as Lucasta's is to become a vegetable. In 'The Garden' this briefly seemed a desirable fate, but as the experience of it continues in the wood the inversion of the natural order it involves is revealed as a disturbing and unacceptable mode of existence for a man, and as he acts it out Marvell finds out the inadequacy of the solution of his perfect cavalier.

Like the Garden and the Meadow, the Wood is an image for a condition of the imagination, here growing as freely and unshaped as trees in a forest, unassisted by the 'Engines strange' that generated the more artificial images of the meadow. There is perhaps an echo of Cowley's poem on wit:

> In a true piece of Wit all things must be,
>   Yet all things there agree.
> As in the Ark, joyn'd without force or strife,
> All Creatures dwelt; all Creatures that had Life.

(Ode: of Wit, lines 57–60)

Marvell, however, distinguishes the aggressive profusion of the products of an undisciplined Fancy from the neat dualities of perfection:

> Although in Armies, not in Paires.   ('A.H.' line 488)

There is wisdom as well as fantasy in the wood: Lovelace's Lucasta had been taught by Caelia, who

> Makes her conversant in Layes
> Of birds, and swaines more innocent.

Marvell comes even closer to understanding a universal language:

> Already I begin to call
> In their most learned Original:
> And where I Language want, my Signs
> The Bird upon the Bough divines.   ('A.H.' lines 569–572)

His senses are heightened as they were in the Garden:

> No leaf does tremble in the Wind
> Which I returning cannot find. ('A.H.' lines 575–576)

He almost attains to universal knowledge, which is revealed in 'Natures mystic Book' as the forest turns into an animated emblem book. But the world of politics cannot be excluded from the images of the mind even in the depths of the wood. The references are more generalized and more oblique, but this only intensifies the feeling of a dreamlike menace.

> The Oak-leaves me embroyder all,
> Between which Caterpillars crawl:
> And Ivy, with familiar trails,
> Me licks, and clasps, and curles, and hales.
> Under this antick Cope I move
> Like some great Prelate of the Grove ('A.H.' lines 587–592)

The caterpillars are related to the family of emblematic caterpillars, among them to the 'envious Caterpillar' who sat 'On the faire blossoms of each growing wit' in Marvell's prefatory poem to Lovelace, (line 15) but now they have a more than emblematic life over which the recumbent moralist has lost control. The sensations are vivid and repulsive. The ivy is charged with 'vis vegetiva' to perform its emblematic role of sycophant with malevolent vitality. Marvell becomes like an arrested Prelate – another Laud? The next stanza concludes with an image that suggests some such connection, as the beneficent action of the wind changes its character with the inexplicable and horrific rapidity of a nightmare:

> And unto you cool Zephyr's Thanks,
> Who, as my Hair, my Thoughts too shed,
> And winnow from the Chaff my Head. ('A.H.' lines 598–600)

But he might easily be the King as well.

Nature achieves this power by the enervation of man. The intermittent moments of wisdom are achieved at the cost of a dangerous debilitation of the body, and for Marvell this goes along with moral laxity as well. The wood is a Temple but it

> in as loose an order grows,
> As the Corinthean Porticoes ('A.H.' lines 507–8)

Henry Wotton, whose influential writings on architecture Marvell had probably read, observes of this order:

> The Corinthian, is a Columne, laciviously decked like a Curtezane, and therein much participating (as all Inventions doe) of the place where they were first borne[33]

154

Marvell's epithet, 'loose', endorse the judgment. The section ends with the poet unsinewed by the pleasure of the experience.

> Abandoning my lazy Side,
> Stretcht as a Bank unto the Tide;
> Or to suspend my sliding Foot
> On the Osiers undermined Root,
> And on its Branches tough to hang,
> While at my Lines the Fishes twang!   ('A.H.' lines 643–648)

But though the image is literally one of total abandon, a life resting on an 'undermined Root', the self-awareness and self-mockery that created it are activated into a renewed sense of responsibility by the coming of Maria:

> Hide trifling Youth thy Pleasures slight.   ('A.H.' line 652)

The tutor's wry rebuke of himself is not wholly serious, but the poem now moves towards the resolution, in which Maria plays a crucial role.

Though the focus of the poem till now has been on Fairfax, Maria has been a latent presence, and the switch of attention here is not unprepared. In the Garden she was both nymph and flower. In the Wood she makes a brief but significant appearance as a Nightingale:

> The Nightingale does here make choice
> To sing the Tryals of her Voyce.
> Low shrubs she sits in, and adorns
> With Musick high the squatted Thorns.
> But highest Oakes stoop down to hear,
> And listening Elders prick the Ear.
> The Thorn, lest it should hurt her, draws
> Within the Skin its shrunken claws.   ('A.H.' stanza LXV)

Marvell could have got these commonplace details about the nightingale from many sources, but verbal echoes suggest that he took them from the Jesuit Henry Hawkins' book of meditations on the Virgin; and more interesting, that his lines have a parodic relationship to Hawkins'. Hawkins paraphrases Pliny as follows:

> The younger (sayth he) do meditate and receave their verses from the elder to practise, to imitate. The scholars attentively listen, and prove their Notes, and by turnes hold their peace.[34]

If Hawkins is kept in mind Marvell's reference to the 'listening Elders' becomes a deliberate pun. Holland's translation of Pliny called them simply 'old birds'. The pun makes the nightingale stand for Maria as in Hawkins, and the passage becomes a graceful compliment to his pupil, with the 'highest Oakes' probably the Great Lord and his wife, the 'listening Elders' no doubt including her language tutor.

It is initially surprising to find an allusion to such a work in a poem to

155

the sternly Calvinist general, though amongst the books he bequeathed to the Bodleian were works by Hugh of St Victor and St Bernard. If he was to appreciate the wit of the allusion, he must have read Hawkins too. Worse, the allusion seems to associate Mary Fairfax with the Virgin, and assign her the role the nun wished so blasphemously to impose on Isabella. But though Marvell allows the idea to be entertained, he immediately states his resistance to it:

> But I have for my Musick found
> A Sadder, yet more pleasing Sound:
> The Stock-doves, whose fair necks are grac'd
> With Nuptial Rings their Ensigns chast ('A.H.' lines 521–524)

The nuptial ideal of the Stock-doves is to be preferred to the solitary song of the celibate nightingale.

But Maria is present more fully in the great Halcyon passage that has been already discussed.[35] The bird there is an image of a vulnerable but dangerous innocence, a resolution of the future and the past. It symbolises a quality of peace and the only means by which it can be achieved. The echoes of Milton's 'Nativity Ode' help to define the quality of this peace,[36] and keep Maria distinct from both the bird and any blasphemous association with the Virgin. On the day of Christ's birth Milton's Peace

> Strikes a universal peace through sea and land. ('N.O.' line 52)

Peace is an act of positive power over a normally unruly Nature, though its result is a harmony like that at Appleton House:

> The winds with wonder whist
> Smoothly the waters kissed,
>   Whispering new joys to the mild ocean,
> Who now hath quite forgot to rave,
> While birds of calm sit brooding on the charmed wave.
>
> ('N.O.' lines 64–68)

Both Milton's and Marvell's halcyons are heralds of peace, not emblems for the Virgin, and they prepare for an event that will regenerate the earth.

The precise relation of all this to Mary Fairfax, then aged fourteen, is obscure, but it is hard to avoid the conclusion that a specific marriage is in prospect for her, and that the choice for her as for Isabella, between celibacy and marriage, has been decided in favour of marriage. It is not impossible that the agreed spouse was Buckingham, whose whirlwind courtship in 1657 may have been preceded several years before by negotiations,[37] in which Marvell could have even had a hand. But whoever was designated as husband, his role is fixed by the poem, and the total lack of evidence makes any further speculation profitless. The full significance of this section may never be recovered.

But the poem achieves a resolution on the part of the poet as well. Over the course of the poem he has come to his own decision, and can judge the respective merits of the competing kinds of life. Even from the Wood he can write:

> Here in the Morning tye my Chain,
> Where the two Woods have made a lane;
> . . . But, where the Floods did lately drown,
> There at the Ev'ning stake me down.   ('A.H.' lines 617–618, 623–624)

The clear lane between the labyrinthine woods is the proper setting for the morning of his life, but the meadow of public life must be the scene for the action of his maturity, now that the floods of the war seem to have subsided. But the brutal image 'stake me down' suggests how much of him resists the conclusion, and how much of a violation of the self such action seems. 'Ev'ning' suggests that this action must continue in a gathering darkness.

So in spite of the keen sense of the imperfections of the world outside:

> 'Tis not, what once it was, the World:
> But a rude heap together hurl'd;   ('A.H.' lines 761–762)

and his intense affection for the order and beauty to be found at Appleton House:

> You Heaven's Center, Nature's Lap
> And Paradice's only Map   ('A.H.' lines 767–768)

this only Paradise is not for him. The poem closes on an equivocal note:

> Let's in: for the dark Hemisphere
> Does now like one of them appear.   ('A.H.' lines 775–776)

There is nothing joyous about the two monosyllables 'let's in'. The evening is peopled by the absurd but faintly threatening Salmon-fishers, who are at home in both flood and meadow, their coracle-shod heads an image of the inversion in the new microcosm. So Marvell returns to the house, which as in the beginning represents Art, the ordering power of man; and he is aware now that solitude is more painful and destructive than immersion in action, in spite of the pleasure and wisdom to be obtained only alone, for fallen man cannot sustain perfection by withdrawing from all human contact. So In is Out for Marvell, and there is a sense of resignation in his decision, to go out of the gardens and wood, away from the beauty and certainties of the lesser world, Paradise's only map, and into the rude heap of the world outside, which could only be tamed to a simulacrum of perfection by the ruthless energy and action of a Cromwell.

157

(iii) Conclusion

Marvell's may seem a trivial decision, to go into politics rather than continue teaching the children of the aristocracy. But to be a tutor was to be associated with a social order, with the leisured and cultivated way of life of a hereditary ruling class. Nowhere does Marvell recreate his deep affection for that way of life so directly as in this poem whose theme is its rejection. But this aristocracy was isolated from government by a war that had temporarily accelerated the erosion of its power. Time was foreshortened, to repeat Marvell's graphic phrase; the beginning and end of a process were dramatically juxtaposed, the whole process available as experience for Marvell to make into poetry.

Something like this is true in general of Marvell's work. His importance comes from his unique vantage point in an age of revolutions. In many areas of experience, in art, science, politics and poetry, his fundamental alignment was with the future not the past. He wrote out of a vital contact with the age's deepest tendencies, in tune with the sources of its creativity. Yet in spite of this centrality, this urgent engagement with so many aspects of the life of his age, he was not at all concerned to confirm its accredited self-images. He remains a shadowy, withdrawn figure, his poems self-effacing, compressed, pared down, and seeming smaller than they are. Their surface seems to claim so little on their behalf. Sensitive readers have always realized that there is more than these surfaces: 'A tough reasonableness beneath the slight lyric grace' was Eliot's famous formulation.[38] But it is easy to underestimate or misunderstand the depths. Marvell was more than tough and less than reasonable. The enigmatic surfaces mask a formidable analytic intelligence and architectonic powers, and an acute sense of anarchy, unreason, perversity. Occasional images open out suddenly to reveal unexpected depths, occasional lines go opaque with esoteric significance. Otherwise the unassuming yet demanding surfaces absorb attention, as though there was nothing more. So he seems isolated from his contemporaries, unfashionable in many superficial ways, but not because history had passed him by. History passed through him, as it does through the greatest artists of an age.

NOTES

Unless stated otherwise, place of publication is London.

Introduction

[1] T. S. Eliot: "Andrew Marvell" (1921) in 'Selected Essays' (1932).
[2] D. Friedman: 'Marvell's Pastoral Art' (1970), p. 2
[3] In my "Marvell's poems to Fairfax: Some considerations concerning dates" 'M.P.' 1974, I argue that at least 'Hill and Grove at Bilborow' should be dated in the 1660's.
[4] T. S. Kuhn: 'The Structure of Scientific Revolutions' (Chicago 1962), F. G. Pocock, in 'Politics Language and Time' (1972) has also urged that Kuhn's concepts be applied to political history. But cf. the brilliant analysis, praised by Kuhn himself, of M. Masterson. She observes at least 21 slightly different ways the term paradigm is used, which she then organizes under three heads. (In 'Criticism and the Growth of Knowledge', ed. I. Latakos and A. Musgrove, Cambridge, 1970, p. 61).
[5] See e.g. Watkins, Toulmin, Popper and Latakos, in Latakos and Musgrove (edd.) op. cit.
[6] C. S. Peirce: 'Selected Writings' ed. Buchler (1940), pp. 8ff. Peirce did his work in the nineteenth century, which indicates something of the roots of the position that Kuhn argues.

Chapter 1

[1] For the standard account of this development, see W. S. Howell: 'Logic and Rhetoric in England, 1500–1700' (1957).
[2] W. J. Ong: 'Ramus, Method and the Decay of Dialogue' (Harvard, 1958).
[3] P. Miller: 'The New England Mind: The Seventeenth Century' (Harvard, 1954). Esp. pp. 116–153.
[4] See N. W. Gilbert: 'Renaissance Concepts of Method' (N.Y. 1960), especially chapters 5 and 6, for confusions in Ramus's actual exposition of the doctrine.
[5] P. Ramus: 'Dialecticae libri duo' (1574), I.ii (p. 5).
[6] Ibid. II, iv–viii (pp. 53–59).
[7] A. Richardson: 'The Logicians School Master' (1629), p. 15.
[8] Ibid. p. 124.
[9] Ibid. p. 43.
[10] Ibid. p. 66.
[11] J. Milton: 'Artis Logicae . . .' (1972) 'Works', Columbia, 1930. Vol. XI. Milton's connection with Ramism is usually minimized in Milton criticism: cf e.g.

P. Albert Duhamel, 'Milton's alleged Ramism' 'PMLA' LXVII (1952), which makes much of Milton's minor deviations from Ramus. Works that praise Milton's logical powers, like D. Burden 'The Logical Epic (1967), tend not to insist on the distinctive qualities of Ramist logic.

12 In 'Works', Vols. XIV–XVII.
13 Milton: 'de Doctrina', I.l (Vol. XIV, p. 16ff).
14 "Detached axioms" as T. S. K. Scott-Craig calls them in his "The Craftsmanship and Theological Significance of Milton's 'Art of Logic' "; 'Hun. L.Q.', Vol. 17, No. 1 (1953), p. 14.
15 'de Doctrina', I.i (Vol. XIV, p. 181).
16 Ibid. (pp. 179–181).
17 Ibid. p. 181.
18 Ibid. p. 191.
19 Ibid. p. 197.
20 Milton: 'Areopagitica' (1644). 'Works', Vol. IV, p. 310.
21 Ibid. p. 342.
22 This discussion seems harsh to Milton, but I do not see it as an attack on his poetic stature. I think he was incapable of one kind of intellectual subtlety and control that is often claimed for him, by critics who essentially follow C. S. Lewis's 'Preface to Paradise Lost' (1942). However, Milton's integrity as a thinker commands respect, and led him to struggle through to heretical doctrines which represented valuable commitments in poetry and politics. C. Hill 'World Turned Upside Down' (1972) points out his affinities with contemporary theological radicals.
23 Milton: 'Art of Logic', 'Works', Vol. XI, p. 355.
24 Ibid. p. 355.
25 Hobbes: 'Leviathan' (1651), I.ix.
26 ibid. I.iv.
27 Ibid. I.viii.
28 Bishop Bramhall: 'The Catching of the Leviathan' (1658) and Parker, 'Discourse', Chapters IV and V and elsewhere.
29 J. Bowles: 'Hobbes and his Critics' (1951), p. 29.
30 Bramhall op. cit., p. 507.
31 Parker: 'Discourse', p. 140.
32 Ibid. p. 143.
33 Ibid. p. 144.
34 'R.T.', p. 77.
35 Ibid. p. 72.
35 Ibid. p. 74.
37 As argued by B. H. Smith: 'Poetic Closure' (1968), pp. 133–135.
38 cf. the misunderstandings exposed in his exchange with Wallis: J. Wallis, 'Due Correction for Mr. Hobbes' (1656). Hobbes: 'Stigmai Ageoimetrias' (1657) etc.
39 'R.T.', p. 146.
40 In 'R.T. 11', p. 314 he gives Cusa as his source, but vaguely. In 'de Docta Ignorantia', 1.xiii, p. 9. Cusa has: '(dictum est) lineam infinitam esse triangulum maximum, circulum, et sphaeram'. Bruno (who also acknowledges Cusa as source) comes closer to Marvell at a crucial point: 'La linea retta infinite vegna ad esser circolo infinito'. ('de Causa', 'Works', ed. Gentile (1925), Vol. I, p. 261). But in his explanation in 'R.T. 11' Marvell reverts to the less paradoxical 'is' of Cusa, having hinted that the intention of the phrase was to lure Parker into an indiscretion that he did not make. As with all Marvell's apparent affinities

with Bruno (see below, chapters 2 and 3) it is not possible to decide whether Marvell's thinking was actually influenced by Bruno's or merely parallel.

[41] Catullus: 'Poems', ed. Cornish (1962), B. Jonson: 'Song: to Celia'. 'Works', ed. Herford and Simpson (1947), Vol. VIII. R. Herrick: 'Gather ye Rosebuds'. 'Poems', ed. L. C. Martin (1956).

[42] T. Carew: 'To A.L.', lines 41–4. 'Poems' ed. R. Dunlop, Oxford (1949).

[43] F. R. Leavis: 'Revaluation' (1936), pp. 30, 32.

[44] Eliot, op. cit. pp. 292, 303.

Chapter 2

[1] cf. Kuhn op. cit. pp. 111–112.

[2] Main secondary works consulted for the period have been: Whinney and Millar: 'English Art 1625–1714': (1957), Ellis Waterhouse: 'Painting in Britain 1530–1790': (Oxford, 1953), and David Piper: 'English Painting' (1965). To David Piper I am also indebted for a useful conversation. For more general notions I have derived most help from E. H. Gombrich: 'Art and Illusion': (1962) and G. T. Buswell: 'How People Look at Pictures' (1935).

[3] Plates from A. M. Hind: 'Tudor and Stuart Engravings' (1952, 58, 64).

[4] Ibid. Vol. 1, p. 113.

[5] Two recent works, K. Scoular: 'Natural Magic' (Oxford, 1965) and R. Colie: 'My Ecchoing Song' (Princeton, 1970) contain many emblems which seem relevant to Marvell.

[6] The connection with Hugo is certain. See K. Scoular Datta: "New Light on Marvell's "A Dialogue between the Soul and Body" ": 'Ren. Q.' XXII, 3 (1969): 242–256. The case for a connection with Hawkins is more circumstantial and cumulative. See M. Bradbrook and M. Lloyd Thomas 'Andrew Marvell' (Cambridge, 1940), pp. 57–60, and the discussion below.

[7] The best guide to the English emblem tradition is still R. Freeman, 'English Emblem Books' (1948). The following account is in general agreement with her book.

[8] See L. L. Martz's authoritative 'Poetry of Meditation' (Yale, 1954), Chapter IV, though Martz emphasises more than I would the common ground between catholic and protestant.

[9] See G. Haight: "The Source of Quarles's Emblems": 'The Lib.', Vol. XVI (1936).

[10] For attribution to Hawkins see Freeman op. cit.

[11] Hawkins op. cit. p. 66.

[12] 'Ros' lines 1–2 (Translation here and throughout W. A. McQueen and K. A. Rockwell, "The Latin poetry of Andrew Marvell"', 'University of N. Carolina Studies in Comparative Literature, 34 (1964).

[13] cf. Legouis 'Andrew Marvell' (Oxford, 1965), p. 4.

[14] T. Browne: 'Pseudodoxia Epidemica'. Book V 'Works' ed. G. Keynes (1928), Vol. 11, pp. 338ff.

[15] G. Wither: 'A Collection of Emblems' (1635), p. 179.

[16] R. Hooke: 'Micrographia' (1665). Schema XXXV.

[17] 'Last Instructions', lines 16–18. (In Margoliouth's opinion, the most certainly Marvellian poem from the restoration satires attributed to Marvell.).

[18] 'The Nymph Complaining . . .', lines 83–92. The overall meaning and intention of this poem is much disputed (see e.g. E. S. Le Comte: "Marvell's 'The Nymph' . . ." 'M.P.', 50 (1952), K. Williamson: "Marvell's 'Nymph': a Reply" 'M.P.', 51 (1954) etc.). Bradbrook and Lloyd Thomas argued that "the love of the girl for her fawn is taken to be a reflection of the love of the Church for Christ" (op cit. p. 50). I am sure that the poem has an esoteric meaning of this kind, but no particular uncoding suggested so far seems convincing, and I have no alternative to offer.

[19] See eg. C. Butler 'Rhetoricae libri duo' (1929), a ubiquitous rhetorical handbook in the seventeenth century. See Howell op. cit. p. 262.

[20] F. A. Yates: 'The Art of Memory' (1966) to which this section is greatly indebted.

[21] T. Wilson: 'The Arts of Rhetoricke' (1553), p. 240.

[22] Peter of Ravenna: 'The Art of Memory' (Trans. Copland 1548), pp. 7r, 12r.

[23] Wilson op. cit. p. 241.

[24] Ibid. p. 243.

[25] T. Watson: 'Compendium Memoriae Localis' (1585?), c.VIII.

[26] A. Dickson: 'de Umbra' . . . (1583). (See Yates op. cit. p. 273 for evidence of connection with Bruno.) Dickson was one of the speakers in Bruno's dialogue 'de Causa, Principe ed Uno' (trans S. Greenberg, Columbia 1950).

[27] G.P.: 'Antidicsonus' (1584). (For identification of G.P. see Yates op. cit. esp. pp. 268ff. The proof is not conclusive.)

[28] Dickson op. cit. pp. 81–82.

[29] G. Bruno: 'Ars Reminiscendi . . .' (1584?), II.i.2.s

[30] G.P. op. cit. p. 35. For Bruno's connections with Ramus see D. W. Singer: 'Giordano Bruno, his life and thought' (1950), p. 22. There is unlikely to be much direct debt. But Dickson was educated at Edinburgh University, a centre of Ramism; cf. J. Durkan: "Alexander Dickson and the STC 6828" 'The Bibliothek', Vol. iii, No. 5 (1962).

[31] G.P. op. cit. p. 36.

[32] Ibid. p. 45.

[33] Ibid. p. 45.

[34] Dickson op. cit. p. 62.

[35] Ibid p. 48.

[36] G.P. op. cit. p. 37.

[37] Martz op. cit. chapter IV, sees Baxter as a decisive figure in the development of Puritan kinds of meditation.

[38] Wallace op. cit. p. 240.

[39] Hobbes: 'The Answer to the Preface', p. 57. With Sir W. Davenant's: 'Gondibert' (1651).

[40] Hobbes, 'Leviathan', I.iii.

[41] Ibid. I.iii.

[42] Davenant op. cit. p. 8. Parker was another Hobbist who adopted this pose; see Preface (p. 2) and elsewhere, mocked by Marvell 'R.T.', p. 11 ff.

[43] Davenant op. cit. p. 6.

[44] Hobbes: 'Answer', p. 57.

[45] Davenant op. cit. p. 20.

[46] Hobbes, 'Leviathan', I.viii.

[47] Dryden: 'An Account of the Ensuing Poem'. (Prose 'Essays' ed G. Watson (1962), Vol. I, p. 98).

[48] Hobbes, 'Leviathan', I.iii.

[49] Dryden op. cit. p. 98.

[50] See especially K. Scoular's account of the poem from this point of view in her 'Natural Magic'.

[51] W. Empson: "Marvell's Garden". In 'Some versions of Pastoral' (1935).

[52] P. Legouis: "Marvell and the new Criticis": 'R.E.S.' (1957).

[53] Empson op. cit. pp. 124–125 (see also the three meanings listed by F. Kermode "The Argument of Marvell's 'Garden' ": 'Essays in Crit.', Vol. 2 (1952), p. 236).

[54] Browne: 'Works', Vol. II, p. 242.

[55] Hawkins op. cit. p. 235.

[56] Ibid. p. 84.

[57] See Lucretius: 'de Rerum Natura', II, 1058ff.

[58] Newton: 'Opticks' (1704).

[59] Hooke: op. cit. pp. 74–75.

[60] Ibid. p. 77.

[61] Ibid. p. 58. If Marvell was directly using Hooke, obviously 'The Garden' would have to be dated much later than is usual, but the parallel is not strong enough to force us to do this.

[62] 'In eandum', line 7. (See also 'A.H.', line 639).

Chapter 3

[1] M. A. Nicolson: 'The Breaking of the Circle' (1950), p. xix. The myth of the antagonism between science and poetry has a direct bearing on education today. See for instance the famous "Two Cultures" debate, initiated by Sir Charles Snow's 1959 Rede Lecture 'The Two Cultures and the Scientific Revolution', attacked by F. R. Leavis in 'Two Cultures? The Significance of C. P. Snow' (1962). On Marvell and science cp. the representative view of Bradbrook and Lloyd Thomas: 'During the later seventeenth century natural science removed the supports from this older conception of Nature: and Marvell ceased to write poetry'. op. cit. p. 55.

[2] L. Thorndike: 'History of Magic and Experimental Science' (Columbia 1941, 58). Vol. V, p 494.

[3] Ibid. Vol. VIII, p. 589.

[4] Thorndike op. cit. Vol. V, p. 13.

[5] M. Boas: 'The Scientific Renaissance' (1962), Chapter VI.

[6] F. Yates: "The Hermetic Tradition in Renaissance Science", in 'Art, Science and History in the Renaissance', ed. C. S. Singleton (John Hopkins, 1967).

7 With apologies to Masterson, who has used the same word in a different sense (Latakos (ed.) op. cit. p. 65).

[8] (Categories following the analysis of G. W. Kitchin: in Preface to Everyman ed. of 'Advancement of Learning' (1915).).

[9] Bacon: 'Advancement', II.xvii.12 (In 'Works', ed. Spedding, Ellis and Heath, 1857–74).

[10] cp. L. C. Knights' important essay, "Bacon and the Dissociation of Sensibility", in 'Explorations' (1964).

[11] Bacon: "Great Instauration: Plan to the Work". 'Works', p. 27.

[12] Ibid. p. 27.

[13] Bacon: 'Nov. Organum', I.lix (p. 61).

[14] Bacon: 'Advancement', II.xiv. II.

[15] Bacon: 'Nov. Org', I.lix (p. 61).

[16] Ibid. I.cxxii (p. 109).
[17] Bacon: 'Nov. Org'. Preface p. 40.
[18] W. Gilbert: 'de Magnete' (1600). Preface p. 1.
[19] Ibid. I.iii.
[20] Bacon: 'Advancement', II.i.5.
[21] Gilbert op. cit. II.34.
[22] Ibid. II.4.
[23] Ibid. III.xii.
[24] Ibid. II.iv.
[25] Ibid. Preface p. 2.
[26] Ibid. p. 2.
[27] Ibid. p. 2.
[28] Bacon 'Nov. Org.,', I.lxx (p. 71).
[29] Ibid. I.liv (p. 59).
[30] Gilbert op. cit. p. 1.
[31] Galileo: 'Dialogues . . . concerning two new Sciences' (Trans. Crew and de Salvio, N.Y. 1912), p. 276.
[32] Newton: 'Principia' (1686), ed. Cajori (California, 1960), III, rule ii (p. 398).
[33] Newton: 'Opticks', Book III, Q.31 (p. 401).
[34] G. Porta: 'Magia Naturalis' (1550). Trans as 'Natural Magicke', 1658. Heading to Chapter X. Book I (p. 15).
[35] Ibid. I.vii (p. 9).
[36] Gilbert op. cit. V.12.
[37] Ibid. III.6.
[38] Newton, 'Principia'. Definition III (p. 2). (He also refers to magnetic phenomena to illustrate definitions V–VIII).
[39] Gilbert op. cit. I.10.
[40] J. Primerosius: 'de Vulgi . . . Erroribus' (1638). Trans. R. Wittie, 'Popular Errors' (1651).
[41] Ibid. p. 418.
[42] O. Crollius: 'Philosophy reform'd . . .' (Trans. H. Pinnell, 1657), pp. 41–42.
[43] Primrose op. cit. p. 416.
[44] Gilbert op. cit. I.i: Bacon: 'Parasceve', viii. ('Works', IV, p. 260).
[45] Porta op. cit. Book VII.xlviii (p. 212).
[46] P. Rossi: 'Francis Bacon: From Magic to Science'. (Trans. Rabinovitch, 1968).
[47] Bacon 'Advancement', II.ix.1.
[48] Ibid. II.ix.2.
[49] Bacon: 'de Augmentis', IV.iii (p. 398, 401).
[50] Ibid. IV.iii (p. 398).
[51] Ibid. p. 402.
[52] Ibid. p. 402.
[53] Bacon: 'Plan', p. 26.
[54] 'Nov. Org.', I.L (p. 58).
[55] Hooke op. cit. 'Dedication'.
[56] Ibid. Preface, p. 3.
[57] Hooke: 'A General Scheme . . .' (In 'Posthumous Works', ed. Waller, 1705), p. 40.
[58] Ibid. p. 41.
[59] Ibid. p. 38.
[60] See discussion above, Chapter 2, Section iv.
[61] See Margoliouth (8 references to Browne, 4 to Gerard's 'Herball').
[62] Pliny: 'History of the World' (trans. Holland, 1634), Vol. II, Book xxxii (pp. 425–426).

[63] A. Kirchner: 'Magnes . . .' (1659), p. 763.
[64] See also 'The Coronet', line 22, and 'Defence of John Howe' ('Works' IV, p. 177) where Marvell professes to find the word multiply ambiguous.
[65] See above, previous section.
[66] Hooke: 'Micrographia', pp. 116ff.
[67] Marvell: 'Last Instructions' (of c. 1667 – see Margoliouth, p. 268) lines 345–346: 'A.H.' lines 357–358 and 619–620.
[68] S. Hales: 'Vegetable Staticks' (1727), p. 3.
[69] Ibid. p. 76.
[70] Vergil, 'Aeneid', VI.726, see McQueen and Rockwell op. cit. ad. loc.
[71] Bacon: 'Advancement', II.xvi.4.
[72] Bacon: 'de Augmentis', VI.i (p. 442).
[73] Donne: 'The Good-Morrow' line 11, 'The Canonization', lines 10–11, 'The Sunne Rising', lines 21–22.
[74] Pliny op. cit. I.x.32 (p. 287).
[75] For Torricelli, see A. Rupert Hall: 'From Galileo to Newton: 1630–1720' (1963), pp. 250–251. Boyle 'New Experiments . . . Touching the Spring of the Air' (1662) and Hooke, 'Micrographia', Preface and elsewhere.
[76] See above, Chapter 2, Section iv.

Chapter 4

[1] J. M. Wallace 'Destiny his Choice' (Cambridge, 1968), Chapter 1. Wallace has also assembled a useful bibliography in his "The Engagement Controversy, 1649–52. An Annotated List of Pamphlets"; 'Bull. N.Y. Pub. Lib', LXVII (1964). In addition, this chapter in an earlier version has benefitted from Professor Wallace's valuable criticisms.
[2] In S. R. Gardiner: 'The Constitutional Documents of the Puritan Revolution, 1625–1660' Oxford, 1908.
[3] Bishop Sanderson: 'A Resolution of Conscience' (1649) and "Of the Engagement", (Case VI in 'Nine Cases of Conscience', pub. 1685). On Sanderson's logic, see Howell op. cit. p. 299.
[4] Sanderson: 'A Judgment concerning Submission to Usurpers' (Pub. 1678), pp. 15–16.
[5] A. Ascham: 'Of the Confusions and Revolutions of Governments' (1649). (A key figure for both Wallace op. cit. and Q. Skinner: "History and Ideology in the English Revolution"; 'Hist. J.' 8 (1965). See also P. Zagorin 'Political Thought in the English Revolution' (1965).
[6] W. Ames: 'de Conscientia' (1631), 'Conscience with the power and cases thereof' (1639), R. Baxter: 'A Christian Directory . . .' (1673).
[7] Ascham op. cit. pp. 32, 33.
[8] Sanderson: 'Resolution', p. 6.
[9] Ibid. p. 3.
[10] Ibid. p. 5.
[11] Op. cit. (See discussion Chapter 2, Section ii.)
[12] Ascham op. cit. p. 5.
[13] Ramus: 'Dialecticae', II.iv.
[14] cf. Wallace: 'Destiny', p. 32.
[15] Ascham op cit. p. 21.
[16] Ibid. p. 29. On the emergence of this kind of attitude to man and society in the

seventeenth century see C. B. MacPherson: 'The Political Theory of Possessive Individualism: Hobbes to Locke' (Oxford, 1962).

[17] Ibid. p. 25.
[18] Ibid. p. 25.
[19] Sanderson: 'Engagement', pp. 90–91.
[20] See above, Chapter 2, Section iv.
[21] See Wallace, 'Engagement Controversy', under Hobbes.
[22] McPherson op. cit.
[23] Hobbes: 'Leviathan', II.17.
[24] Ibid. II.29.
[25] See above, Chapter 1, Section i.
[26] R. Hooker: 'Of the Lawes of Ecclesiastical Politie' (1593), I.iii.5 (p. 161).
[27] Ibid. I.iii.2. (p. 157).
[28] Hobbes: 'Leviathan', II.19.
[29] Wallace: 'Destiny', Chapter 3.
[30] The importance of Millenarian thinking in the poem is discussed by J. A. Mazzeo: "Cromwell as Davidic King" in 'Renaissance and Seventeenth Century Studies', 1964. On the millenarian strain in Hobbes also, see Pocock op. cit.
[31] Margoliouth ad. loc., p. 243.
[32] Ibid. ad loc., p. 247.
[33] Marvell Sr.: 'Sermons', Hull Lib. Ms. B. 64359 (unpaginated).
[34] Ibid.
[35] Cf. 'Flecknoe' and Margoliouth's discussion ad loc.: and Legouis op. cit., pp. 9ff.
[36] For dates see Margoliouth ad loc. (p. 243).
[37] C. Brooks: "Marvell's 'Horatian Ode'." (1948) (In 'Seventeenth Century English Poetry', ed. W. Keast (1962), p. 324. There is a possibility that 'Tom May' was partly written after the Restoration, but at most this would only be certain lines (esp. 85–90). See Margoliouth ad loc. The omission of the poem from the Bodleian MS. Eng. poet d.49 is certainly "puzzling" (Margoliouth, Additiorfal Notes to 2nd Edition p. xv) but is hardly unequivocal enough evidence to suggest that the poem is not by Marvell.
[38] R. Wild: 'The Tragedy of Mr Christopher Love'. Act IV (In 'Inter Boreale' (1670), p. 26).
[39] E.g. use of dramatic analogy: and Charles' demeanour on the scaffold, 'Tragedy' Act II, p. 24) with 'H.O.', lines 61–64.
[40] Sir R. Fanshaw: 'Selected Parts of Horace' (1652). I.v.ix: II, xiv: II.vii: IV.iv. s
[41] J. S. Coolidge: "Marvell and Horace", (M.Phil), 63 (1965), p. 118.
[42] Fanshaw (with 'Translations of Pastor Fido' (1648)). He may have been working on this project for many years: cf. W. Simeone 'N. & Q', Vol. 197, 1952, pp. 316–318.
[43] Cf. J. B. Leishman: 'The Art of Marvell's Poetry' (1966), p. 284.
[44] Wild op. cit. epilogue, p. 28.
[45] T. May: 'Lucans Pharsalia' (1635), Il.33ff.
[46] See R. H. Syfret's excellent discussion: "Marvell's Horation Ode", 'R.E.S.' (n.s.), 12 (1961).
[47] May's 'Lucan', Il.240ff.
[48] Cf. Margoliouth's note ad loc. (pp. 237–238).
[49] Hobbes, 'Leviathan', I.14, p. 68.
[50] Brooks op. cit. p. 331.
[51] Fanshawe: 'A Short Discourse of the Civil Wars'. (Attached to 'Translation of Pastor Fido'), p. 304 (Translating Paterculus).

52 Wild op. cit. esp. p. 23.
53 Milton: 'Defensio Prima'. In 'Works', Vol. VII, p. 17.
54 Margoliouth ad loc., (p. 239) suspects a pun on the Latin 'acies', eyesight and blade. The word could also mean intellectual keenness, or a debate.
55 Milton 'Works', IV, p. 645.
56 Pliny op. cit. Vol. II, p. 295.
57 Livy: 'Annals' (trans. P. Holland, 1600), I, p. 38.
58 Clarendon: 'History of the Rebellion' (1849), Vol. vi, p. 106 (xv.151).
59 See the subtle discussion to this effect of L. Hyman: "Politics and Poetry in Andrew Marvell": 'PMLA' LXXIII, Vol. 2 (1958), though he sees the poem finally as a skilful argument in favour of Cromwell.
60 See the perceptive account of the poem from this point of view by C. K. Stead: "The Actor and the Man of Action: Marvell's 'Horatian Ode' ". 'Crit. Survey' (1967).

Chapter 5

1 E.g. D. C. Allen: in 'Image and Meaning' (Baltimore, 1960) and M. O'Loughlin: "This Sober Frame", in 'Andrew Marvell', ed. G. de F. Lord (1968).
2 This account can all be found in the 'D.N.B.' article on Fairfax, unless an alternative source is given.
3 Clarendon op. cit. Vol. IV, p. 244 (X.88).
4 Ibid. V, p. 159 (xiii.20).
5 C. R. Markham: 'A Life of the Great Lord Fairfax' (1870), p. 363.
6 See Chapman op. cit. p. 90.
7 Brian Fairfax wrote a prefatory poem – which was not published – for a book by Witty in 1681. ('BM. E. 2146'). This is of course considerably later than the date of Marvell's tutorship: otherwise it would be strong evidence for Witty's standing in the Fairfax family and his potential influence in such an appointment.
8 Margoliouth, p. 229.
9 The mistaken view behind M-S. Rostvig "Andrew Marvell's 'The Garden': A Hermetic Poem": 'E. Studies' LX (1959), which used this work to elucidate Marvell's thought in the shorter poem.
10*Fairfax: 'The Divine Pimander' (BM Autog. MS. 25, 447), p. 5v. Fairfax has mainly relied on the translation of J. Everard: 'The Divine Pymander' (1650).
11 Ibid. p. 6v.
12 J. Calvin: 'Institutio' (Trans. T. Norton). III.iii.10.
13 Ibid. III.ii.17.
14 Leed Library: 'Philips Mss. 10690'.
15 Fairfax: 'Memorials of Thomas Lord Fairfax' (in 'Antiquarian Repertory', Vol. III, 1808, communicated by E. Lodge).
16 Ibid. p. 1.
17 Letter headed Marston, June 4th, 1645. In 'Fairfax Correspondence', Vols. III and IV, ed. R. Bell, 1849. Vol. III, p. 228.
18 Ibid., headed Ragland Aug. 10th, 1646 (III, p. 316).
19 Fairfax: 'Memorials', p. 4.
20 Ibid. p. 4.
21 Ibid. p. 6.
22 John Raymond: 'An Abridgment of the Life of Julius Caesar' (1649). (Copy in Bodleian).

[23] Fairfax: 'Memorials', p. 3.
[24] Cf. G. R. Hibbard: "The Country House Poem of the Seventeenth Century", 'J. Warburg and Courtald Institute', Vol. XIX, and, with an admirable awareness of the social context of these poems, R. Williams in 'Country and City' (1973).
[25] Wallace: 'Destiny', p. 239ff.
[26] As also in 'Coronet', lines 10–16.
[27] Quoted Margoliouth ad loc.
[28] See above, section i. The antiquarian Dodsworth, whom Fairfax assisted financially, was interested in monasteries of Yorkshire.
[29] See Markham op. cit.
[30] 'The Poems of Thomas Lord Fairfax', ed. Bliss Reed (1909).
[31] Story in J. Rushworth 'Historical Recollections' (6 volumes, 1703), Vol. V, p. 52. Rushworth acted as Fairfax's secretary during the period, and is a reliable source.
[32] Lovelace 'Poems', ed. Wilkinson, 1930, p. 117.
[33] H. Wotton: 'The Elements of Architecture' (1624), p. 37.
[34] Hawkins op. cit. p. 150.
[35] See above, chapt. 3, section ii.
[36] See Allen op. cit. for the parallels, though he interprets them differently.
[37] D. Underdown: 'Royalist Conspiracies in England, 1649–1660', (1960), pp. 118–119, suggests that Fairfax in 1653 was insisting on Buckingham as his contact with the King. See also Chapman op. cit. p. 91 for contemporary rumours of a Buckingham–Fairfax alliance in the early 1650's.
[38] Eliot op. cit. p. 293.

INDEX

Allen, D, 168
Ames, W, 99
Amphion, 108–112
Aristotle, 75, 76
Art of memory, 48
Ascham, A, 99–104, 123, 130
Aubrey, J, 94
Augustus, 119

Bacon, Francis, 70–80, 82, 91
Baxter, Richard, 54–56, 60–61, 99, 138
Boas, M, 69
Bowles, J, 18
Boyle, Robert, 94
Bradshaw, John, 113
Bradbrook, M (and Lloyd

Thomas, M), 161, 162, 163
Bramhall, Bishop, 18–19, 101
Brooks, C, 116, 117, 123, 125
Browne, Thomas, 41, 65, 85, 164
Bruno, Giordano, 24, 50, 51, 57, 61, 62–63, 65, 67, 160
Buckingham, Duke of, 134, 156, 168
Burden, D, 160

Calvin, 136
Carew, Thomas, 24–25, 142
Casuistry, 97, 99
Catullus, 25

Chapman, H, 168
Charles I, 118, 124, 125–131, 133, 136, 137, 139, 141
Christina, Queen of Sweden, 67
Clarendon, Earl of, 21, 127, 133, 134
Claudius Nero, 119
Cockson, Thomas, 30–32, 35, 47, 58, 62
Colie, R, 161
Connex syllogisms, 8
Cooper, Samuel, 35–36
Copernicus, 69
Cowley, Abraham, 23, 94
Crollius, 80, 81
Cromwell, 6, 15, 67, 96, 104, 106–114, 116–117,

119, 121–131, 133, 141, 151, 157
Cusa, Nicholas of, 24, 160

Davenant, William, 56, 58–59, 61, 63, 142, 143–144
Datta, K Scoular, 161, 163
le Maniban, J, 90–91
Dichotomies, 8
Dickson, Alexander, 50–54, 63, 67, 93
Disjunctive syllogisms, 8
Dobson, William, 36
Dodsworth, John, 136
Donne, John, 16, 48, 85, 93, 95
Drusus Nero, 118, 129
Dryden, John, 46–48, 60–61, 94
Duhamel, P A, 160
Dutton, William, 113

Eliot, T S, 1, 26, 158
Emblems, 36
Empson, W, 63
Engagement Oath, 97
Erasmus, 49
Everard, J, 167

Fairfax, Brian, 167
Fairfax, Mary, 94, 134, 135, 155–156
Fairfax, Thomas Lord, 30, 63, 116, 118, 119, 129, 132–141, 144–151, 155–156
Fane, Mildmay, 118
Fanshawe, Richard, 118–121, 124, 132
Fracastoro, 69, 70
Freeman, R, 161

Galileo, 65, 77, 95, 123
Gerard, 85, 164
Gilbert, N, 159
Gilbert, William, 69, 74–80, 81, 82, 83, 85, 89, 94, 95
Glover, George, 32–34
Goring, George, 127
Grotius, 101

Hales, Stephen, 89–90
Hannibal, 119, 120, 129
Hawkins, Henry, 36, 39–43, 46, 55, 65, 155–156
Hermetic texts, 135
Herrick, Robert, 142
Hill, C, 160
Hilliard, Nicholas, 27, 35–36
Hobbes, Thomas, 7, 17–19, 23, 56–63, 65, 68, 73, 84, 100, 101–102, 104–108, 111, 123, 130, 138
Hooke, Robert, 44, 62, 66, 83–85, 89, 94, 95, 163
Hooker, Richard, 99, 107–108, 112
Horace, 118–121
Hugh of St Victor, 156
Hugo, Herman, 36, 37–39, 41
Hyman, L, 167

Ireton, Henry, 151

Jonson, Ben, 88, 142–144
Julius Caesar, 121, 122, 129, 139

Kepler, 69, 95
Kermode, F, 163
Keynes, G, 69
Kirchner, 86
Kitchin, G, 163
Knights, L C, 163
Kuhn, T, 2–5, 8, 27, 28, 70

Lambert, General, 134
Laud, Archbishop, 154
Laws of justice, wisdom and truth, 8
Leavis, F, 26, 163
Legouis, P, 63–64
Lely, Peter, 36
Lewis, C S, 160
Livy, 126
Locke, John, 10, 55, 68
Love, Christopher, 117
Lovelace, Richard, 114–115, 116, 152–153, 154
Lucan, 116, 120, 121, 122

Lyly, John, 85

MacPherson, C, 104
MacQueen (and Rockwell), 67
Magic, 69
Margoliouth, H, 66, 113, 129, 134, 161, 166, 167
Markham, C, 134
Marlowe, Christopher, 95
Marshall, William, 30–32, 38
Martz, L, 161, 162
Marvell, Andrew, senior, 115
Marvell, Andrew, the poet, works cited in the text,
Ad regem Carolum Parodia, 115, 118
Bermudas, 88–89
Character of Holland, The, 113
Dialogue between the Soul and Body, A, 16, 38
Dignissimo Suo Amico, 90
Elegy upon the Death of My Lord Francis Villiers, An, 114
First Anniversary, The, 15–16, 106–113, 114, 123, 125, 130
Garden, The, 63–67, 87–88
Horatian Ode, An, 113, 116, 117–131, 132
Hortus, 66
In effigiem, 67
In legationem, 116
Last Instructions to a Painter, The, 43
Letter to Doctor Ingelo, 67, 113–114
Match, The, 91–92
Nymph Complaining for the Death of her Faun, The, 43–47
On a Drop of Dew, 40–41
Rehearsal Transpros'd, The, 18, 20–22, 24, 141

To a gentleman, 90–91
To Doctor Witty, 90
To his Coy Mistress, 22–26, 86
To Lovelace, 114–115
Tom May's Death, 116, 117
Upon Appleton House, 42, 56, 61–63, 85, 86, 93–94, 116, 118, 132, 141–157
Masterson, M, 159, 163
May, Thomas, 116, 117, 120, 122, 135, 142
Mazzeo, J, 166
Metaparadigm, 70
Miller, P, 7
Milton, John, 7, 11–16, 18, 87, 96, 106, 113, 124, 126, 134, 156
Monck, George, 134

Nero, 119–120
Newton, Isaac, 66, 69, 77–78, 79, 95, 164
Nicolson, M, 68
Normal science, 3, 5

Ong, W, 7
Ovid, 16
Owen, John, 18

Paracelsus, 75
Paradigm, 3–4, 5, 7
Parker, Samuel, 18–22, 54, 160, 162
Peirce, C S, 4
Perkins, William (GP), 50–54, 55, 74
Peter of Ravenna, 49, 51, 53
Picasso, P, 27
Plato, 135
Pliny the younger, 85–86, 88, 94, 126, 155
Pocock, F, 159, 166
Poemander, The, 135
Porta, G, 78, 82
Primerose, James, 80–82, 85

Quarles, Francis, 38

Ramus, 7, 8, 10, 16, 55, 71, 101
Remora (also echeneis), 85–86
Renaissance art, 28
Richardson, Alexander, 10–11, 14, 71
Rockwell, K (and Mc-Queen, W), 67
Rossi, P, 82
Rostvig, M-S, 167
Rubens, 36
Rushworth, John, 168

Salmasius, 124
Sanderson, Bishop, 98–101, 115
Scepticism, 99–100
Scott-Craig, T, 160
Shakespeare, William, 48, 95, 111
Simeone, W, 166
Simpson, W, 166
Singer, D, 162
Smith, B, 160
Snow, C, 163
Spenser, Edmund, 46–48, 49, 58, 63
Stead, C, 167
Syfret, R, 166

Tarquin, 126
Thorndike, L, 69–70, 75
Thompson, Captain, 128
Thurloe, John, 134
Thwaites, Isabella, 145–146, 148, 150
Torricelli, 94
Trinity, Milton's doctrine of, 13

Underwood, D, 168

Van den Keere, 32–34, 35
Van Dyke, Anthony, 36
Vulgar errors, 80, 85

Wallace, J, 56, 97, 99, 104, 111, 142, 165
Wallis, John, 160
Weapon-salve, 80
Wild, Robert, 117–118,

119, 124, 132
Williams, R, 168
Wilson, Thomas, 48, 49, 50, 51
Wither, George, 41–42
Witty, Robert, 90, 135, 167
Wootton, Henry, 154

Yates, F, 48, 69, 161